TRAJECTORIES

TRAJECTORIES

A Gospel-Centered Introduction
to Old Testament Theology

BRYAN C. BABCOCK,
JAMES SPENCER,
& RUSSELL L. MEEK

PICKWICK *Publications* · Eugene, Oregon

TRAJECTORIES
A Gospel-Centered Introduction to Old Testament Theology

Pickwick Publications
An Imprint of Wipf and Stock Publishers
199 W. 8th Ave., Suite 3
Eugene, OR 97401

www.wipfandstock.com

PAPERBACK ISBN: 978-1-4982-3284-5
HARDCOVER ISBN: 978-1-4982-3286-9
EBOOK ISBN: 978-1-4982-3285-2

Cataloging-in-Publication data:

Names: Babcock, Bryan C., author | Spencer, James, author | Meek, Russell L., author.

Title: Trajectories : a gospel-centered introduction to Old Testament theology / Bryan C. Babcock, James Spencer, and Russell L. Meek.

Description: Eugene, OR: Pickwick Publications | Includes bibliographical references.

Identifiers: ISBN: 978-1-4982-3284-5 (paperback) | ISBN: 978-1-4982-3286-9 (hardcover) | ISBN: 978-1-4982-3285-2 (ebook).

Subjects: LCSH: Bible. Old Testament—Theology.

Classification: BS1192.5 S66 2018 (print) | BS1192.5 (ebook).

Manufactured in the U.S.A.   03/01/18

CONTENTS

PREFACE

The authors of this book set out to meet a current need in both undergraduate and graduate level courses. Too often courses and textbooks in Old Testament theology focus on the end product of Old Testament theology. Readers see the results, but the writer's thought process is not always made transparent. This text seeks to make the thought process of the author clear by including the author's exegesis, as well as including the author's perspective on the theological theme in question framed within a discussion of the gospel.

In addition, Old Testament theologies often pay little attention to the ongoing role of Old Testament theological themes in the New Testament. Rather than simply pointing to passages in which Old Testament themes are explicitly utilized, this text provides a discussion of how the Old Testament themes inform our understanding of New Testament texts.

Trajectories addresses those challenges for students through a biblical orientation to the study of Old Testament theology. Thematically organized chapters address many of the major themes of the Old Testament. Each chapter analyzes key biblical passages that inform the theme in question so that the textbook may serve as a companion study guide to courses in the Old Testament. In addition, the exploration of thematic topics allows the study to better provide a link to the New Testament and the contemporary church.

Each chapter addresses a single theological topic of the Old Testament through exegetical and theological analysis of relevant biblical texts. By including three scholars whose research emphases complement each other, the text brings multiple evangelical voices to the table and provides examples of the manner in which different scholars develop Old Testament themes. The chapters conclude with an assessment of how each theological theme may be applied to the contemporary Christian church, along with questions for group discussion and reflection.

Finally, *Trajectories* seeks to situate Old Testament theology in relation to global and generational trends influencing the church and evangelical theology. The implications of globalization and the rise of the millennials on Old Testament theology are specifically addressed.

In sum, this theology Old Testament approaches the Old Testament as a theological text. Each essay presumes that humanity has become confused about God, about human nature, about the problems and solutions people face, and about the world they inhabit. This disorientation often encourages activities counter to the reign of God. The Old Testament, however, also describes a reality in which God participates. Humanity is not left alone, but given the opportunity to see beyond what appears to be insurmountable constraints and to live a life of obedience to God. As a counterpoint to humanity's misperceptions and misdirected desires, the Old Testament offers a vision of reality in which God governs, sustains, tests, calls, protects, disciplines, delivers, and transforms those who are faithful to Him.

ACKNOWLEDGMENTS

"He who finds a wife finds a good thing,

and has obtained favor from Yahweh"

(PROV 18:22)

We would like to dedicate this book to our wonderful wives Brittany Meek, Betsy Babcock, and Kim Spencer, who have encouraged us to pursue our passions for research, writing, and to increasingly be in fellowship with God. We want to thank them for the countless hours that they entertained our families so we might engage in writing. And we want to thank our mentors Rick Hess, Gordon Wenham, Walter McCord, Jon Monson, Dick Averbeck, and Mark Boda for allowing us to sit at their feet and learn from giants. Russell also thanks Louisiana College and its faculty development committee for providing funding for research for this book.

ABBREVIATIONS

ABD	*The Anchor Bible Dictionary*
AcOr	*Acta orientalia*
AOTC	Abingdon Old Testament Commentary
Atl Mon	The Atlantic
AUSS	*Andrews University Seminary Studies*
BA	*Biblical Archaeologist*
BAR	*Biblical Archaeology Review*
BASOR	*Bulletin of the American Schools of Oriental Research*
BASORSup	Bulletin of the American Schools of Oriental Research: Supplement Series
BBR	*Bulletin of Biblical Research*
BBRSup	Bulletin of Biblical Research Series Supplement Series
BDB	Francis Brown, S. R. Driver, and Charles A. Briggs, *A Hebrew and English Lexicon of the Old Testament*. Oxford: Clarendon, 1907
BHS	*Biblia Hebraica Stuttgartensia*. Edited by K. Elliger and W. Rudolph. Stuttgart, 1983
BI	*Biblical Illustrator*
Bib	*Biblica*
BibOr	*Biblica et orientalia*
BSac	*Bibliotheca sacra*
BZAW	Beihefte zur Zeitschrift für die alttestamentliche Wissenschaft

CBQ	*Catholic Biblical Quarterly*
COS	*The Context of Scripture.* 4 vols. Edited by William W. Hallo. Leiden: Brill, 1997-2017
CJT	*Canadian Journal of Theology*
ConJ	*Concordia Journal*
CTJ	*Calvin Theological Journal*
CTR	*Criswell Theological Review*
DBSJ	*Detroit Baptist Seminary Journal*
DHQ	*Digital Humanities Quarterly*
EBib	*Etudes bibliques*
EvQ	*Evangelical Quarterly*
ExAud	*Ex Auditu*
FAT	Forschungen zum Alten Testament
HBC	*Harper's Bible Commentary.* Edited by J. L. Mays et al. San Francisco, 1988
HBT	*Horizons in Biblical Theology*
HOTE	Handbook of Old Testament Exegesis
HS	*Hebrew Studies*
HTR	*Harvard Theological Review*
IJOE	*Innovate: Journal of Online Education*
Int	*Interpretation*
JAAR	*Journal of the American Academy of Religion*
JBL	*Journal of Biblical Literature*
JBQ	*Jewish Bible Quarterly*
JBR	*Journal of Bible and Religion*
JEP	*Journal of Education Policy*
JETS	*Journal of the Evangelical Theological Society*
JQR	*Jewish Quarterly Review*
JNES	*Journal of Near Eastern Studies*
JNSL	*Journal of Northwest Semitic Languages*
JRelS	*Journal of Religious Studies*

JSOT	*Journal for the Study of the Old Testament*
JSOTSup	Journal for the Study of the Old Testament Supplement Series
JTS	*Journal of Theological Studies*
JTI	*Journal of Theological Interpretation*
KEL	Kregel Exegetical Library
MSJ	*Master's Seminary Journal*
NIBC	New International Bible Commentary
NAC	New American Commentary
NCBC	New Cambridge Bible Commentary
NICNT	New International Commentary on the New Testament
NICOT	New International Commentary on the Old Testament
NIDNTT	New International Dictionary of New Testament Theology. Edited by C. Brown. 4 vols. Grand Rapids, 1975–1985
NIVAC	NIV Application Commentary
NovT	*Novum Testamentum*
NSBT	New Studies in Biblical Theology
NTL	New Testament Library
Or	*Orientalia (NS)*
OrAnt	*Oriens antiquus*
OTL	Old Testament Library
OTS	*Old Testament Studies*
PEQ	*Palestine Exploration Quarterly*
PrPe	*Priests and People*
PTSB	*Princeton Theological Seminary Bulletin*
ProE	*Pro Ecclesia*
RB	*Revue biblique*
RelSoc	*Religion and Society*
ResQ	*Restoration Quarterly*
SJOT	*Scandinavian Journal of the Old Testament*
SS	*Studies in Spirituality*

TDNT	*Theological Dictionary of the New Testament.* Edited by Gerhard Kittel and Gerhard Friedrich. Translated by Geoffrey W. Bromiley. 10 vols. Grand Rapids, 1964–1976
TDOT	*Theological Dictionary of the Old Testament.* Edited by G. Johannes Botterweck and Helmer Ringgren. Translated by John T. Willis, Geoffrey W. Bromiley, and David E. Green. 15 vols. Grand Rapids, 1974–2006
TOTC	Tyndale Old Testament Commentaries
TynBul	*Tyndale Bulletin*
Vid	*Vidyajyoti*
UF	*Ugarit-Forschungen*
VT	*Vetus Testamentum*
VTSup	Supplements to Vetus Testamentum
WBC	Word Biblical Commentary
WTJ	*Westminster Theological Journal*
ZAW	*Zeitschrift für die alttestamentliche Wissenschaft*

INTRODUCTION

JAMES SPENCER

APPROACHING THE OLD TESTAMENT THEOLOGICALLY

As a student at Wheaton College, I had the privilege of taking a class from Paul House. After reading my paper examining the Davidic innocence motif in the book of Samuel, Dr. House asked me a question that has shaped my perspective on the theological task to this day: "Where is the theology?" The question caught me off-guard as I truly believed that I had done some solid theological work in describing the text's strategies for distancing David from violence against other Israelites. The problem, Dr. House explained, is that I had said nothing about God. Observations about David, explanations of literary techniques, and theories as to why the author took pains to distance David from wrongdoing are all important, but they aren't (yet) theology. What did the portrayal of David convey about God? How did it showcase God's character? Needless to say, I had some revisions to make after meeting with Dr. House.

The moral of the story is that Old Testament theology is first and foremost about God. Investigating ancient Near Eastern history and culture, evaluating Hebrew grammar and syntax, and analyzing archaeological or geographical data are not ends in themselves. They are the means by which we more faithfully understand God through his word. An Old Testament theology that does not finally offer a portrayal of God is incomplete because an Old Testament theology's primary task is that "of presenting what the Old Testament says about God as a coherent whole."[1]

Presenting this "coherent whole" requires those engaging in Old Testament theology to look at the Old and New Testaments as a whole book and to synthesize the various portrayals of God. This synthesis represents the synchronic dimension of Old Testament theology. Old Testament theology must attend to the manner in which specific books develop, expand on, and introduce new facets of God's character. In other words, there is a diachronic element to Old Testament theology, which recognizes the progress of revelation through time.

In addition, Old Testament theology must not lean solely upon conceptualization, or on the abstraction of so-called universal principles. Such approaches rightly recognize that the Old Testament is the enduring word of God relevant and beneficial across all times, places, and cultures. Yet, focusing on principles alone can also distract God's people from the inherently relational intent of the text, which seeks to lead us toward a greater knowledge of the God who creates, redeems, delivers, forebears, and supplies.[2] Old Testament theology requires a constant movement between more particular depictions of God in Scripture and the combination of those biblical depictions to develop a broader canonical understanding of God.

To assert that Old Testament theology is first and foremost about God is not intended to deny theology the role as a means of articulating, or re-articulating, understandings of humankind, time, place, the world, or a host of other topics. Rather, the assertion that Old Testament theology is first and foremost about God suggests that these other topics may only be understood rightly in relation to or through the lens of a faithful rendering of God's identity. As we view the various aspects of our world and our activity within it in relation to God as He is revealed in the Old Testament, we engage in the task of Old Testament theology. This task is an act of worship, a means of proclaiming God to the Church and the world, and a way of

1. Zimmerli, *Old Testament Theology*, 12. For examples of the various methods used in the production of Old Testament theology up to the early 2000s, see Ollenburger, *Old Testament Theology*.

2. While principles do arise from the biblical text, there can be a tendency to separate principles from the theological context of the broader Israelite narrative. For instance, the rationale behind the prohibition against muzzling oxen while they are treading grain is that Israel has a God willing and able to supply for the needs of the community. Allowing oxen to eat while treading grain is a theological act which recognizes and proclaims God's sufficiency. There is not so much a general principle here as there is an understanding of God that has implications for particular acts within the context of the Israelite community and, later, for the church in Corinth (1 Cor 9:9–12). Contrast this reading with that offered by Kaiser, "A Principlizing Model," 7–8.

establishing the criteria for distinguishing true and false witness to the God of the Old Testament.[3]

While Old Testament theology surely begins in the Old Testament and its discrete witness of God, it does not end in the Old Testament. Rather, it is necessary to recognize that, with the coming of Christ, Old Testament theology constitutes one element within a reciprocal theological "loop" in which the New Testament reinforces and expands upon the theology of the Old Testament even as the Old Testament informs and provides a crucial framework for the New Testament.

Respecting and studying the discrete witness of the Old Testament cannot be separated from the canonical task of describing the Triune God as he is presented in both the Old and New Testaments. At the same time, it is important to recall that the Old Testament is a Christian Testament. As Barr notes, "Insofar as a position is Christian, it is related to the Old Testament from the beginning."[4] Striking the balance, then, between treatments of the Old Testament separate from the New Testament and the construction of more canonical readings, which look back upon the Old Testament from the standpoint of the New, is essential to the work of Old Testament theology. Ultimately, the Old Testament proclaims the gospel in harmony with the New Testament offering unique revelation of God's plan for restoring his kingdom.

OLD TESTAMENT THEOLOGY AND THE GOSPEL

The gospel encompasses far more than the salvation message though it is surely right for us to identify and celebrate the gospel message as communicating "what we must believe to be saved."[5] As John Goldingay notes, "'Gospel' does not come into being only with the coming of Jesus. In speaking of Jesus' story as 'gospel,' the early Christians were thinking of his story in terms that had already been applied to Israel's story."[6] The point is not to minimize the importance of Christ to the gospel, but to recognize that, as Kevin Vanhoozer suggests, that the gospel entails "a series of divine entrances and exits, especially as these pertain to what God has done in Jesus Christ."[7]

---

3. Williams, *On Christian Theology*, xiii.

4. Barr as quoted in Seitz, *Figured Out*, 5.

5. Goldsworthy, *Gospel-Centered Hermeneutics*, 19.

6. Goldingay, *Old Testament Theology*, 28.

7. Vanhoozer, *The Drama of Doctrine*, 31.

The gospel, the "good news," involves the transformation of social, political, economic, and ecological structures, systems, and relationships in the victory of Christ over sin on the cross. It is the good news that God's order will be restored and the effects of sin will no longer plague God's creation. The gospel entails the realignment of all aspects of the created order according to God's wisdom. While this broader sense of the gospel is prominent within the New Testament, the Old Testament's treatment of the gospel within the context of the nation of Israel and the nations with whom they come into contact offers a distinctive picture of the various intersecting areas of creation impacted by the gospel.

Issues, for instance, of politics, bureaucracy, corporate care of the disenfranchised, as well as the intersection of religious and national leadership, feature prominently in the Old Testament. This prominence should not suggest a sharp distinction between a "corporate" orientation in the Old Testament and an individual orientation in the New. Such characterizations deny the communal, political, and social aspects of the New Testament, as well as the individual spirituality developed within the Old Testament.[8] In truth, even the separation of individual and communal is misleading in so much as it overshadows the interdependent relationship between individuals and the communities of which they are a part.

Another aspect of the Old Testament's unique presentation of the gospel is related to the manner in which the gospel is articulated. Unique depictions of human suffering and emotion may be found in the wisdom, poetic, and prophetic literature of the Old Testament. Job's debates in the midst of suffering, the imprecatory prayers of the Psalter, and the anguished cries voiced by Jeremiah represent raw, impassioned expressions of God's people who struggle to reconcile their situation with their understanding of God. God's faithfulness and single-minded desire to restore a right relation between himself, his people, and his creation demonstrates his worthiness, compassion, and empowering presence among those who believe in him.

Old Testament theology provides present-day believers with resources to align their lives with God's character and to participate with Him as he transforms creation. The Old Testament serves as one of the resources available to present-day believers as they seek to live theologically in modern-day contexts by looking back and remembering the past acts of God amongst his people. Engaging in Old Testament theology is an act of memory in so much as "memory is the central faculty of our being in time . . . the negotiation of past and present through which we define our individual and collective

---

8. For a helpful analysis and survey of Old Testament spirituality, see Adam, *Hearing God's Words*, 47–80. Note also Sheriffs, *The Friendship of the Lord*.

selves."[9] In other words, as believers engage in Old Testament theology, they seek to understand themselves, the historical community of faith of which they are a part, and the whole of creation in light of and in relation to God.

INTRODUCTION TO THIS OLD TESTAMENT THEOLOGY

The manner in which an Old Testament theology is structured has an impact on the overall theology itself. The current volume has been organized based on Old Testament themes arranged to follow the general storyline of the Old Testament as it appears in the protestant canon with two additional chapters discussing Old Testament theology in light of the contemporary interests in the increasing influence of multiethnic discourse and the growing influence of digital technologies in today's world. Themes will be addressed through a broad, synthetic treatment of the theme and its appearance throughout the Old Testament, as well as through a more focused treatment of the theme within a key passage in which the topic is developed. The theme will then be discussed in relation to the New Testament with a particular emphasis placed on the relation of these themes to the gospel. Finally, each chapter will examine the implications for the modern-day believer and community of faith.

The thematic chapters are arranged with the intention of communicating the storyline of the Old Testament. Chapter 2 addresses the Old Testament's treatment of creation with an exegesis of Genesis 1. This discussion of creation is followed by the ancillary themes of "abundance and faithfulness" (chapter 3), structural evil (chapter 4), and covenant (chapter 5). These four chapters provide an overview of the primordial history and transition into the patriarchal age with the formation of the covenant. This portion of the Old Testament theology seeks to establish a basis for understanding God as benevolent creator whose love and care for His creation endures despite human rebellion.

Chapters six through nine address themes deriving from Israel's initial liberation from Egypt (chapter 6) to the establishment of God's temple (chapter 9) with intervening chapters related to Torah (chapter 7) and the messiah in the psalter (chapter 8). These themes were chosen as they represent key events in the formation of the nation of Israel and the definition of Israel's relationship to God. This section of this book demonstrates the distinct character of God as Sovereign over Israel, as well as the potential for Israel to live a unique, God-empowered life with God amongst the nations through obedience to God's commands.

---

9. Olick. *States of Memory*, 15.

The final thematic section discusses the enduring presence of God among his people (chapter 10), as well as the sort of loyalty and trust required of God's people during times of turmoil and transition (chapter 11). Human suffering (chapter 12) will be examined alongside the themes of hope (chapter 13) and renewal (chapter 14). This final thematic section demonstrates God's continued presence with His people despite difficult circumstances. It also addresses the manner in which God safeguards His people in order to usher in renewal.

Following the thematic section, the multiethnic church and the impact of the digital age will be addressed. "Old Testament Theology for a Multiethnic Church" will offer an introductory exploration of the possibilities and challenges of involving global voices in the task of Old Testament theology. The chapter focuses Old Testament theology as an academic field offering possibilities for stronger connections between the church and the academe.

"Old Testament Theology and the Digital Age" will explore the ways in which the thinking and learning is changing in the digital age and the manner in which these changes influence Old Testament theology. The rise of digital natives and digital immigrants has introduced new cultural perspectives and means of communication that may inform the presentations, if not the methods, of Old Testament theologians. Digital natives have a seemingly limitless amount of information at their fingertips. The potential benefits and pitfalls of such access are explored in this final chapter.

Old Testament Theology provides an often undervalued role in the life of the church. The Old Testament's portrayal of God provides a rich picture of God's interactions with his fallen creation while anticipating the redemption of that creation in the New Testament. Any treatment of Old Testament theology must surely acknowledge the unique witness of Old Testament, as well as the Old Testament's connection to the New Testament. As Seitz notes, "The Old Testament tells a particular story about a particular people and their particular God, who in Christ we confess as our God, his Father and our own, the Holy One of Israel. We have been read into a will, a first will and testament, by Christ."[10] The Old Testament is not a book foreign to the Christian faith, but an integral part of that faith. It is not a book set apart, but an essential chapter in the full story of God and His people. In this sense, the study of Old Testament theology must maintain a highly Christian character deeply rooted in the contemporary church.

---

10. Seitz, *Word Without End*, 11.

BIBLIOGRAPHY FOR CONTINUED STUDY

Adam, Peter. *Hearing God's Words: Exploring Biblical Spirituality*. Downers Grove, IL: InterVarsity, 2004.

Kaiser, Walter C., Jr. "A Principlizing Model." In *Four Views on Moving beyond the Bible to Theology*, 19–50. Grand Rapids: Zondervan, 2009.

Goldingay, John. *Old Testament Theology: Israel's Gospel*. Downers Grove, IL: InterVarsity, 2015.

Goldsworthy, Graeme. *Gospel-Centered Hermeneutics: Foundations and Principles of Evangelical Biblical Interpretation*. Downers Grove, IL: InterVarsity, 2010.

Olick, Jeffrey K. *States of Memory: Continuities, Conflicts, and Transformations in National Retrospection*. Durham: Duke University Press, 2003.

Ollenburger, Ben C. *Old Testament Theology: Flowering and Future*. Winona Lake, IN: Eisenbrauns, 2016.

Sheriffs, Deryck. *Friendship of the Lord*. 1996. Eugene, OR: Wipf & Stock, 2004.

Seitz, Christopher R. *Figured Out: Typology and Providence in Christian Scripture*. Louisville: Westminster John Knox, 2001.

———. *Word without End: The Old Testament as Abiding Theological Witness*. Grand Rapids: Eerdmans, 2002.

Vanhoozer, Kevin J. *The Drama of Doctrine: A Canonical Linguistic Approach to Christian Doctrine*. Louisville: Westminster John Knox, 2005.

Williams, Rowan. *On Christian Theology*. Oxford: Blackwell, 2000.

Zimmerli, Walther. *Old Testament Theology in Outline*. Translated by Davied E. Green. Louisville: Westminster John Knox, 1978.

1

CREATION

RUSSELL L. MEEK

INTRODUCTION

Creation undergirds the Old and New Testaments. If Yahweh did not create the heavens and the earth—and all within them—then we should abandon the rest of the Bible as well. If Yahweh is not creator, then he also is not redeemer. If Yahweh is not creator, then there is no exodus, no giving of Torah, no judgment through exile, no restoration through repentance, no future hope in the Messiah, no incarnation, no cross, no resurrection. If Yahweh is not creator, then indeed, "we are of all people most to be pitied" (1 Cor 15:19b ESV).

This chapter will look primarily at the creation accounts in Gen 1–2 to illustrate the Old Testament's view of creation. We will also examine creation texts in the wisdom and prophetic books in order to demonstrate how Genesis's creation account informs the theology of the Old Testament, particularly with regard to its description of Yahweh's character and the connection between creation and redemption in the Old Testament. Next, this chapter examines how the New Testament, in particular the good news of Jesus's death, resurrection, and ascension, informs the Old Testament's creation theology. We will find that the Bible begins with God's creating the universe and placing humans in the garden of Eden and ends with God's recreating the universe and placing humans in a new garden of Eden—a place of perfect fellowship with him. This redemption—and new creation—occurs through the work of Christ on the cross and is founded on Yahweh's creative work in the first chapters of Genesis. Before that time, though, we will see that Christians wait longingly for Jesus's ultimate redemption and work to restore the created order through reclaiming humanity's role as priest-kings. The church would not properly understand this responsibility without a clear understanding of the Old Testament's theology of creation. First, however, we will briefly contemplate the relationship between creation and the gospel.

CREATION AND THE GOSPEL

My faith tradition has no problem recognizing the personal implications of Jesus's death and resurrection and the consequent sanctification that occurs as Christians continually submit to Christ's lordship. We likewise stand strong on the doctrine of Yahweh's creation *ex nihilo* of the universe as depicted in Genesis. We preach Christ crucified, urge sinners to repent, promise new life in him—both in this world and the next—and yet often fail to acknowledge the implications of the gospel on our doctrine of creation. I don't mean that the gospel should impact our view of how God created or that God created or when God created. Rather, I mean that we sometimes forget that the gospel impacts all of theology, including—perhaps *especially* including—how we view creation.

Jesus Christ makes all things new. This applies not only to the personal implications of a life surrendered to his lordship but also to how we understand and relate to the theology of creation today. First, redemption rests on creation. If there is no creation, there is no redemption. The statement sounds silly, but it's nonetheless true. It's true first of all because, of course, Yahweh had to create in order to redeem. There can be no *new* heavens and *new* earth if there's no *old* heavens and *old* earth. If there's no one for whom to die, then of course Christ doesn't die. But it's also true because Yahweh's power to create is the same power to redeem.

Do you ever wonder if God is faithful to save those who call upon his name in faith? You only have to look out your window (or maybe walk through park if you live in an urban area) to see he's powerful to save. That tree and that grass and that flower and that bird and that squirrel—Yahweh created those. Their presence in this world declares God's faithfulness and goodness toward us, the crowning of his work in creation.[1]

Creation affirms that God is powerful enough to enact the gospel.[2] We may think for a moment that maybe God can't forgive us, that maybe our sins are too great, or we're just out of his reach. We may think—if only briefly—that the grip of sin or the world or the old man is too great for God to overcome. If we think such thoughts, we only have to observe the mountains, the rivers, the seas to know our doubts are unfounded. These most powerful things in the world—waves that engulf, rivers that run wild, mountains that tower above us—God created them. He's more powerful than the sturdiest mountain, the wildest sea, the fastest river. When we look around and behold the world's natural wonders, we can know that God is more powerful than them because God created them. And if he's more powerful than the strongest created things, then surely he's powerful enough to save us frail humans.

Creation makes us without excuse. With Paul in Romans we can look at creation and affirm that "his invisible attributes, namely his eternal power and divine nature, have been clearly perceived, ever since the creation of the world, in the things that have been made" (Rom 1:20 ESV). And because of that we, like Paul says, are without excuse. So creation does three things (and probably a lot more): it quells our doubts if we wonder about God's faithfulness; it denies our concern that God is not powerful enough to rescue us; and it makes us all without excuse on that day.

ANALYSIS OF GENESIS 1:1—2:4

Genesis 1–2 contains two accounts of creation. The first (1:1—2:4) broadly overviews Yahweh's creative activity in first six days (seven if we count the first Sabbath). The second (2:5–25) narrows its focus to the jewel of Yahweh's creation: man and woman. These two accounts have much to say about Yahweh, his character, his creation, humans, and human purpose.

A Few Important Differences

The Bible opens with the simple statement that "in the beginning, God created the heavens and the earth."[3] This is most certainly a faith statement,

---

1. See Goldingay, *Israel's Gospel*, 69.

2. Ibid., 71. See also Brueggemann, 150–54.

3. Unless otherwise noted, Scripture quotations in this chapter are the author's

a polemical stance taken against the "gods" of Israel's neighbors.[4] Other ancient Near Eastern cultures had their own creation stories, stories that narrated the beginning quite a bit differently.[5] First, our creation account has only one protagonist: God himself. There's no other god Yahweh must battle. He goes about his creative work alone. That the Bible does not even mention rival gods highlights the fact that God has no rivals. He is a singular God, the only God who creates, the only God in existence.

Second, creation doesn't result from a battle between God and his enemies. Verse 2 paints a dim picture of universe before Yahweh sets things in order—it's formless, void, and dark—but there's not even a hint at a cosmological struggle between Yahweh and the waters or chaos or any other god.[6] Other ancient Near Eastern creation stories, such as *Enuma Elish*, portray the epic struggle to create vividly, with one god winning out over others and ascending to the top of the pantheon. In Yahweh's case, though, there is no such struggle because there are no rival gods to fight.[7]

A Crucial Similarity

One key similarity exists between the Genesis creation account and the other ancient Near Eastern creation accounts: all of the texts presuppose the existence of deity. Those in the ancient Near East would think it absurd even to consider that there could be an explanation for creation that excluded God/gods. The ancient Near Eastern audience, whether followers of Yahweh or not, would agree with the psalmist that "a fool says in his 'there is no God'" (Ps 14:1). Likewise, the creation accounts contain no speculation about God's/gods' origin because such speculation would be foolishness.[8]

translation.

4. On the polemical nature of Gen 1, see Hasel, "Polemical Nature," 81–102.

5. For comparisons between ancient Near Eastern creation accounts and Genesis, see, e.g., Gunkel, "Influence of Babylonian Mythology," 25–52; Millard, "New Babylonian 'Genesis Story,'" 3–18; Hasel, "Significance of the Cosmology of Genesis 1," 1–14; Fisher, "Creation at Ugarit," 313–24; Clifford, "Cosmogonies in the Ugaritic Texts," 203–19. The most recent treatments of this issue come from John Walton. See Walton, *Ancient Near Eastern Thought*, 165–202; Walton, *The Lost World of Genesis 1*; Walton, *The Lost World of Adam and Eve*.

6. Johnston, "Genesis 1," 179. Levenson (*Creation and the Persistence of Evil*, 66) acknowledges the lack of battle in Gen 1 but proposes its absence indicates it has already been won. See also Brueggemann, *Old Testament Theology*, 147.

7. Dyrness, *Themes*, 65.

8. See ibid., 63.

This crucial similarity between the creation accounts is important for Christian theology in the West today because we are so interested in the origins debate. We of course hold firmly that Yahweh created the entire universe just like Genesis testifies that he did. But, in an increasingly post-Christian West, rather than arguing over the *how* of creation—this author holds to a literal seven-day creation—perhaps we should emphasize the *who* of creation, just as the biblical account does. Yahweh himself, the same God who sent his son Jesus to die for our sins, created the entire universe.

Yahweh's Word and Work

Rather than creation resulting from a cosmological battle, creation results from the "word and work" of the creator God.[9] He speaks, and existence happens. Yahweh creates by divine command for the first five days of creation. He simply speaks to bring into existence another piece of the puzzle: light, the heavens, dry land, vegetation, the sun and moon, fish and birds. On each of these days Yahweh created by his very word. He only had to speak and all of the world came forth. As Dyrness has stated, God displayed "creative power that is completely without analogy."[10] And perhaps this is why the Hebrew term *bārā'* only appears in the Old Testament with God as its subject, with the "creative endeavors of human beings being expressed by other verbs."[11]

Finally, on the sixth day God creates by work. Rather than speaking humanity into existence, he "makes" man in his image (Gen 1:26). The overview of creation in Gen 1:1–2:4 gives only the scantest details about this creative work, but the more focused account of humanity's creation in Gen 2:5–25 completes the picture. Here we learn that Yahweh "formed" man from the dust (Gen 2:7) and later fashioned the woman out of his rib. Yahweh took a personal interest in creating humans, stooping to form us from the earth. Yahweh created humans in his own image. Yahweh breathed life into humans. And Yahweh gave humans dominion over the earth. Each these aspects of the creation of humanity has enormous implications for the Christian life specifically and the human life more generally.

Humans, crafted in God's image, are God's image bearers in the earth. That means we participate in the same type of work Yahweh participates in—creative rule. As Goldingay has stated, "Genesis 1–2 imply that

---

9. Ibid., 65.

10. Ibid., 66.

11. Merrill, *Everlasting Dominion*, 101.

humanity's chief and highest end is to work for God in the world."[12] That work certainly involves creation care—humans are stewards of the rest of creation. And since the fall that work also involves priestly work, or mediating between God and other humans as Yahweh's image bearers. Of course, Jesus Christ is the one Mediator between God and man (1 Tim 2:5), and yet Christians today must also boldly proclaim the gospel so that humans may be reconciled to God. These two roles—mediator and ruler—are entrusted to us at the very beginning of time.

CREATION IN THE OLD TESTAMENT

Creation in Job

The book of Job presents Yahweh as all-powerful creator both in Job's speeches about Yahweh and in Yahweh's response to Job. After Job's horrific attacks from the accuser (Satan) and consistent defense of his innocence in the face of his interlocutors, Yahweh confronts Job in chapter 38. Yahweh fires off a series of questions in chapters 38–41 that highlight his power in creation and resulting sovereignty over all things. He laid the earth's foundations, he put the stars and moon and sun in place, he said to the sea, "thus far and no more," he set light and darkness in its place, he ordained rain and snow and hail, he feeds the animals and gave them their distinctive features and instincts. What's more, he created Behemoth and Leviathan—beasts humans cannot contain—thus demonstrating his great power. Yahweh's point is clear: we humans are "not as strong as we think we are."[13] As we cower before animals we cannot overpower, so we should submit to the power and sovereignty he displayed in creation.

Creation in Psalms

Several psalms extol the Lord for the attributes he displayed in creation: wisdom, power, sovereignty, faithfulness. Psalm 33, for example, connects God's work in creation with God's faithful love, or *hesed*. The psalmist here sees God's love and faithfulness to Israel expressed in creation itself.[14] The grand narrative of Yahweh's special relationship with his people therefore did not begin with his covenant with Abraham in Genesis 12. It began much

12. Goldingay, *Israel's Gospel*, 110.

13. Rich Mullins, "We Are Not as Strong as We Think We Are," *Songs* (Reunion, 1996).

14. Golding, *Israel's Gospel*, 57.

earlier than that, when Yahweh spoke and the heavens and earth and all within them came forth. Psalm 33 further indicates that Yahweh's creation was not a static event, a one-time display of greatness and mercy. No, Yahweh's creative work is ongoing as he fashions the hearts of all the earth's inhabitants (Ps 33:14–15). Verse 8 points out the appropriate response of humans in light of Yahweh's creative work: to fear him.[15]

Psalm 89 likewise extols the majesty of Yahweh because of his work in creation. This psalm declares that the heavens and earth—and all within them—belong to Yahweh because he created them (Ps 89:11). However, it quickly moves in a different direction. After proclaiming Yahweh's faithfulness and sovereignty in creation, the psalmist reminds the Lord of his covenant with David, thus connecting Yahweh's faithfulness in creation with his faithfulness to the people of Israel.[16] Yahweh's care and faithfulness and sovereignty in creation assures his people of his care and faithfulness and sovereignty in their lives. Yet the psalmist laments in vv. 38–45 that the Lord has rejected the Davidic servant for a time, then asks in 46–51 how long God will be distant from his people and implores him to remember. The psalm ends with a bold declaration of praise.

The wonder of this psalm—and its importance for a theology of creation—is that it connects Yahweh's work in creation with Yahweh's concern for his people. The psalmist honestly reflects on the current crisis—there is no Davidic ruler in Israel, God is silent, the covenant seems demolished—and bases his certainty that Yahweh will hear on the very fact that Yahweh created all things. The psalmist proclaims that we can know that Yahweh hears, remembers, and acts on behalf of his people because he created this whole world. This clear connection between Yahweh's *hesed* in creation and his *hesed* toward his people is a sure foundation on which the people of Israel—and we today—stand. Indeed, "Blessed be Yahweh forever. Amen and amen."

15. Wilson, *Psalms*, 558.
16. See Clifford, "Psalm 89," 44–47.

Creation in Proverbs

Proverbs contributes to the Old Testament understanding of creation by highlighting that Yahweh crafted the world through wisdom. Yahweh did not create haphazardly. He did not set about building a tower before counting the cost, as the foolish are wont to do (Luke 14:25–33). No, Proverbs tells us that Yahweh "fathered [wisdom] at the beginning of his deeds" (8:22).[17] Wisdom was there before Gen 1:1 (Prov 8:23–24). Birthing wisdom was the first of his acts, and the rest of creative activity flowed out of it.[18] Importantly, personified wisdom does not create, thus further clarifying that wisdom itself is not a goddess but rather one of Yahweh's many attributes that elicit worship and awe from his creation.[19]

Thus, whereas Psalms assures us that creation displays Yahweh's faithfulness to his people, Proverbs tells us that it also displays his wisdom. This is not so difficult to see when we look at the world around us. Trees and animals and bugs all create after their kind. The world works together in an infinitely complex ecosystem. Rains water the earth. The earth produces food. Life continues. These things happen not by chance but by the wisdom of our creator. It is not haphazard; it is not an accident. It is Yahweh's wise work, Prov 8 assures us.

Consequently, humans also should seek wisdom. As Garrett points out, Prov 8:26 indicates that, "Humans, as dust, are part of the created world and cannot live contrary to the order by which the world was created. By Wisdom the formless, chaotic dust became Adam, the human race. People who reject Wisdom, therefore, are certain to return to their prior state."[20] Creation assures us of Yahweh's goodwill toward us, and it also assures us of the proper path to take in life—the path of wisdom, the path marked out in Prov 1–9. Bartholomew and O'Dowd rightly point out that "God has built, or etched, an order into the world, and wisdom, personified as a woman, is the key to discerning it . . . She can guide us in walking wisely in this life because she knows the places that God carved out for us."[21] A failure to

---

17. Some early Christian scholars were quick to equate the personification of wisdom in Prov 8 with Jesus Christ. However, this connection is highly problematic theologically and not easily defended exegetically. For discussion, see Waltke, *Proverbs 1–15*, 127–30. For a brief history of interpretation of Prov 8:22 in early Christianity and Judaism, see Clifford, *Proverbs*, 98–99.

18. See Garrett, *Proverbs*, 108.

19. Clifford, *Proverbs*, 100. Contra Perdue, *Proverbs*, 142.

20. Garrett, *Proverbs*, 109.

21. Bartholomew and O'Dowd, *Wisdom Literature*, 89.

recognize Yahweh's faithfulness, Yahweh's wisdom, and our proper role in light of these two features exhibited so clearly in creation is a dire failure indeed.

Creation in Isaiah

The book of Isaiah, particularly chapters 43–45, is rife with creation theology.[22] Having proclaimed judgment on God's people for their idolatry and waywardness, the prophet now encourages the exiles in Babylon with a word of hope that he bases on Yahweh's creation of the entire world and his special creation of Israel as a nation.

There are several important items to note in these passages that impact how the people of Israel, and we today, should understand the theological importance of creation. First, Yahweh states plainly that he is the only true God (43:10–12), a fact attested previously in the creation account. Second, Yahweh indicates that he has the right to discipline his people because he created them (43:14–15).[23] By extension, his role as creator gives him the right to do what he will with his creation. Third, Yahweh uses creational language—e.g., "seas" and "waters"—to describe his creation of Israel.[24] In doing this Yahweh demonstrates that his care in creating the world is consistent with his care in creating Israel. Further, he shows that just as he made the entire world in a special, spectacular event, so he formed Israel in a unique way and for a unique purpose. Just as the entire world was created for a particular purpose by his word, so Israel was created for a purpose through his word.[25]

Fourth, because Yahweh created the world—and Israel in particular—his people can be assured of his continued care for them. In 44:2–5 he bases his comforting words on the very fact of his creation. This should not be lost on readers today: because Yahweh is the creator, he is the caregiver. He

22. For discussion of Isaiah's theology of creation in Isa 40–55, see Mangum, "Creation Traditions in Isaiah 40–55."

Mangum rightly argues that Isaiah utilizes creation themes in order to demonstrate Yahweh's superiority over other so-called gods in the ancient Near East. Also helpful is Lessing, "Yahweh versus Marduk," 234–44.

23. Note also that Yahweh's discipline is for his people's good (Isa 43:14). He is not a sadist who punishes for the sake of punishment. This sentiment is repeated several times in the Bible (e.g., Prov 3:12; Heb 12:6; Rev 3:19).

24. For more discussion on the creation motif as it relates to the creation of the nation of Israel, see Schnittjer, *The Torah Story*, 232–34; Enns, *Exodus*, 39–42.

25. On the interrelated themes of creation and exodus in the latter half of Isaiah, see Harner, "Creation Faith in Deutero-Isaiah," 298–306; Ollenburger, "Isaiah's Creation Theology," 54–71.

is not a distant God who set the world on its own after creation. Instead, his creation of the world confirms his care of the world. He is a benevolent lord who will see to the protection of his people, his special creation. Fifth and finally, Isaiah 43–45 argues on the basis of creation that the proper response to God is worship. That is, because Yahweh is the only God, the God who disciplines his people with their best interests in mind, the God who fashioned the nation of Israel, and the God who cares for his people, Israel should worship him and him alone.[26] In sum, in these three chapters Yahweh makes a progressive case based on his creative work that he alone is to be worshiped. The theology of creation, then, should impact our theology of worship, for by virtue of his creative work—and all it entails—Yahweh alone is worthy of adoration and adulation.[27]

CREATION AND THE GOSPEL

What, then, becomes of the doctrine of creation when we move into the New Testament? How does the Old Testament's theology of creation impact our understanding of the birth, death, and resurrection of Jesus Christ? Should we read the New Testament differently, or for that matter the Old Testament differently, because of how we understand God's creative work as depicted in the Old Testament? We will address these important matters through examining three aspects of the New Testament's theology of creation: 1) Jesus Christ is creator; 2) creation is groaning in anticipation for the day of full redemption; and 3) Jesus Christ is redeemer.

Jesus Christ Is Creator

John 1:1–3 (ESV) states, "In the beginning was the Word, and the Word was with God, and the Word was God. He was in the beginning with God. All things were made through him, and without him was not any thing made that was made."[28] The author of Hebrews confirms John's view of Jesus as creator when he states, "Long ago, at many times and in many ways, God

26. Note the sarcasm of 44:9–20, where Yahweh points out the absurdity of worshiping the created thing instead of the creator.

27. Lessing ("Yahweh Versus Marduk," 234) points out that worship causes humans to become like that which we worship. We are always imaging *something* and, as creatures of Yahweh, it is crucial that we worship him alone. See also Beale, *We Become What We Worship.*

28. For a discussion of John's reliance on Genesis for crafting John 1:1–18, see Borgen, "Creation, Logos, and the Son," 88–97.

spoke to our fathers by the prophets, but in these last days he has spoken to us by his Son, whom he appointed the heir of all things, through whom also he created the world" (Heb 1:2 ESV). Paul concurs: "yet for us there is one God, the Father, from whom are all things and for whom we exist, and one Lord, Jesus Christ, through whom are all things and through whom we exist" (1 Cor 8:6 ESV).

Polhill points out that John 1:1 "contains three basic affirmations that are fundamental to Christian theology": the Word existed before all things, there is a "relational difference" between the Word and God, and the Word and God are one.[29] Having established the preexistent nature of Christ (John states that Christ is the Word in v. 14) as well as the unity of and distinction between the Father and Christ, John addresses Christ's role in creation: Christ is the agent through whom all of creation came into existence (John 1:3). This confirms the unity of the Trinity, but also demonstrates the Son's separate role in creation as its agent. Further, Ridderbos points out, "The range of action of God-in-Christ at the creation coincides with the range of action of the Word in his incarnation. Therefore Christ is the light of the world (cf. 8:12) and by his coming into the world enlightens *every* person (1:9)."[30] Thus, our theology of creation impacts our understanding of Christ's work his incarnation, for they reflect each other.

First Corinthians 8:6 confirms our understanding of the unity of the Father and Son in stating that the all things are *from* the Father and *through* the Son. Paul furthers our understanding of the Son's role in creation by stating we exist through Christ. Thus, not only did the Father create us through the Son but also the Son's creative work is ongoing. All humans who have breath in their nostrils are current recipients of Christ's grace in upholding creation. This is called common grace and is true whether or not a person knows Christ personally. It is one more indication of God's great care for creation both in its initial conception during those six days at the beginning of time and also now.

In sum, the New Testament witness fully confirms that Jesus Christ is the creator of all things. The Trinitarian implications of Christ as creator cannot be overlooked: when John and Paul and the author Hebrews proclaim Christ as the creator of all things they identify him with the Father and give a small insight into the mystery of the Trinity. Genesis testifies that God created all things, and the New Testament teaches that through Christ all things were created—indeed, the Father and the Son are one. All the

29. Polhill, *John*, 102.

30. Ridderbos, *John*, 36.

praise and honor owed to the Father for his faithfulness and goodness in creation should be likewise given to the Son.

Creation is Groaning

Work is hard. Famine is a real concern in many parts of the world. Blights and locusts and droughts destroy crops. The land doesn't yield to humans like we want it to. Genesis lets us in on why things are the way they should be: Adam and Eve sinned against our good and gracious God. God created all things "good," even "very good." He told Adam to work the ground and it would yield to him. Adam and his wife could eat from whatever tree they wanted—that is, whatever tree except the one tree. And we know the rest of the story. They ate from the tree and God punished them and here we are today where work is hard and bad things happen.

The New Testament says something about our relationship with the rest of creation—we caused it a lot of pain. Our sin through Adam resulted in the cursing of the ground and now creation is groaning:

> For the creation waits with eager longing for the revealing of the sons of God. For the creation was subjected to futility, not willingly, but because of him who subjected it, in hope that the creation itself will be set free from its bondage to corruption and obtain the freedom of the glory of the children of God. For we know that the whole creation has been groaning together in the pains of childbirth until now. And not only the creation, but we ourselves, who have the firstfruits of the Spirit, groan inwardly as we wait eagerly for adoption as sons, the redemption of our bodies. (Rom 8:19–23 ESV)

Scholars have interpreted this passage myriad ways,[31] but the overall intent is clear: creation suffers along with the rest of humanity because of *our* sin. And like us, creation anticipates that day when Christ will set all things right. We will return to this crucial issue in discussing how creation relates to the Christian church today; for now it suffices to note the inter-relatedness of human sin and the suffering of creation.

---

31. For an overview of patristic interpretation of this passage, see Tyra, "When Considering Creation," 251–73. See also Tyra, "All Creatures Are Martyrs," 27–53.

Christ Is Redeemer

Finally, the New Testament clearly shows Jesus Christ as the redeemer of both humanity and the created world (e.g., Matt 1:21; Luke 2:11; 19:10; Acts 4:12; 13:23; 1 Tim 1:15; Titus 2:13; etc.). The narrative arc of the Bible is that God—in Christ—created a good world, humans bungled it all by rebelling against God's Word, and then God set about a plan of redemption that climaxed in the death, resurrection, and ascension of his own Son, the one through whom creation was made.

Christ inaugurated his redemptive work two millennia ago when he lived a sinless life and died a sinner's death. He took upon himself all of God's wrath so that those who believe in him would experience God's forgiveness and kindness toward sinners (Rom 5:9; 2 Cor 5:21; 1 Thess 5:9). In this present moment, we can experience the forgiveness of sins and new life in Christ; however, we also experience the sting of death in this life, in this creation damaged by our sin. But Jesus promises that he will one day return and create a new heavens and a new earth, a place where there is no sin and no death and no mourning (Rev 21). Christ the Creator and Christ the Redeemer will re-create all that we have destroyed. Maranatha!

CREATION AND THE CHRISTIAN LIFE TODAY

How should Christians live differently in light of the Trinity's work in creating and sustaining the world? Our discussion of Genesis indicated that God's original intent for humans was that we function as priest-kings in right relationship with him. This was certainly the case with Adam and Eve, who lived in Yahweh's presence in the garden of Eden, exercised dominion over creation, and enjoyed right relationship with each other. Of course, all that changed when they asserted their own authority and ate from the forbidden tree.

Genesis 3:15 sets the stage for the rest of the biblical narrative: a seed will come who will crush Satan's head. That seed, we now know, is Jesus Christ, who indeed conquered death and crushed Satan's head through his own death, burial, and resurrection. Being in Christ means, at least in part, that we have returned to that original role as priest-kings (see, e.g., Exod 19:6; 1 Pet 2:9). There is much to explore about how a theology of creation impacts the church's role as priest-kings—not the least of which is the high priority we should place on creation care[32]—but here we will focus only on worship.

As we saw above, the Old Testament is filled with adulation for God because of his creative work. Creation displays God character, power, might, majesty, wisdom, sovereignty, and lovingkindness toward his people. Several months ago I stood on a beach and beheld the wonder of the Pacific Ocean. Such sights may be old hat for people who live close to the ocean, but for a guy from central Arkansas, it was breathtaking. I was overcome by the sheer beauty and majesty and danger of those waters that crashed against the beach. I had no choice but to praise the God who said, "as far as here you may come, but no farther" (Job 38:11). Such was the posture of the biblical writers, and we do well to remember God's work in creation and worship him for it.

Our worship, however, must be properly focused. My father was the type of man who loved to be outside hunting or fishing, tinkering with this or that, and sometimes just sitting there, enjoying the hot sun or cool night. Whenever I would talk to my dad about Jesus, he always told me he wasn't interested in Jesus or church because he experienced God outdoors. I'm sure there are many people just like him, people who marvel at creation but do not know the Creator. In essence, the worship the thing that was made rather than the One who made it (see Rom 1). Knowing Christ means knowing *who* created the waves, the birds, the trees. Thus, it is not enough simply to marvel at creation. We must allow creation to fulfill its proper role in pointing us toward the One worthy of worship. Likewise, we fulfill part of our role as priest-kings as we point others toward the One who created this magnificent world.

QUESTIONS FOR DISCUSSION

1. How does God's creation in the first few chapters of Genesis set the tone for the rest of the biblical witness?

2. What does it mean that all things were made through and for Christ? What is a practical way that Christ's work in creation applies to the Christian life today?

32. There are many excellent resources on how Christians should care for creation. See, among others, Bouma-Prediger, *For the Beauty of the Earth*; Liederbach and Bible, *True North*; Berry, ed., *The Care of Creation*; Snyder and Scandrett, *Salvation Means Creation Healed*; Moo and White, *Let Creation Rejoice*.

3. Why should Christians work to develop a theology of creation? How does creation impact what we do on a daily basis?

4. How and why does a proper view of creation impact how Christians understand the gospel?

BIBLIOGRAPHY AND RECOMMENDED READING

Bartholomew, Craig G., and Ryan P. O'Dowd. *Wisdom Literature: A Theological Introduction*. Downers Grove, IL: InterVarsity, 2011.

Beale, Greg. *We Become What We Worship: A Biblical Theology of Idolatry*. Downers Grove, IL: IVP Academic, 2008.

Berry, R. J., ed. *The Care of Creation: Focusing Concern and Action*. Downers Grove, IL: IVP Academic, 2000.

Borgen, Peder. "Creation, Logos, and the Son: Observations on John 1:1–18 and 5:17–18." *ExAud* 3 (1987) 88–97.

Bouma-Prediger, Steven. *For the Beauty of the Earth: A Christian Vision for Creation Care*. Engaging Culture. Grand Rapids: Baker Academic, 2010.

Brueggemann, Walter. *Theology of the Old Testament: Testimony, Dispute, Advocacy*. Minneapolis: Fortress, 1997.

Clifford, Richard J. "Cosmogonies in the Ugaritic Texts and in the Bible." *Or* 53 (1984) 203–19.

————. *Proverbs: A Commentary*. OTL. Louisville: Westminster John Knox, 1999.

————. "Psalm 89: A Lament over the Davidic Ruler's Continued Failure." *HTR* 73 (1980) 35–47.

Dyrness, William A. *Themes in Old Testament Theology*. Downers Grove, IL: InterVarsity, 1977.

Enns, Peter. *Exodus*. NIVAC. Grand Rapids: Zondervan, 2000.

Fisher, Loren R. "Creation at Ugarit and in the Old Testament." *VT* 15 (1965) 313–24.

Garrett, Duane A. *Proverbs, Ecclesiastes, and Song of Songs*. NAC 14. Nashville: Broadman & Holman, 1993.

Goldingay, John. *Old Testament Theology*. 3 vols. Downers Grove, IL: IVP Academic, 2003.

Gunkel, Hermann. "The Influence of Babylonian Mythology upon the Biblical Creation Story." In *Creation in the Old Testament*, edited by Bernhard W. Anderson, 25–52. Issues in Religion and Theology 6. Philadelphia: Fortress, 1984.

Harner, Phillip B. "Creation Faith in Deutero-Isaiah." *VT* 17 (1967) 298–306.

Hasel, Gerhard F. "The Polemical Nature of the Genesis Cosmology." *EQ* 46 (1974) 81–102.

————. "The Significance of the Cosmology of Genesis 1 in Relation to Ancient Near Eastern Parallels." *AUSS* 10 (1972) 1–14.

Johnston, Gordon H. "Genesis 1 and Ancient Egyptian Creation Myths." *BibSac* 165 (2008) 178–94.

Lessing, Reed. "Yahweh versus Marduk: Creation Theology in Isaiah 40–55." *Concordia Journal* 36 (2010) 234–44.

Levenson, Jon. *Creation and the Persistence of Evil*. Princeton: Princeton University Press, 1988.

Liederbach, Mark, and Seth Bible. *True North: Christ, the Gospel, and Creation Care.* Nashville: B&H Academic, 2012.

Mangum, Douglas T. "Creation Traditions in Isaiah 40–55: Their Origin and Purpose." Paper presented at the annual meeting of the Upper Midwest Region of the SBL. St. Paul, MN. 27 March 2009.

Merrill, Eugene H. *Everlasting Dominion: A Theology of the Old Testament.* Nashville: B&H Academic, 2006.

Millard, Alan R. "A New Babylonian 'Genesis Story.'" *TynBul* 18 (1967) 3–18.

Moo, Jonathan A., and Robert S. White. *Let Creation Rejoice: Biblical Hope and Ecological Crisis.* Downers Grove, IL: IVP Academic, 2014.

Ollenburger, Ben C. "Isaiah's Creation Theology." *ExAud* 3 (1987) 54–71.

Perdue, Leo G. *Proverbs.* Interpretation. Louisville: Westminster John Knox, 2012.

Polhill, John B. *John.* NAC 26. Nashville: Holman Reference, 1992.

Ridderbos, Herman N. *The Gospel of John: A Theological Commentary.* Translated by John Vriend. Grand Rapids: Eerdmans, 1997.

Schnittjer, Gary E. *The Torah Story: An Apprenticeship on the Pentateuch.* Grand Rapids: Zondervan, 2006.

Snyder, Howard A., and Joel Scandrett. *Salvation Means Creation Healed: The Ecology of Sin and Grace. Overcoming the Divorce between Heaven and Earth.* Eugene, OR: Cascade Books, 2011.

Tyra, Steven W. "All Creatures are Martyrs: Martin Luther's Cruciform Exegesis of Romans 8:19–22." *WTJ* 76 (2014) 27–53.

———. "When Considering Creation, Simply Follow the Rule (of Faith): Patristic Exegesis of Romans 8:9–22 and the Theological Interpretation of Scripture." *JTI* 8 (2014) 251–73.

Waltke, Bruce K. *Proverbs 1–15.* NICOT. Grand Rapids: Eerdmans, 2004.

Walton, John H. *Ancient Near Eastern Thought and the Old Testament: Introducing the Conceptual World of the Hebrew Bible.* Grand Rapids: Baker Academic, 2006.

———. *The Lost World of Adam and Eve: Genesis 2–3 and the Origins Debate.* Downers Grove, IL: IVP Academic, 2015.

———. *The Lost World of Genesis 1: Ancient Cosmology and the Origins Debate.* Downers Grove, IL: IVP Academic, 2009.

Wilson, Gerald H. *Psalms.* NIVAC. Grand Rapids: Zondervan, 2002.

2

BE FRUITFUL AND MULTIPLY

BRYAN C. BABCOCK

INTRODUCTION

During the creation narrative, God blesses the first couple saying "be fruitful and increase in number." This phrase is repeated by God when addressing Noah and Abraham and always in the context of an increasing population. At first reading, the blessing makes total sense. God is addressing the first created humans and the world needs to be populated for mankind to survive and flourish. However, the blessing (conveyed as a command) is repeated to other key figures in the biblical narrative after survival of mankind is secured.

So, what is the intent of the blessing? A literal reading might imply that one is blessed if they have lots of children. If this is the case, then in a modern Western context very few are blessed, as most families have a maximum of two or three children while the biblical norm is eight to twelve. Would the opposite apply? If a couple is not able to have children are they somehow less blessed (or cursed)? Are those families who limit the size of their families blocking or limiting God's blessing?

These are difficult questions. The key to understanding the phrase "be fruitful and multiply" is through a hermeneutical examination of the passage. The methodology demonstrated in this chapter will explore the use of the phrase "be fruitful and multiply" across the entire canon of Scripture. The goal is to illuminate the intended meaning of the phrase for the initial Old Testament audience. Then to interpret that meaning for a modern Christian reader in light of the New Testament. In other words, what did God mean when he inspired the original author and how should we apply these passages to our modern lives?

FRUITFULNESS AND THE GOSPEL

To begin this study, it is helpful to understand whether the blessings given to Adam, Noah, and Abraham are still relevant in light of the gospel message. Essentially, is the blessing to have children a command for us to have children? Or is this a blessing but not a command? There are religious traditions that take the blessing from Gen 1:28 prescriptively and seek to produce as many children as God allows. If Gen 1:28 is prescriptive today, then the New Testament should support this idea. Therefore, let's turn to the New Testament and determine in the teachings of Jesus whether there is support this position.

While it is clear that having children does constitute a blessing from God, it is less clear whether the New Testament commands Christian couples to produce children. Jesus lived thirty-three years and did not marry or have children. Galatians 4:4 notes that Jesus was "born under the law."[1] In Matthew 5:17 Jesus declares that he came to fulfill the law, yet Jesus did not marry or have children. Finally, when speaking with Pharisees about marriage and divorce, Jesus mentions that choosing a celibate life or remaining single is a viable option (Matt 19:12). If having children was commanded by God then Jesus, who fulfilled all of God's commands, would at a minimum have supported this position in his teaching.

The notion that it is acceptable to serve God and not have children is further supported in Paul's teaching. 1 Corinthians 7:38[2] states that it may be better to stay single and devote one's life to the ministry of God than to be married. In fact, the Apostle Paul's life stands in conflict with the idea that everyone is commanded to marry and have children as he never marries or produces offspring.

---

1. Unless otherwise noted, Scripture quotations in this chapter are the author's translation.

2. Cf. 1 Cor 7:25–31.

A final note is the topic of infertility. If it is a command for all married couples to have children, then is being infertile somehow a sin or a curse? Nowhere in the Bible does it mention that the inability to have children constitutes a sin or breach of God's commands. There are examples like with Sarah and Abraham where God choses to delay conception for a specific reason. However, nowhere in the Bible is this mentioned as a response to sin.

Therefore, an initial review of the New Testament reveals that the command to "be fruitful and increase in numbers" must have a deeper meaning than merely a call to have lots of children. To uncover the intent of God's blessing upon Adam and Eve we must more closely examine where and how these words are used.

ANALYSIS OF "BE FRUITFUL AND INCREASE IN NUMBER" IN GENESIS

Now that we have completed a brief review of the theme of fruitfulness in the gospel let's turn to explore some of the key early references where God says to be fruitful and increase in number (multiply).

Adam and Eve (Gen 1:28)

The first reference to being fruitful occurs during the creation account of mankind. The NIV translation of the passage begins in v. 26 with "Then God said, 'Let us make mankind in our image, in our likeness, so that they may rule over the fish in the sea and the birds in the sky, over the livestock and all the wild animals, and over all the creatures that move along the ground.'" The passage continues in v. 28 with "God blessed them and said to them, 'Be fruitful and increase in number; fill the earth and subdue it. Rule over the fish in the sea and the birds in the sky and over every living creature that moves on the ground.'" The passage concludes by describing the breadth of mankind's dominion over all created plants and animals.

In this passage, God creates mankind as the first couple—Adam and Eve. God blesses the two with the promise of children and describes mankind's role in the stewardship of the earth. The key to understanding God's blessing is to focus on the broad theological purpose and not merely the act of procreation.

God's blessing upon Adam and Eve is similar to v. 22 for the created animals. Verse 22 reads: "God blessed them and said, 'Be fruitful and increase in number and fill the water in the seas, and let the birds increase on the earth.'" This passage concludes day five of creation and there is no further responsibility of the animals beyond increasing in number.

In contrast, the passage concerning the creation and blessing of mankind has two additional components. First, the verse adds that "God said to them," thus drawing attention to the personal relationship between God and mankind. Second, the first couple are told to subdue and rule over the earth and all the created plants and animals thereby fulfilling their role as God's image-bearer on earth (cf. v. 26).[3]

The focus here is not merely to increase in number—that would make mankind the same as the animals (cf. v. 22). Here, the focus is on *why* mankind is instructed to multiply and fill the earth. Bruce Waltke states that "Humanity is given a twofold cultural mandate: to fill the earth and to rule creation as benevolent kings (cf. Gen 9:2; Ps 8:5–8; Heb 2:5–9)."[4] God's purpose in creating mankind was that they should rule over God's other creations on God's behalf. To effect this purpose Adam and Eve must "be fruitful and multiply." It is important to note that the verb used to relate God's blessing is an imperative—thus the blessing is also a command to mankind.

Wenham adds that the dominion of mankind over nature does not give license for the unbridled exploitation and subjugation of nature. While mankind was given a kingly status, this role included the ideal of stewardship and not exploitation. "Ancient oriental kings were expected to be devoted to the welfare of their subjects, especially the poorest and weakest members of society (Ps 72:12–14). By upholding divine principles of law and justice, rulers promoted peace and prosperity for all their subjects."[5] In the same way, acting as God's representative over creation, mankind is instructed to rule over the environment and all the animals as benevolent kings.

Therefore, the blessing to be fruitful and multiply is not a stand-alone command. The blessing is an agency/task to fulfill God's purpose of filling the earth with enough people for mankind to act as God's steward over all of the Lord's creation. The blessing is given to Adam and Eve before their fall from grace and establishes them as God's viceroy over creation.

---

3. Wenham, *Genesis 1–15*, 33.

4. Waltke, *Genesis*, 67.

5. Wenham, *Genesis*, 33.

Noah (Gen 9:1–7)

Now let's turn to explore the third occurrence where God blesses mankind and tells them to "be fruitful and multiply."[6] Chapter 9 of Genesis begins with Noah and his family leaving the ark and providing an offering to God for bringing them to dry ground after the flood waters have receded. The last time God blessed mankind was before the Fall in Gen 3. Between Gen 3 and Gen 8 we learn of the depravity of mankind. Violence and reciprocal killing characterized the communal life of mankind. According to Gerhard von Rad this raised theological questions. After the fall and with the total depravity of mankind did the first command of creation, "be fruitful," still hold (Gen 1:28)? Did mankind, who had fallen from God's garden, still have God's will on its side?[7] The theological answer is clearly stated—Yes. God, despite all mankind's sin, renews his blessing on the new humanity. Similar to the blessing in Gen 1, the verb used to denote the blessing is an imperative relying that the blessing is a command upon mankind.

Verses 1–3 read: "Then God blessed Noah and his sons, saying to them, 'Be fruitful and increase in number and fill the earth. The fear and dread of you will fall on all the beasts of the earth, and . . . they are given into your hands. Everything that lives and moves about will be food for you. Just as I gave you the green plants, I now give you everything.'"

The content in this passage is like the initial blessing of mankind in Gen 1. God gives a blessing upon the new humanity using the same language to be fruitful, to increase in number, and to fill the earth that was present in Gen 1:28. Derek Kidner finds that while mankind is still in the image of God and humanity still acts as heaven's viceroy, the effects of sin have darkened the scene. Mankind's "regime will (now) be largely one of fear (v. 2), his fellow-creatures are now his food (v. 3), and violence will be abroad in the earth (v. 5, 6)."[8] The passage ends with a reminder that mankind is created in God's image (v. 6) and an echo of the command to "be fruitful and increase in number; multiply on the earth and increase upon it." (v. 7)

The context of the Noahic blessing is the same as the blessing for Adam. God is granting stewardship over all creation to Noah and his descendants. Similarly, the intent for the increase in population is to create sufficient heirs to affect God's purpose—not merely more people for the sake of increasing the world's population or because having children is a rewarding exercise.

---

6. Cf. 8:17.

7. Rad, *Genesis*, 131.

8. Kidner, *Genesis*, 100–101.

Abraham (Gen 17:1–27)

Chapter 17 conveys God's covenant with Abraham. Verses 1–6 read: "When Abram was ninety-nine years old, the Lord appeared to him and said, 'I am God Almighty; walk before me faithfully and be blameless. Then I will make my covenant between me and you and will greatly increase your numbers.' Abram fell facedown, and God said to him, 'As for me, this is my covenant with you: You will be the father of many nations. No longer will you be called Abram; your name will be Abraham, for I have made you a father of many nations. will make you very fruitful; I will make nations of you, and kings will come from you.'"

This chapter is linked to our investigation by the inclusion of two phrases. First in v. 2 with the promise by God that God himself will greatly increase Abraham's numbers (multiply) and then again in v. 6 where God will make Abraham very fruitful. Before we unpack the meaning in chap. 17, we need to first understand the earlier call of Abraham.

Chapter 17 is the ratification of a covenant that God established earlier in Gen 12. In this earlier passage, God promised Abraham the he would become a great nation with a great name (12:2), all the families of the earth would find blessing in him (v. 3), and he would prosses a land (vv. 1–2, 7). Now God is ratifying and further clarifying that promise through a covenantal address.

It is worth tracing these three aspects of the promise from the call to the covenant in order to demonstrate how chapter 17 brings the promises into sharper focus. Going to a land "that I will show you" in 12:1 becomes "this land" in v. 7. The scope of the gifted land is expanded in 13:15 to "all the land which you can see" and again in 15:18 to "from the river of Egypt to the great river, the river Euphrates." While these passages provide a general outline for the land granted to Abraham, the nation of Canaan is first explicitly mentioned in 17:8 when God states that "[t]he whole land of Canaan, where you now reside as a foreigner, I will give as an everlasting possession to you and your descendants after you."

At the beginning of chapter 12 Abraham is told that he will become a great nation. In 13:16 this promise is explained that Abraham's descendants will be as numerous as the dust of the earth and again in 15:5, where his descendants will be as many as the stars. The promise begins to be fulfilled in chapter 16 where Abraham fathers a child through whose offspring innumerable offspring would follow. Now in chapter 17 that promise is expanded and explained that Abraham will not just found a great nation (e.g., one nation), but he will father a "multitude of nations" and "kings will be descended from you" (17:4–6).

The nature of the covenant relationship is also defined more clearly in chapter 17 than previously. In 12:3 there was a vague guarantee of protection: those who bless Abraham will be blessed and his disdainers cursed. But this too becomes more explicit. Chapter 15 predicts Egyptian slavery and exodus, but 17:7 announces an eternal covenant with Abraham and his descendants, "in order to be your God and your descendants' God."

To mark these great promises, the names of Abram and Sarai are changed to the more familiar Abraham and Sarah, and the national rite of circumcision is instituted as a sign of the covenant between God and Abraham's descendants. The changing of Abram's name is significant because names convey meaning. In this case, the original name of Abram was the fusion of two Hebrew words *'Ab* (father) and *rām* (exalted).[9] The changing of the name brings a new component *hamôn* (multiple). Therefore, the original meaning of Abram's name was "he is exalted as to his father" (likely referring to God as father); however, it is also possible that the name refers to Abraham as "exalted father." God is now changing the name to "the exalted father of a multitude" (likely referring to Abraham as the father).

Moving back to explore the linkage to our study of being fruitful and increasing in number, the key is found in 17:6 when God states "I will make you very fruitful . . ." Here the Hebrew root *prh* (fruit), regularly paired with *rbh* (multiply), reappears, linking this verse with v. 2. To "be fruitful and increase in numbers" was the first command given to mankind (1:28) and was repeated to Noah in 8:17 and 9:1, 7. Wenham finds that a similar remark is made to Abraham, who like Adam and Noah, stands at the beginning of an epoch in human history. God's original purpose for mankind, thwarted by the fall and faltering again in the post-Noah period, is eventually to be achieved by Abraham's descendants.[10] Unlike the prior two passages we discussed, the verb used to relate God's message is no longer an imperative but a reflexive verb. This changes the action from a command on mankind to an action that will be conducted and completed by God himself. Wenham notes that "this change of conjugation suggests that Abraham will be given divine power to achieve this fertility, whereas his predecessors. Left simply to themselves, failed."[11]

The key to understanding the passage begins with God's second speech. Abraham is not simply to become a great nation (12:2) but to become the

9. The name Abram is attested throughout the second- and first-millennium BC Akkadian and Ugaritic texts with the meaning noble birth and he is exalted as to his father. The Akkadian root for *rāmu* can mean "to love," which adds "loving father" as a possible (but less likely) translation.

10. Wenham, *Genesis 16–50*, 22.

11. Ibid.

father of a multitude of nations. His name is changed to confirm that this action, to "father of a multitude" as a lasting guarantee of God's covenant, will be performed by God. Adam and Noah had simply been told to be fruitful (1:28; 9:1). Here the action is changed so that God will complete what he commands. Abraham will be enabled to achieve the impossible through divine aid. Furthermore, through Abraham God's plans for humanity will be realized. Indeed, kings will now descend from Abraham. The strong suggestion is that Abrahams offspring will fulfill the other aspect of mankind's original mandate to have dominion over creation (1:28).

Just as important, however, are the fresh remarks about the covenant (vv. 7–8). Already implicit in 12:1–3 and 15:18, it is now defined more precisely with a view to its confirmation or ratification. This covenant is not simply between God and Abraham but between God and Abraham's descendants "after you throughout their generations." It is to be an "eternal covenant." Similar to the covenant made with Noah, the nature of the covenant demonstrates that a permanent relationship is envisaged, as durable as life itself (cf. 8:20–22; 9:11). This relationship with Abraham's descendants is to be unique because, unlike the other nations, Israel enjoys a unique relationship with the one true God.

A key feature of the covenant with Abraham and his descendants is their required response. God has taken upon himself the difficult task of providing land, descendants, nations, and kings. All that is left for Abraham and his descendants is to provide a demonstration of acceptance. Abraham is to institute the circumcision of all the males in his household. While this practice was well known in Canaan and the ancient Near East, God commands the practice for those accepting the covenant—investing a singular significance in the practice. The enduring mark of circumcision reflects the eternity of the covenant, the permanent bond between God and Abraham's descendants (17:13). Most importantly, it is a sign of the covenant (v. 11) that reminds the Israelites of their special spiritual relationship and of their obligation to walk before God and be perfect.

Essentially, circumcision as the sign of the covenant becomes synonymous with being a descendant of Abraham and heir to God's promises. Therefore, one who is circumcised is grafted into the covenant and the promise of being fruitful, increasing in number, having land, becoming a nation, and being associated with kings.

As with the prior two passages we are left with the hermeneutical question—so what is the point? Is Abraham to be fruitful and increase in numbers merely so that he might possess land, found nations, and produce kings? Waltke argues that God's promise to make Abraham a father of many nations should be understood, on the one hand, in a purely biological sense.

Through Hagar, Abraham physically "begets" the Ishmaelites (cf. 17:20; 21:13; 25:12–18); through Keturah, the Midianites, among others (25:14). Through Isaac and Rebekah, the Edomistes (cf. 25:23; 36:1–43). This interpretation is validated by the genealogies of Keturah (25:1–4), Ishmael (25:12–18), and Edom (chap. 36).[12]

Waltke goes on to argue that the promise should also be understood as a reference to the nations that reproduce his faith. Essentially, the descendants of Abraham are the people who follow the theological teaching of God. This cannot be said of the Ishmaelites, the Edomites, or the descendants of Keturah. Significantly, whereas God says that kings will be born from Abraham's loins, God does not say that of the nations' Abraham will father.[13] Therefore, this passage continues to support and further clarifies that the theological intent is that Abraham will multiply and produce kings so that mankind may act as God's viceroy and agents on the earth. In addition, that the descendants of Abraham will theologically reach out to all nations of the earth.

If this is correct, then we should be able to identify the theme of the descendants of Abraham as God's agents on earth throughout the balance of the Old Testament and into the New Testament.

UNITY OF FRUITFULNESS AND INCREASING IN NUMBER IN THE OLD TESTAMENT

Several passages in the balance of the Old Testament continue the theme of fruitfulness and increasing in number. In the previous section, we found that the theme of fruitfulness was closely tied to the Abrahamic Covenant. This meant that to be fruitful and increase in number is linked to God's promise that Abraham's descendants would poses the land given by God, form nations, and generate kings. The sign of this relationship is circumcision. Let's now turn to explore how this theme of fruitfulness, God's covenant with Abraham, and the sign of the covenant are lived out in the rest of the Old Testament.

The theme is evident with Abraham's heir and continuing throughout the Pentateuch. In Gen 26:4 God repeats the Abrahamic promises to Isaac saying "I will make your descendants as numerous as the stars in the sky and will give them all these lands, and through your offspring all nations on earth will be blessed." This passage clearly links the blessing of Adam's

12. Waltke, *Genesis*, 47.

13. Ibid.

fruitfulness with the ongoing Abrahamic covenant. These promises are then relayed to Jacob/Israel and Joseph (Gen 28:3; 35:11; 47:27; 48:4).

The Bible continues the theme through the time of Moses. As the narrative of Exodus begins, the narrator affirms that "the Israelites were exceedingly fruitful; they multiplied greatly, increased in numbers and became so numerous that the land was filled with them" (Exod 1:7). When giving the Law to Moses, God affirms the link between fruitfulness and the covenant when he states that "I will look on you with favor and make you fruitful and increase your numbers, and I will keep my covenant with you" (Lev 26:9).

The psalmist supports this interpretation. Below, Ps 87:4–6 anticipates the nations becoming part of the people of God by rebirth:

> "I will record Rahab and Babylon
>> among those who acknowledge me—
> Philistia too, and Tyre, along with Cush—
>> and will say, 'This one was born in Zion.'"
> Indeed, of Zion it will be said,
> "This one and that one were born in her,
>> and the Most High himself will establish her."
> The Lord will write in the register of the peoples:
>> "This one was born in Zion."

This passage supports our theme in two ways. First, biologically the passage demonstrates that the blessing given to Adam and Noah is realized as all the people of the earth are still under God's dominion. Second, theologically the passage supports the connection to Abraham that those nations who have rebelled against God can be grafted into the promise of Abraham through faith.

The theme continues into the prophetic texts. The prophet Jeremiah was likely born during the reign of king Manasseh (645 BC) and prophesied from the time of king Josiah's positive reforms through the downfall and deportation of the Judahites into the Babylonian Exile. Toward the end of Jeremiah's prophetic activity and just before Judah goes into exile, God foreshadows the exile declaring that the scattering of the Judahites and Israelites is due to the sinful actions of the people and especially the sin of the leaders. However, all is not lost as God will bring them home. God tells Jeremiah "I myself will gather the remnant of my flock out of all the countries where I have driven them and will bring them back to their pasture, where they will be fruitful and increase in number" (Jer 23:4). God ties the promises made to Adam, Noah, and Abraham to the remnant of Israelites that will be brought home from exile in Babylon and provides a clear metaphor that God will gather true believers to himself.

Ezekiel is a sixth-century BC prophet who was taken into exile in Babylon with the first wave of Judeans in 597 BC. The prophet speaks the word of God to the people who were living in Babylon during the time of the exile. As the exilic period ends, Ezekiel shares a message from God to the people. In this prophecy, God is speaking to the mountains and ground in Israel and Judah about the fate of the exiles. God affirms that the mountains and the landscape have suffered from a lack of attention (because the people were removed). The Lord continues by assuring the fields and trees that a time will come where they are productive again. In v. 11 God begins to discuss the role of the returning exiles and says, "I will increase the number of people and animals living on you, and they will be fruitful and become numerous. I will settle people on you as in the past and will make you prosper more than before. Then you will know that I am the Lord." This passage continues the link between being fruitful and filling the land that we found with Adam. At the end of the statement we find the "so what" of the prophecy. The fruitfulness and increasing in numbers is not an end in itself. The point is twofold. First, and most importantly, it is so the entire created order will know more about and be in relationship with God. Secondly, the land needs a steward to care for God's creation. This passage clearly shows that mankind will return to the land so the creation of God may reach its potential.

The theme of being fruitful and increasing in number is evident throughout the Old Testament. Usually this theme is found in close connection to the Abrahamic covenant and God's promise of land, progeny, nationhood, and kings. The sign of the covenant is circumcision and it is relevant for us to spend a little time exploring the meaning and relationship of circumcision in the balance of the Old Testament.

Shortly after the time of the Patriarchs, God speaks to Moses and about the circumcision of the heart as the key sign of the covenant with Abraham (Lev 26:41). In this way, the people of Israel need to repent and commit themselves to God in order to be in relationship. This sentiment is echoed in Deuteronomy when the Lord speaks to Moses from the mountain on what is required to be in relationship. Verses 12–16 read:

> And now, Israel, what does the Lord your God ask of you but to fear the Lord your God, to walk in obedience to him, to love him, to serve the Lord your God with all your heart and with all your soul, and to observe the Lord's commands and decrees that I am giving you today for your own good? To the Lord your

> God belong the heavens, even the highest heavens, the earth and
> everything in it. Yet the Lord set his affection on your ancestors
> and loved them, and he chose you, their descendants, above all
> the nations—as it is today. Circumcise your hearts, therefore,
> and do not be stiff-necked any longer.

The key to the covenant is not a physical act of circumcision. Instead,
God is looking for an act of faith as confirmation of the promises given to
Abraham. This circumcision of the heart is again mentioned at the end of
God's covenant with Moses where God will "circumcise your hearts and the
hearts of your descendants, so that you may love him with all your heart and
with all your soul, and live" (Deut 30:6).

The connection between the circumcision of the heart and relationship with God through the Abrahamic covenant is echoed in the prophets.
Turning again to Jeremiah and Ezekiel we find a similar message. In Jeremiah when the people are being warned to repent God calls to Judah and
Jerusalem, saying to "[b]reak up your unplowed ground and do not sow
among thorns. Circumcise yourselves to the Lord, circumcise your hearts,
you people of Judah and inhabitants of Jerusalem, or my wrath will flare up
and burn like fire because of the evil you have done—burn with no one to
quench it" (Jer 4:3–4). This sentiment is repeated when Jeremiah prophesies
about a new covenant of the heart (31:31–34). Similarly, Ezekiel equates
unbelievers as "uncircumcised in the heart" (Ezek 44:7–9).

This brief review of fruitfulness in the Old Testament confirms several
conclusions. First, God's promise for mankind to be fruitful and increase
in number is supported throughout the Old Testament. Second, the intent to increase in number is in a greater context than just multiplying the
population. Third, there is a clear link between God's promise to increase in
number and God's covenant with Abraham. Therefore, there is also a link
between the symbol of circumcision as the sign of the Abrahamic covenant
and fruitfulness. Finally, fourth, the intent of increasing in number to become a steward of the earth finds support in the prophetic books.

IMPLICATIONS FOR READING THE NEW TESTAMENT

Turning to the New Testament, we need to understand how the Abrahamic
covenant is fulfilled. The promises of the covenant are effective upon Abraham's heirs. The Jews at the time of the New Testament understood this
literally, either 1) to be under the covenant one had to be born a Jew or 2)
one could come under the covenant if they were physically circumcised. The

New Testament teaches that anyone could be grafted into the descendants of Abraham (and therefore into the family of God) if they believed in Jesus.

Jesus serves as the link between the people of God (i.e., the spiritual offspring of Abraham) and Abraham's physical offspring promised in the Abrahamic covenant. At the end of Matthew Jesus asserts his authority over all nations and commissions his disciples to make disciples of all nations, teaching them to obey everything he had commanded them (Matt 28:18–20). Similarly, Mark records a scene where Jesus's physical mother and brothers stand outside the house where Jesus is teaching. To those seated in the circle around him he asks, "who are my mother and my brothers?" Looking at this same group of people Jesus rhetorically responds, "Here are my mother and brothers! Whoever does God's will is my brother and sister and mother" (Mark 3:33–35). In Luke, Jesus forecasts through the parable of the tenants that God will take the vineyard (i.e., the right to be the people chosen to mediate his moral rule) away from Israel and give it to the Gentiles (Luke 20:9–19). In John, Jesus speaks of having other sheep (i.e., the Gentiles) who "are not of this sheep pen" (i.e., physical Israel) (John 10:16). Each of these establishes that all mankind (including Gentiles) can be part of the family of Abraham if they have faith in Jesus.

Paul and Barnabas fulfill what Jesus predicts. Abraham's physical offspring had the first opportunity to represent God's rule and mediate the blessing (Acts 3:25). But when the Jews reject the gospel, Paul turns away from them to the Gentiles (Acts 13:46; 18:6). By the second century the church was composed almost entirely of Gentiles. In Galatians, Paul refers to the seed God covenanted to give Abraham as finding fulfillment uniquely in Jesus (Gal 3:15–29).

In Romans, Paul interprets God's promise to make Abraham a father of many nations in the sense that they reproduce his faith. The church at Rome undoubtedly had representatives from many nations at the center of the Roman Empire. To them the apostle writes,

> Therefore, the promise comes by faith, so that it may be by grace and may be guaranteed to all Abraham's offspring—not only to those who are of the law but also to those who have the faith of Abraham. He is the father of us all. As it is written: "I have made you a father of many nations." He is our father in the sight of God, in whom he believed—the God who gives life to the dead and calls into being things that were not. (Rom 4: 16–17)

Paul goes on in Rom 16:20, likely identifying the promised seed of Eve with the church at Rome, which represents the nations subject to his rule: "The God of peace will soon crush Satan under your feet." However,

Paul adds in Romans that God is not yet finished with Abraham's physical progeny. God always retains a remnant among them who also reproduce Abraham's faith. Indeed, the apostle implies that they may again become the dominant group among the people of God (see Rom 11).

Finally, using language reminiscent of Gen 17, Rev 7:9 envisions, "there before me was a great multitude that no one could count, from every nation, tribe, people and language, standing before the throne and before the Lamb. They were wearing white robes and were holding palm branches in their hands" praising God. This passage brings us full circle from the beginning of creation to the fulfillment of the blessing to be fruitful and increase in number. Under the new covenant, Abraham's spiritual seed fulfills God's plan to have mankind increase in number and act as God's viceroy on earth. Most importantly, all of mankind comes together to praise God. This review of the New Testament demonstrates that to "be fruitful and increase in number" is closely tied to the evangelistic goal of spreading the gospel message and increasing the number of believers in Christ.

IMPLICATIONS FOR AND IDENTITY WITH
THE MODERN CHRISTIAN CHURCH

One test remains for our analysis, and that is to take the exegetical information that we found in our analysis of the theme of "be fruitful and increase in number" and determine how that theme should be applied to the modern church. In Gen 1:28 God blessed Adam and Eve and said to them, "Be fruitful and increase in number; fill the earth and subdue it. Rule over the fish in the sea and the birds in the sky and over every living creature that moves on the ground." At face value the blessing is straight forward and simple—go and be fruitful and increase in number—in other words, go have babies.

Therefore, our first hermeneutical take-a-way from the study is that children are a blessing from God. This finding is supported in several passages including Ps 127:3, which explores the theme of legacy and the necessity for God at the center of life. The passage reads: "Children are a gift from the Lord. They are a reward from [God]" (cf. RNIV, Ps 113:9). This theme of children as a gift from God and legacy for the family is echoed in Prov 17:6: "Grandchildren are like a crown to older people. And children are proud of their parents." In another example, Joseph gives God the credit for providing children when Joseph introduces his children to Israel (his father), who passes along the family blessing (Gen 48:9; cf. 33:5).

Children are clearly a blessing from the Lord and they bring joy to a family and a sense of legacy. However, the core meaning of Gen 1:28 goes deeper. The imperative command of the blessing is to have children *so that* mankind can 1) fill the earth, 2) subdue creation, and 3) rule over God's creation. Let's focus on the second and third points, which are ongoing commands. Our second hermeneutical finding is that the modern church needs to act as God's stewards over creation.

But what does that mean? When we talk about dominion (rule over), it's helpful to think of it this way: As God's image bearers in creation, we were commanded to act as his representatives. We were designed, in a very real way, to show the world what God is like (see Gen 1:26). So, when God gave us the command to rule over the earth, the expectation was to do so in a way that reflected his character. Ezekiel 34:4 unpacks God's expectation of stewardship. In a tirade against Israel's kings, God says through the prophet, "You have not strengthened the weak or healed the sick or bound up the injured. You have not brought back the strays or searched for the lost. You have ruled them harshly and brutally."

The dominion that God desires is one that protects the defenseless and gives justice to the oppressed. Applying this to the command for humanity to exercise dominion over creation, we can see that while we rule over creation, we're called (as stewards) to protect it. The Bible outlines the role of the king in an ancient Near Eastern context. As an ancient Near Eastern king accepts tribute or taxes from his subjects, so too we may receive a bountiful sustenance from the fruits of creation. Yet also as a king should take care of the weak and poor in his kingdom, so too we are called to guard natural beauty, preserve endangered species of God's creatures, and even to restore the places that we have too often ruled "harshly and brutally."

Finally, and perhaps most importantly, we need to explore the enduring understanding of being fruitful and increasing in number. As we traced the idea of being fruitful and increasing in number through Adam and Noah to Abraham it became clear that the first fulfillment of God's promise to Adam was in the Abrahamic covenant.

However, the ultimate fulfillment of the Abrahamic promise for descendants and kings is fulfilled in Christ. With the coming of Jesus as the Messiah, the New Testament demonstrates several points of relationship to the Abrahamic Covenant. First, Jesus is viewed as the one whom God sent to effect the deliverance of Israel from her enemies according to his promises to Abraham (Luke 1:54–55, 68–75). Keith Essex argues that "this deliverance will be accomplished, and the Abrahamic Covenant fully fulfilled, when the Messiah causes the Israelites to repent (Acts 3:25–26). It will be at the time of Israel's repentance which will lead to the period of restoration of all things spoken by the prophets, including Israel's possession of and prosperity in the land of Canaan (Acts 3:19–24)."[14]

Second, the New Testament portrays the nation of Israel as descendants of Abraham's seed (cf. Luke 16:24; 19:9; John 8:37; Acts 13:26; Rom 11:1). However, being the physical "seed" of Abraham does not necessarily mean that they will experience the fulfillment of the blessings associated with the promise (Matt 8:11; Luke 13:28). Just as with Gentiles, an Israelite must come to faith leading to repentance to experience the Lord's deliverance and blessing (Acts 3:19–26).

Third, the New Testament calls Gentile believers "the seed of Abraham" because of their adoption by Jesus through faith (Gal 3:6–29). Galatians 3:16 reads, "The promises were spoken to Abraham and to his seed. Scripture does not say 'and to seeds,' meaning many people, but 'and to your seed,' meaning one person, who is Christ." This passage specifies that Jesus, as the Messiah, is the seed described in the covenant and the one who conveys the blessings of the Abrahamic covenant to both the Israelites and the Gentiles (cf. Gen 22:17b–18). According to Essex, the church today experiences in Christ some spiritual benefits that Israel and the nations will experience (with physical results) in the future when Jesus implements fully the blessings of the Abrahamic Covenant. The New Testament, like the Old, views the complete fulfillment of the Lord's promises to Abraham as a future event (Matt 8:11; Acts 3:19–26; Rom 11:25–32).[15]

Therefore, the individuals in the church enter into the promises of blessing given to those in Christ and to this extent are the *spiritual* children of Abraham. This is expressly stated in Gal 3:7: "Understand, then, that those who have faith are children of Abraham." The passage continues: "Scripture foresaw that God would justify the Gentiles by faith, and announced the gospel in advance to Abraham: 'All nations will be blessed through you.' So those who rely on faith are blessed along with Abraham, the man of faith" (Gal 3:8–9). In other words, those who believe in Jesus are grafted into the promises and blessings given to Adam, Noah, and Abraham.

Galatians 3:7–9 also provides the link for understanding "be fruitful and increase in number" to the modern church. One of the primary goals to increasing in number for the Abrahamic covenant is to enlarge the number of believers in God. This aspect of the promise is now identified with Jesus and with spreading the gospel message and creating a multitude of believers (Rev 7:9). Therefore, perhaps the most important enduring interpretation for "be fruitful and increase in number" is to expand the number of

14. Essex, "The Abrahamic Covenant," 211.
15. Ibid., 212.

Christians through evangelism, as Matt 28:18–20 commands: "Then Jesus came to them and said, 'All authority in heaven and on earth has been given to me. Therefore, go and make disciples of all nations, baptizing them in the name of the Father and of the Son and of the Holy Spirit, and teaching them to obey everything I have commanded you. And surely I am with you always, to the very end of the age.'"

QUESTIONS FOR FURTHER STUDY

Discussion Questions

1) After reading the chapter and in light of Gen 1:28, should the church hold a position on the use of contraception methods after marriage?

2) After reading the chapter and considering Gen 1:28, what should the Christian position be on protecting the environment?

3) The Apostle Paul chose not to have children. Did he violate God's command in Gen 1:28 to "be fruitful and increase in number"?

Assignments

1) Word Study: be fruitful

   There are twenty-nine occurrences of verb to be fruitful (*prh*) in the Old Testament. Create a chart and identify each of the occurrences with the translation of the verse where the verb is used. In a column to the right of the verse summarize the intent of the use of the verb and whether this use can be linked to the use in Gen 1:28. Below the chart add a concluding paragraph that summarize the different ways that the verb might be translated and the best understanding of the word in Gen 1:28. You may want to use the following link to help with your study: http://biblehub.com/hebrew/6509.htm

2) Word Study: Subdue/Dominion/Rule over

   Genesis 1:28 uses two verbs to describe the relationship between mankind and God's creation. The verb for "subdue" (*kbsh*) is found in Gen 1:28 and fourteen other places in the Old Testament. Similarly, there are twenty-seven occurrences of verb to "rule over" (*rdh*) in the Old Testament. Create a chart and identify each of the occurrences with the translation of the verse where the verbs are used. In a column to the right of the verse summarize the intent of the use of the verb and whether this use can be linked to the use in Gen 1:28. Below the chart add a paragraph summarizing the different ways that the verb might be translated and the best understanding of the word in Gen 1:28. You may want to use the following link to help with your study: http://biblehub.com/hebrew/7287.htm and http://biblehub.com/hebrew/3533.htm

3) Comparative Theological Study

Complete a study on the use of Gen 1:28 in different denominations. Summarize the interpretations by three or four different denominations/theological traditions on contraception and the development of families—especially where the theological positions rely upon Gen 1:28 for support. At a minimum, include the Catholic tradition, one Protestant tradition, and the Mormon tradition. Then provide a conclusion with your personal interpretation of Gen 1:28 and how the passage should impact a family's decision to have children.

4) Interviews

Read Gen 1:28 to five friends (preferably from your church) and ask them what is the meaning of the passage for: 1) Adam and Eve; and 2) the modern church. Summarize their answers and outline where your friends were correct and where they might be wrong in their interpretation.

BIBLIOGRAPHY AND RECOMMENDED READING

Blaising, Craig A., and Darrell L. Bock. *Progressive Dispensationalism.* Wheaton, IL: BridgePoint, 1993.

Essex, Keith H. "The Abrahamic Covenant." *MSJ* 10 (1999) 191–212.

Kidner, Derek. *Genesis: An Introduction and Commentary.* TOTC. Downers Grove, IL: InterVarsity, 1967.

Rad, Gerhard von. *Genesis.* Rev. ed. OTL. Philadelphia: Westminster, 1972.

Saucy, Robert L. *The Case for Progressive Dispensationalism: The Interface between Dispensational & Non-Dispensational Theology.* Grand Rapids: Zondervan, 1993.

Waltke, Bruce K. *Genesis: A Commentary.* Grand Rapids: Zondervan, 2001.

Wenham, Gordon J. *Genesis 1–15.* WBC 1. Dallas: Word, 1987.

———. *Genesis 16–50.* WBC 2. Dallas: Word, 1994.

3

THE FALL

JAMES SPENCER

INTRODUCTION

The fall of humanity has been the subject of a great deal of theological reflection. The narration of the disobedience of the first human couple is a core component of Israel's national narrative. This chapter will examine the fall through an analysis of the dynamics of Gen 3:1–7 in relation to structural evil. Though it is not often treated in a formal, systematic, or even explicit, fashion, structural evil is available in the works of several theologians. Augustine, for instance, describes the difficult interplay that exists between individuals and society by noting his experience in positions that "require the holder to be loved and feared by men." Such positions have the capacity to diminish one's potential and hold one captive to humanity's praise. In this manner, the joy that Augustine once placed in the truth is transferred to the "deceitfulness of men." Augustine's experience reveals the difficulty of separating from social conventions and the dynamics that govern them. It is the difficulty of escaping humanity's "well done, well done." The presence of sin in this case is evident in the social practices that inspire individuals "to be loved and feared, not for Thy sake, but in Thy stead" (*Confessions* 36.59).

Cornelius Plantinga suggests that structural evil is intimately connected to personal evil and "comprises a vast historical and cultural matrix that includes traditions, old patterns of relationship and behavior, atmospheres of expectation, social habits."[1] In describing social or structural evil, Plantinga does not absolve humanity from responsibility for sin. Instead, he extends individual culpability for evil by highlighting the impact of individual acts of evil on the world around us. He notes,

> Though we cannot always measure culpability for it, we do know that sin possesses appalling force. We know that when we sin, we pervert, adulterate, and destroy good things. We create matrices and atmospheres of moral evil and bequeath them to our descendants. By habitual practice, we let loose a great, rolling momentum of moral and spiritual evil across generations. By doing such things, we involve ourselves deeply in what theologians call corruption.[2]

While we do not fully comprehend the extent of our individual acts and ongoing participation in evil, whether knowingly or unknowingly, we are not innocent in the creation of the world around us or in the evil that occurs within it.

It is important to note that evil is not confined to intentionally evil acts. Surely intentional acts of evil contribute to structural evil in a variety of ways, but structural evil also comes "through ignorant if well-intentioned choices."[3] The reciprocal relationship between personal and structural evil, as well as the often unintentional complicity that perpetuates structural evil underscores the complexities involved in identifying, examining, avoiding, resisting, and counteracting structural evil. Individuals live within a series of relationships. They live in relationship to the natural world, to other humans, to institutions and organizations, to governments, and to God. Charles Taylor describes the way people understand these relationships in terms of "social imaginaries," or "the ways people imagine their social existence, how they fit together with others, how things go on between them and their fellows, the expectations that are normally met, and the deeper normative notions and images that underlie these expectations."[4]

Individual and corporate social imagination provides a sort of logic or sense through which humans navigate complex interactions on a day-to-day

1. Plantinga, *Not the Way It's Supposed to Be*, 25.

2. Ibid., 27.

3. Murphy, "On the Priority of Personal to Structural Evil in Catholic Social Teaching," 150.

4. Taylor, *Modern Social Imaginaries*, 23.

basis. Such imagination is inspired by human notions of order, fairness, and, ultimately, fitting participation within a given social imaginary. In other words, the social imaginary provides the background for behaviors and those behaviors reinforce the social imaginary. As such, behaviors often betray aspects of individual or corporate social imaginaries, which "begins to define the contours of their [the participants'] world and can eventually come to count as the taken-for-granted shape of things, too obvious to mention."[5]

Thinking about structural evil in terms of Taylor's concept of social imaginaries offers a new means of describing the phenomenon of structural evil that recognizes the interdependence of the background understandings that provide context for actions and for the actions themselves.[6] Structural evil does not excuse intentional acts of evil, nor does it bracket out one's culpability for unintentional evil acts. Instead, structural evil recognizes that evil acts, whether intentional or unintentional, individual or collective, are undergirded by common understandings of how society is ordered, as well as reinforcing or otherwise influencing that common understanding. At root, structural evil is a theological problem whereby the underlying order of things is misrecognized resulting in a number of distortions some of which we notice and others which we don't.

THE FALL, STRUCTURAL EVIL, AND THE GOSPEL

While the gospel is often rightly discussed in terms of individual forgiveness of sins, the gospel entails far more than the salvation of individuals. It also impacts the manner in which those individuals relate to one another and to the world around them. If, as argued above, structural evil is the misrecognition of the fundamental order of God's creation, the gospel is the good news that proclaims the true order of things and gives a sure hope to all creation that God's order will be restored.

Salvation by grace through faith has implications for the individual soul and for the whole of creation. Living in light of the gospel means more than acting ethically or morally. Rather, living in light of the gospel means that God empowers us to be at peace finding strength and solace in the knowledge that our troubles are "light and momentary. . .achieving for us an eternal glory that far outweighs them all" (2 Cor 4:17). We have, through the gospel, a hope that allows us to break away from the misrecognized order

---

5. Taylor, *Secular Age*, 176.

6. Ibid., 29–30.

of structural evil in order to represent God faithfully by conforming to the image of Christ.

The gospel is the slap in the face we need to dismiss our delusions about ourselves and the world. It reminds us of the leveling power of depravity and the common ground that all humanity finds in the need for God's grace (Eph 2:8–22). It reminds us that the powerful serve at the will and whim of our God. It reminds us that we do not belong to this world, but that "our citizenship is in heaven, and from it we await a Savior, the Lord Jesus Christ" (Phil 3:20). Ultimately, the gospel calls and empowers God's people to align with God participating with him as he reorders creation according to his perfect will and wisdom.

ANALYSIS OF GENESIS 3:1–7

After narrating the creation of the world and all things in it, the book of Genesis focuses in on a set of specific events in the garden. We find the serpent conversing with the woman who has been placed in the garden with man. The serpent is characterized as "crafty." This English translation does not preserve the ambiguity of the Hebrew term (*arum*), which is not always used with negative connotations (Prov 12:23; 13:8; 14:15). As modern readers, we know the story and recognize that the serpent is an agent of chaos. Within the narrative, however, it is important to allow the character of the serpent to emerge since it is not necessarily clear that the woman automatically recognizes the serpent as her enemy.[7] Part of what the woman is trying to determine is whether the serpent represents life or death.

The serpent's line of questioning takes advantage of this ambiguity. While the first question has often been understood as clarifying the content of God's command to the human couple, there is good reason to understand the question in a slightly different manner. The Hebrew construction that begins the serpent's question in Gen 3:1 may be better understood as a rhetorical interjection that highlights the exaggerated nature of the statement. In other words, it is not so much that the serpent is trying to clarify the original content of the command. Instead, the serpent is attempting to highlight the absurdity and severity of that command.[8]

7. Joines states that "the serpent in Gen 3 represents the embodiment of a strange combination of life, wisdom, and chaos" (Joines, "Serpent in Gen 3," 9). When the woman looks at the serpent, she does not necessarily see it as a symbol of evil and chaos, but of wisdom and life.

8. Hamilton takes a similar view (*Book of Genesis*, 186). Speiser also concludes that 3:1 is not a question suggesting that the combination is a "half-interrogative, half-reflective exclamation." See Skinner, *Genesis*, 73.

Reading the initial question in this manner, the serpent's words might be paraphrased as "What more could God demand! Has he said, 'You shall not eat from any of the trees in the garden!?!" In essence, the serpent is implying that by denying the human couple the fruit from the tree of the knowledge of good and evil, God is withholding something essential and might as well starve the human couple. The serpent has accused God of being less-than fully benevolent in keeping the human couple from eating the fruit of the tree of the knowledge of good and evil.

In this light, the woman's response is not a misquotation, but an interpretation of the command. The woman does not doubt God's benevolence, but suggests that God has prohibited the tree's fruit for the good of her and her husband. The combination of "eat" and "touch" is found again in legislative contexts which prohibit the handling or eating of various unclean animals (Lev 11:8; Deut 14:8). The use of this language suggests that the woman is drawing a connection between the nature of the tree (i.e. that it is unclean) and the rationale for God's prohibition. The tree has some inherent flaw that makes it deadly to the human couple.

Having listened to the woman's explanation, the serpent now makes explicit his accusation against God. There is nothing wrong with the tree. God's prohibition is motivated by self-interest and a desire to deprive the man and woman so that they do not reach their full potential. God wants to keep them under his thumb. The man and the woman will never achieve their highest stature unless they break loose from God's command and begin to fulfill their own destiny.[9]

As the woman examines the tree, the plausibility of her explanation begins to fade. The tree was "good for food" and "a delight to the eyes" (Gen 3:6). Being persuaded by the serpent's wisdom and trusting now that the serpent is indeed an agent of life, she also recognizes that the tree offers wisdom (v. 6). Unfortunately, the woman misjudges the serpent. Rather than bringing life and wisdom, the serpent points the human couple toward chaos. By choosing to believe that God's order was wrong and that they should somehow be able to transcend their position in the cosmos to be equal with God, the human couple disobey God's command. They misrecognize their place in the world, doubt God, and, as a consequence, must

---

9. Sailhamer states, "The centerpiece of the story is the question of the knowledge of the 'good'. The snake implied by his questions that God was keeping this knowledge *from* the man and the woman, while the sense of the narratives in the first two chapters has been that God was keeping this knowledge *for* the man and the woman" (Sailhamer, *The Pentateuch as Narrative*, 103–4). Walton's analysis is similar, though he identifies conceptual parallels within ancient Near Eastern literature (204–6).

now live a cursed existence in which God, humanity, and the rest of creation are not rightly related.

THE FALL AND STRUCTURAL EVIL
IN THE OLD TESTAMENT

Pharaoh's efforts to curtail the multiplication of Israel not only represents the evil musings of one man, but also the sort of evil that derives from a particular societal order. The purpose of the increased labor and genocide implemented by Pharaoh against Israel was to curtail the growth of the nation and to prevent Israel from joining Egypt's enemies in the event of an attack. The comparison of the previous Pharaoh and the Pharaoh "who knew not Joseph" highlights the second Pharaoh's dismissal of God. The systematic oppression of the Israelites reflects the Pharaoh's dependence on his own power to provide security for Egypt. That this dependence manifests itself in the inhumane treatment of Israel is rooted in the underlying assumption that what Pharaoh has built must be protected at all costs.

Pharaoh's program against Israel is rooted in taken-for-granted assumptions about the world and God's activity in it. The political and economic dimensions of Pharaoh's activities are not simply an individual perversion, but the extension of the logic of a system dependent on tyranny, military strength, and material production. In other words, Pharaoh has no viable choice, but to oppress Israel because of his commitment to a particular way of life. Egypt could not stand unless Pharaoh had a workforce that was constantly working to produce wealth. Similarly, this workforce had to be constrained because Egypt's security was guaranteed not by its faith in the one true God, but by its military capacity to defeat those who opposed it. This way of thinking denies God's ability to provide without labor and to protect without military might. Pharaoh, despite being given alternatives, would have been hard pressed to shake off the logic of the system that he had seen build Egypt into an impressive empire.

Structural evil is also evident in the pronouncements of the prophets against the established systems of power which exhibit and are guided by human rather than divine wisdom.[10] The frequent condemnation of oppressive practices designed to increase personal wealth and security, injunctions related to the perversion of religious practice, and general dismissal of God's

---

10. VanGemeren discusses the *real politic* and the *vox populi* as standing in opposition, in many ways, to each other and to divine revelation. VanGemeren, *Interpreting the Prophetic Word*. The conflict between *real politic* and *vox populi* and divine revelation suggests the presence of social or structural evil.

power through dependence on political alliances, characterize a social system with underlying assumptions concerning the value of material wealth and militaristic strength. Worse still is the false theology that, at times, arose in relation to religious structures. At various points in Israel's history, the people and their leaders attempted to use spiritual disciplines such as fasting and Sabbath to manipulate God as if he were obligated to respond to their piety. Similarly, the people and their leaders also mistakenly thought that God was somehow tied to Israel in a way that precluded judgment.

Jeremiah 7, for instance, critiques the underlying assumptions related to the association of the physical temple with God's continued blessing and protection of Israel. The false sense of security fostered by the existence of the temple reinforces the practice of false worship and the continuation of . God's continued presence, as witnessed by the physical temple, was seen as an implicit legitimation of Israelite practice. The role of the prophet in this case is to correct and reorient the community's vision by helping them to recognize rightly their misplaced assumptions and providing them with appropriate theological perspectives which would reshape their character and motivate faithful action.

THE FALL AND STRUCTURAL EVIL
IN THE NEW TESTAMENT

Romans 1:18–32 demonstrates a dynamic similar to that described regarding structural evil. Here the natural is exchanged for the unnatural as a consequence of human disobedience. This exchange and God's subsequent giving over of humanity to a "depraved mind" resulted not only in the development of a disposition toward wickedness, but in the approval of those who practice such wickedness (v. 32). This approval may well be akin to what Augustine identified as the "Well done! Well done!" of mankind in relation to Jas 4:4. He references the "well done" again in his discussion of offices. Concerning the "third kind of temptation" which involved being "feared and loved of men," Augustine notes,

> Because now certain offices of human society make it necessary to be loved and feared of men, the adversary of our true blessedness layers hard at us, every where spreading his snares of "well-done, well-done"; that greedily catching at them, we may be taken unawares, and sever our joy from Thy truth, and set it in the deceivingness of men; and be pleased at being loved and feared, not for Thy sake, but in Thy stead . . .[11]

11. *Confessions*, 36.59 (trans. Pusey, 173).

As Augustine clearly recognizes, the affirmation of humankind can become a hindrance to the pursuit of God. On first examination, however, such affirmation does not appear pernicious, but, as Augustine's description makes clear, these affirmations are deceptively damaging to one's desires, potentially misdirecting them toward creaturely praises and away from true praise of God.

The gospels offer what are possibly the most significant instances of structural evil in the New Testament through the depiction of Jesus's work amongst those who are ostracize by society and through his ongoing critique of the religious establishment. Jesus refuses to play by the rules established by the Pharisees, Saducees, or scribes. Instead, he points to the true order of things and what it means to be God's people. His engagement of those outside of spheres of power and influence and his condemnation of the religious leaders of his day demonstrate Jesus' confrontation of structural evil. He was not only seeking to address the sins of individual believers, but to overturn the a system that was not representing God faithfully despite claiming to do so.

THE FALL AND STRUCTURAL EVIL
IN THE CHRISTIAN LIFE TODAY

As believers, we are responsible for our own actions and activities, but these actions and activities are not disconnected from the broader communities of which we are a part. All of us influence and are influenced by broader social, cultural, and organizational contexts. Like the woman in the garden, we find ourselves trying to discern the truth and, if my own experience is normative, often failing to do so. Christians, both as individuals and groups, have misrecognized the order of things throughout history and will continue to do so until Christ's return. The fact that we will continue to fail until that time, however, does not negate the call to live lives worthy of Christ.

Understanding that structural evil persists, in part, because we continually misrecognize the order of things, requires believers, both individually and corporately, to critically examine underlying assumptions about the way the world supposedly works. The presence of structural evil should not produce within us an isolationist posture. We must continue to engage our fallen world and our imperfect church. We must, however, be diligent in our reflection on the Scriptures and on Christian practice. We must look beyond our normal community norms and resist the sort of conformity that does not call us to mimic Christ, but an incomplete articulation of him. In short, the fall has limited our vision and made us less sensitive to the disorder of our world. Reflection on the fall and the structural evil that has resulted from it should cultivate within us a dependence on the one who is willing and able to change our fallen hearts and minds.

QUESTIONS FOR DISCUSSION

1. Describe some specific areas of life that the fall has impacted?

2. How is it significant to understand the fall as an event that puts all of humanity on the same level in light of the gospel?

3. What examples of structural evil in the Old Testament can you think of?

4. What might be some examples of structural evil in today's world?

BIBLIOGRAPHY AND RECOMMENDED READING

Emmrich, Martin. "The Temptation Narrative of Genesis 3:1–6: A Prelude to the Pentateuch and the History of Israel." *EvQ* 73 (2001) 3–20.

Hamilton, Victor P. *The Book of Genesis: Chapters 1–17*. Grand Rapids: Eerdmans, 1990.

Joines, Karen R. "The Serpent in Gen 3." *ZAW* 87 (1975) 1–11.

Moberly, R. W. L. "Did the Serpent Get It Right?" *JTS* 39 (1988) 1–27.

Augustine. *The Confessions of Saint Augustine*. Translated by Edward Bouverie Pusey. London: Aeterna, 2015.

Sailhamer, John H. *The Pentateuch as Narrative: A Biblical-Theological Commentary*. Grand Rapids: Zondervan, 1992.

Scullion, John J. *Genesis: A Commentary for Students, Teachers, and Preachers*. Collegeville, MN: Liturgical, 1992.

Skinner, John. *A Critical and Exegetical Commentary on Genesis*. International Critical Commentary. New York: Scribner, 1910.

Speiser, E. A. *Genesis*. Garden City, NY: Doubleday, 1964.

Summer, George R. "'You Have Not Yet Considered the Gravity of Sin': A Key Retrieval for Our Time." *ProE* 25 (2016) 261–73.

Townsend, P. Wayne. "Eve's Answer to the Serpent: An Alternative Paradigm for Sin and Some Implications in Theology." *CTJ* 33 (1998) 399–420.

Trible, Phyllis. *God and the Rhetoric of Sexuality*. Overtures to Biblical Theology. Philadelphia: Fortress, 1978.

Vogels, Walter. "Like One of Us, Knowing *tôb* and *ra*'." *Semeia* 81 (1998) 144–57.

Wenham, Gordon J. "Sanctuary Symbolism in the Garden of Eden Story." *Proceedings from the 9th World Congress of Jewish Studies, Jerusalem*. Jerusalem: World Union of Jewish Studies, 1986.

———. *Genesis 1–15*. WBC 1. Waco: Word, 1987.

4

GOD'S COVENANT WITH DAVID

BRYAN C. BABCOCK

INTRODUCTION TO GOD'S COVENANTS

The theme of covenant is essential to understanding the Bible's meta-narrative. Rolf Rentdorf argues that covenant presents God's desire to enter into a promissory relationship with men and women created in his image. This is reflected in the repeated covenant refrain, "I will be your God and you will be my people" (Exod 6:6–8; Lev 26:12 etc.).[1] Alistair Wilson adds that "covenant is all about relationship between the Creator and his creation. The idea may seem simple; however, the implications of covenant and covenant relationship between God and humankind are vast."[2]

When God reaches out to humans at key points in history, the result of that communication is often recorded in covenantal language. In fact, it is impossible to appreciate the progression of humanity's relationship with God without focusing through the lens of covenant. Michael Horton unpacks this idea when he argues that covenants are "the architectural

---

1. Rendtorff, *The Covenant Formula*, 12. All Bible translations are original unless otherwise noted.

2. Wilson, "Introduction," 12. Also quoted in Gentry, *Kingdom through Covenant*, 1.

structure that we believe the Scriptures themselves to yield. . . . It is not simply the concept of the covenant, but the concrete existence of God's covenantal dealings in our history that provides the context within which we recognize the unity of Scripture amid its remarkable variety."[3]

THE MEANING OF COVENANT

To best understand God's use of covenants, we must explore the biblical meaning of a covenant. Daniel Lane defines covenant (*berît* in Hebrew) as "an enduring agreement which establishes a defined relationship between two parties involving a solemn, binding obligation to specified stipulations on the part of at least one of the parties toward the other, which is taken by oath under threat of divine curse, and ratified by a visual ritual."[4] Gordon Hugenberger, who explores the meaning of covenant in the context of marriage contracts, found that a covenant included four parts: a relationship; with a nonrelative; that involves obligations; and is established through an oath.[5]

The term *berît* is found over eighty times in the Pentateuch in reference to two broad types of covenant.[6] The first is an interpersonal agreement between two people. For instance, Gen 21:27 reads, "so Abraham brought sheep and cattle and gave them to Abimelech, and the two men made a treaty (*berît*)" (see also Gen 14:13; 21:32; 26:28; 31:44; Exod 23:32; 34:12; Deut 7:2).

A second type of covenant is divine-human. Examples from the human-human covenants help us to understand that a covenant is a solemn obligation between two parties including the guarantee of obligations between one or both parties. In this way a covenant may be a promise of one party to fulfill an obligation to another party, or both parties may hold obligations to the other. In addition, a covenant may be unconditional—where one party must perform the obligation regardless of the action of the other party. Finally, the covenant may be conditional: one party is only obligated if the other party fulfills its obligation. Paul R. Williamson adds that the divine-human covenants "not only occupy a pivotal place within the Pentateuch itself but are also clearly fundamental for the revelation that unfolds in the rest of the Bible."[7]

---

3. Horton, *God of Promise*, 13.

4. Lane, "Meaning and Use of the Old Testament Term for 'Covenant,'" 314.

5. Hugenberger, *Marriage as a Covenant*, 11.

6. 285 times in the Old Testament.

7. Wiliamson, "Covenant," 139.

Ancient Near Eastern Context

Exploring how the word and concept of covenant was used in the context of other ancient Near Eastern cultures will help us understand its meaning in the Old Testament. Kenneth Kitchen finds that *berît* is attested as a loan-word in Egyptian texts as early as 1300 BC. This usage demonstrates that the word was already well established before the time of Moses.[8] The word may come from the Akkadian *beritu*, meaning *to bond* or to *fetter*.[9] Gentry adds that "covenants or treaties either identical or similar to those mentioned in the Old Testament were common all across the ancient Near East, in lands and regions known today as Egypt, Iraq, Syria, and Turkey. Two types of treaties in the ancient Near East are especially noteworthy: 1) the suzerain-vassal treaty and 2) the royal charter or land grant."[10]

The suzerain-vassal treaty is a diplomatic treaty between two nations. The greater power and initiating nation is called the suzerain, and the lesser power is identified as the vassal. The Hittite version of this treaty is structed with six sections that outline the agreement, including: (1) preamble, which introduces setting and occasion; (2) historical prologue, which states the rights of the ruler; (3) general stipulations, or principles of the relationship; (4) specific stipulations, or regulations in the form of apodictic laws; (5) blessings and curses, or statement of rewards and sanctions; and 6) witnesses. While the vassal swore allegiance to the suzerain, the suzerain was primarily responsible for protection of the vassal.

The royal land grant involves an endowment of an item of importance from a greater power (usually the king or god) to a lesser power. This type of grant may involve the transfer of property title or may grant a privileged position (e.g., priestly or royal office). The key to this type of treaty/grant surrounds the interpersonal relationship between the two parties. Moshe Weinfeld described the differences between the vassal-treaty and the royal grant in this way:

> While the "treaty" constitutes an obligation of the vassal to his master, the suzerain, the "grant" constitutes an obligation of the master to his servant. In the "grant" the curse is directed towards the one who will violate the rights of the king's vassal, while in the treaty the curse is directed towards the vassal who will violate the rights of his king. In other words, the "grant" serves mainly to protect the rights of the servant, while the treaty comes to

8. Kitchen, "Egypt, Ugarit, Qatna and Covenant," 453–64.

9. This origin is debated, with the Akkadian preposition *birit* (meaning "between") and another Hebrew root meaning "to eat" or "to select" as possibilities.

10. Gentry, *Kingdom through Covenant*, Loc. 3159.

protect the rights of the master. What is more, while the grant
is a reward for loyalty and good deeds already performed, the
treaty is an inducement for future loyalty.[11]

In addition to the differences between the grants and treaties, Gentry
and Weinfeld find that there are important similarities as well: "While the
grant is mainly a promise by the donor to the recipient, it presupposes the
loyalty of the latter. By the same token the treaty, whose principal concern
is with the obligation of the vassal, presupposes the sovereign's promise to
protect his vassal's country and dynasty."[12]

Contract vs. Covenant

Before we turn our attention to a theological and hermeneutical review of
the biblical covenant, it is appropriate to spend a few minutes outlining the
sections of a covenant and its differences from a contract. Elmer Martens
provides a comparison between covenant and contract that clarifies and
sharpens our understanding of the biblical idea of a covenant relationship.
He finds the following points of similarity and difference:[13]

Category	Contract	Covenant
Form/Literary Structure	1. Date 2. Parties 3. Transaction 4. Investiture 5. Guarantees 6. Scribe 7. List of witnesses	1. Speaker introduced 2. History of relationship 3. General command 4. Detailed stipulations 5. Document statement 6. Witnesses 7. Blessings and curses
Occasion	Expected benefit	Desire for relationship
Initiative	Mutual agreement	Stronger party
Orientation	Negotiation, Thing-oriented	Gift, Person-oriented
Obligation	Performance	Loyalty
Termination	Specified	Intermediate
Violation	Yes	Yes

11. Ibid, Loc. 3166.
12. Ibid, Loc. 3173.
13. Adapted from Martens, *God's Design*, 73.

Martens adds that "the occasion for contract is largely the benefits that each party expects. Thus for a satisfactory sum one party agrees to supply a specified quantity of some desired product for the other party. The contract is characteristically thing-oriented. The covenant is person-oriented and, theologically speaking, arises, not with benefits as the chief barter item, but out of a desire for a measure of intimacy."[14]

In a contract negotiation, arriving at a mutually satisfactory agreement is important. However, negotiation has no place in a covenant. The greater party initiates the process and offers his help. According to Martens, a

> "gift" is descriptive of covenant as "negotiation" is descriptive of contract. Both covenant and contract have obligations, but with this difference. The conditions set out in a contract require ful-fillment of terms; the obligation of a covenant is one of loyalty. A covenant is often eternal; a contract for a specified period. A ticking off of terms in check-list fashion can reveal a broken contract, and the point of brokenness can be clearly identified. A covenant, too, can be broken, but the point at which this tran-spires is less clear, because here the focus is not on stipulations, one, two, three, but on a quality of intimacy. Of all the differ-ences between covenant and contract, the place in covenant of personal loyalty is the most striking.[15]

Based upon this argument, Gentry concludes that "at the heart of cov-enant, then, is a relationship between parties characterized by faithfulness and loyalty in love. In the Hebrew of the Old Testament there is a word pair which is consistently used to express this: ḥesed and 'ĕmet. Neither word has a convenient and simple equivalent in English. The first, ḥesed, has to do with showing kindness in loyal love. The second, 'ĕmet, can be translated by either *faithfulness* or *truth*. As a word pair, the meaning of the whole cannot be reduced to the sum of its constituent parts, just as one cannot explain the meaning of butterfly in English by describing butter and fly. This word pair operates, then, within covenant relationships and has to do with demonstrating faithful loyal love within the covenant context.[16]

Armed with a better understanding of the meaning of a covenant, we will turn to examine the Davidic covenant.

14. Ibid.

15. Ibid.

16. Gentry, *Kingdom through Covenant*, Loc. 3317.

ANALYSIS OF KEY PASSAGE: 2 SAMUEL 7

To better understand and illustrate God's use of covenants we now turn to explore the agreement or covenant which God initiated with David, king of Israel. The Davidic covenant functions in the metanarrative of Scripture in several significant ways. First, for the people and nation of Israel, the covenant inaugurates a divinely designed model for kingship. Second, the agreement inaugurates Yahweh as king over his people at a deeper and higher level. Third, the Davidic covenant addresses the intentions and purposes of God expressed in the Israelite covenant and, even further back, in the covenant with Abraham.[17]

To better understand the Davidic covenant, we will first analyze the historical context for the institution of kingship. Then we will examine 2 Sam 7 and the covenant with David.

Historical Context of Kingship

Moses led the people of Israel out of bondage and oppression in Egypt to the boundary of the land promised to Abraham and his descendants. God established Moses's position as leader and God was actively involved with the nation. In fact, God's presence in the tabernacle was unprecedented—demonstrating God's immanence. While Moses was the leader of the people, he never assumes the title of king, as God was the king of the nation. However, Moses foreshadows a day when there will be a king over Israel when he writes:

> When you come to the land that the LORD your God is giving you, and you possess it and dwell in it and then say, "I will set a king over me, like all the nations that are around me," you may indeed set a king over you whom the LORD your God will choose. One from among your brothers you shall set as king over you. You may not put a foreigner over you, who is not your brother. Only he must not acquire many horses for himself or cause the people to return to Egypt in order to acquire many horses, since the LORD has said to you, "You shall never return that way again." And he shall not acquire many wives for himself, lest his heart turn away, nor shall he acquire for himself excessive silver and gold.
>
> And when he sits on the throne of his kingdom, he shall write for himself in a book a copy of this law, approved by the

---

17. Ibid., Loc. 3396.

Levitical priests. And it shall be with him, and he shall read in it all the days of his life, that he may learn to fear the LORD his God by keeping all the words of this law and these statutes, and doing them, that his heart may not be lifted up above his brothers, and that he may not turn aside from the commandment, either to the right hand or to the left, so that he may continue long in his kingdom, he and his children, in Israel. (Deut 17:14–20)

As such, Moses is a divinely appointed leader who serves as the liaison between God and the people. God is the king of the people guiding the action.

Joshua was a leader tutored by Moses and promoted into leadership by Yahweh. Joshua led the people into the land promised to the patriarchs in the covenant with Abraham. As the nation is formed, God continued to be the understood king and Joshua his agent. While Joshua acts as the executive leader, the leadership becomes split between Joshua and the increasing role of the Levite tribe as priests. Over time this split in authority between the executive leadership and priestly leadership creates increasing confusion for the people, and the people begin to ask, Who is in charge of the nation of Israel?

The period of the judges is a time of spiritual rebellion by the people and a leadership void for the nation. The Bible records minimal communication of God's word through the people, and leadership becomes fragmented between the tribes. At the same time, the nations surrounding Israel develop strong sovereign identities with aggressive territorial expansion plans. God uses Israel's neighbors to enact his judgment upon the people of Israel for their violations of the covenant.

The writer of the book of Judges portrays a recurring cycle in which (1) the people break the covenant and sin against Yahweh, (2) Yahweh disciplines them by allowing aggression against Israel by foreign nations, (3) there is a call to repentance and a cry for help, and (4) Yahweh raises up a spiritually inspired leader or deliverer, called a judge, who rescues the people from their enemies and rules them for a time.

At the end of the book of Judges the author comments, "In those days there was no king in Israel; everyone did what was right in his own eyes" (Judg 21:25). Gentry finds that the author is really referring to the condition of the people and how the covenant would be preserved. He is saying that, despite the lack of human support which might have preserved a political or religious ideal, in spite of the fact that there was no king and each person followed his own standard, Yahweh, by direct intervention through a series of savior figures, preserved the covenant with Israel at this time. The book of Judges, then, suggests that, in any age, the people of Israel would not owe their existence to political constitutions devised by themselves, such as the monarchy. Israel would owe its survival to the faithfulness of its covenant partner, who would never defect from his obligations to which he was bound by oath and promise.[18]

The lack of leadership and continual threat from other (stronger) nations led the people to ask the prophet Samuel for a king. Samuel responds that God is the king of Israel and that the people should give their allegiance to Yahweh. Despite Samuel's advice, Yahweh acquiesces and tells Samuel to appoint a king over the people, saying "Obey the voice of the people in all that they say to you, for they have not rejected you, but they have rejected me from being king over them. According to all the deeds that they have done, from the day I brought them up out of Egypt even to this day, forsaking me and serving other gods, so they are also doing to you. Now then, obey their voice; only you shall solemnly warn them and show them the ways of the king who shall reign over them" (1 Sam 8:7–9).

God then tells Samuel to appoint Saul as king over the nation. The selection is exactly what the people asked for—Saul looks like a king and acts like a king, just as the people wanted. He has modest military success defending and expanding Israel's boarders. However, he follows his desires for wealth and power, forsaking the spiritual leadership of the people. God rejects this secular king that the people desired and chooses David, a man after God's own heart.

2 Samuel 7

David's reign begins in this context. While Saul possessed all the attributes of the secular king, David had none. He was from a modest family of limited social standing. Within a family, the status of each son was ranked from oldest to youngest and David had several older brothers, thus limiting his standing within the family. While other young men were educated, socialized, and experienced in battle, David was a meager sheepherder. Yet God knew that David had the only characteristic that mattered—a heart for God.

This is not to say that David was without flaws. He was a complex person with serious imperfections. However, God looked beyond the sinful nature of his anointed king and inspired David to accomplish Yahweh's plan. It is during his reign that God reaches out to David to establish a covenant with David and his heirs.

---

18. Gentry, *Kingdom through Covenant*, Loc. 9241.

The main passages in the Old Testament dealing with the Davidic covenant are 2 Sam 7, with its parallel text in 1 Chr 17, and Ps 89 (esp. vv. 3–4 and 19–37). Robert Gordon describes 2 Sam 7 as "an 'ideological summit,' not only in the 'Deuteronomistic History' [Deuteronomy–2 Kings] but also in the Old Testament as a whole."[19] Anderson echoes this sentiment finding that the Davidic Covenant is the theological highlight for the Deuteronomistic History.[20]

While 2 Sam 7 does not use the word *covenant*, several other passages confirm this understanding, including 2 Sam 7:15; 23:5; Jer 33:21; Pss 89:3, 28, 34, 39; 132:12; Isa 55:3; and 2 Chr 13:5. To better understand God's covenant with king David, we will begin by unpacking the literary structure of the text so that we can observe the shaping of this communication.

The passage is structured by several monologues (speeches and prayers) with minimal plot, action, or narration. The text begins with a brief narrative section providing the only background necessary to support the dialogue to follow. Essentially, David intends to build a temple for Yahweh in his new capital city, with support from Nathan the prophet. The mention of David's palace in 2 Sam 7:1 assumes knowledge of the capture of Jerusalem (5:6–9) and the building of a royal palace with Phoenician help (v. 11). The statement that Yahweh had given David rest from all the enemies around him assumes David's success at driving the Philistines out of Israelite territory (vv. 17–25). David's complaint that the ark of God remains in a tent (7:2) recalls the ark's arrival into Jerusalem and its deposition in a temporary tent (6:1–23).[21]

According to Bill Arnold, the previous chapters have been preparing us for this critical moment in the extended narrative. Beyond the immediate context, these verses are also reminiscent of Deut 12:10–11, where the command was given: Once the Israelites had settled in the promised land and enjoyed rest from all their enemies, they were to worship at "the place the LORD your God will choose as a dwelling for his Name." Yahweh has blessed the Israelites with land and peace, and the entrance of the ark of the covenant seems to confirm that the new capital of Jerusalem is that place God chose.[22]

Surely this is a favorable time for the new, successful king to build a permanent structure for God's dwelling. With the reference to David's *house* in 7:1, the narrator introduces the theme word for the chapter, which occurs

---

19. Gordon, *I and II Samuel*, 235.

20. Anderson, *2 Samuel*, 112.

21. Arnold, *1 and 2 Samuel*, Loc. 9612.

22. Ibid., Loc. 9618.

fifteen times 2 Sam 7. Reinforcing its importance, the word recurs several times in the next few verses, all referring to a physical structure, either a royal palace (as here in v. 1) or a temple. David's complaint in 7:2 contrasts the house he lives in with the tent where the ark of God resides. To David's thinking, the time is right to build a permanent structure to house the ark of God. Nathan concurs and encourages David to fulfill his dream. As substantiation, Nathan repeats the sentiment that is an important theme of the extended narrative (7:3): "The Lord is with you" (see also 7:9).[23]

In place of David's proposed house for God, Yahweh has an alternate plan (7:8–17). The plan is stated first generally (7:8–11a) and then specifically (7:11b–17). According to Arnold,

> the general statement emphasizes the special relationship Yahweh has with David, signaled at the outset by the epithet "my servant David" (7:5, 8). In essence, God has done everything for David. He took David "from the pasture and from following the flock" to make him ruler of the people. Yahweh has been with David wherever he went. God himself thus states what the books of Samuel have been emphasizing throughout the extended narrative, that he has been with David. One of the driving theological convictions of the history of David's rise has been that David succeeds where Saul fails because Yahweh has blessed David with his divine presence. (See 1 Sam 16:18; 18:12, 14, 28; 2 Sam 3:1; 5:10; 7:3)[24]

Therefore, David is the legitimate anointed one who appropriately rules God's people because he is the Immanuel figure; God is with him.

God promises to continue these blessings in the future (2 Sam 7:12–13, 16). He will make David's name great, "like the names of the great ones of the earth" (v. 9). This phrase echoes the Abrahamic promise and is the eternal legacy sought after by every great ruler—a permanent place in history. In addition, God will make a place for the nation to live in peace, secure in the knowledge that "violent men shall afflict them no more" (v. 10).

The promise of rest in the land is an important unifying theme throughout the Deuteronomistic History (Deut 12:9–10). It was partially fulfilled in the conquest of Joshua but eventually came to be linked to the central worship of Yahweh in his chosen place. Now that Jerusalem has been established, this chapter introduces the theme of a temple for Yahweh, which means the long-awaited rest is possible. Arnold finds that "this text's

23. Ibid., Loc. 9626.
24. Ibid., Loc. 9645.

references to 'rest' (7:1, 11) reveal that this rest has now been secured in David and will be ensured by his perpetuating dynasty."[25]

Next, Yahweh details his plan more specifically for David (vv. 11–17). At this point the chapter's theme word returns to carry the message. Rather than David's building a house for Yahweh, God declares he instead will build a house for David (v. 11). The message from Nathan continues its use of house as a central theme. The author utilizes the word fifteen times with meanings ranging from a physical building (either palace or temple) to an extended family, clan, or tribe. The wordplay creates meaning by mixing these uses. Allen notes that "David intends to build a physical house for Yahweh, but he is not the right person for that job. Then the oracle contains this surprise. In an ironic twist, Yahweh announces he himself will build an enduring house (read 'royal dynasty') for David because of his special relationship with the new king. David will be succeeded by a son, thus establishing the first royal dynasty in Israel. That son will build the temple (v. 13)."[26]

But this is only part of the promise. David's line will be established *forever* (vv. 13, 16) through additional sons. In fact, the line of David will last eternally (v. 13). Yahweh will be a father to David's descendants, and they will be his sons (v. 14). When they sin, Yahweh will graciously restrict his punishment to that appropriate for humans, but he will never withdraw his steadfast covenant love as he withdrew it from Saul (v. 15). Saul's progeny will not last; David's is forever! The wonderful and surprising promises end with the emphatic sentence: "Your house and your kingdom will endure forever before me; your throne will be established forever" (v. 16).

God therefore vows to protect the line of David and provide leadership for his people through it. A direct understanding of the covenant is that David's sons will sit on the throne over a united Israel for generations. However, within one generation the nation is torn into two parts. Then, after a just a few generations the Davidic rule of Judah is lost. Therefore, Yahweh must intend more from the covenant than merely the Davidic rule. With this in mind, let's turn our attention to how the rest of the Old Testament views God's use of covenants in general, with specific attention to the future interpretation of the Davidic covenant.

25. Ibid., Loc. 9655.
26. Ibid., Loc 9670.

UNDERSTANDING THE THEME OF THE DAVIDIC COVENANT WITHIN THE OLD TESTAMENT

What is the nature of the specific relationship between the Davidic covenant and other covenants in the Old Testament? To best answer this questions it is important to take a step back and explore the context of covenants through Israel's history.

The first explicit mention of the word "covenant" describes God's commitment to Noah (Gen 6:18; 9:1–17). The essence of Noah's covenant was a solemn promise from God to deliver Noah and his family from the flood and to refrain from such devastating floods in the future (reaffirming God's original creation intent). The latter promise was eternal and marked by the sign of the rainbow (bow in the clouds 9:12–17). The occasion for the establishment of the covenant was the offering of sacrifices which appears to be an essential element in ratifying the agreement.[27]

As the first covenant of the Bible, Noah's is universal in scope. It is not limited to Noah and his family but extends to all creation. In this sense, the covenant of Noah establishes God's program of general revelation for all humankind and provides a context for the other covenants of the Old Testament, which will introduce more specific revelation.

The next covenant is established between God and Abraham (Gen 12, 15 and 17). With Abraham, Yahweh fashions a covenant using language of the land-grant (Gen 12:1–3; 15; 17; 22). As with the prior covenant with Noah, God ratifies the agreement with an offering. However, the symbolism changes so that God alone passes between the dissected animals, indicating the covenant's unilateral nature. God alone took on obligations and Abraham remained a passive spectator of the ritual.[28]

Through the covenant, God obligates himself to Abraham and his descendants as Lord, savior, and protector through the promise of a land, a people, and blessings.[29] Israel, in turn, is called to covenant faithfulness (15:6), circumcision (Gen 17), and torah obedience (Exod 19–24). Scot McKnight notes that central to covenant is "divine initiative: humans do not, as pagans do with idols, imagine a covenant; instead, God breaks into history with a revelation of relationship in terms of covenant."[30]

---

27. Williamson, "Covenant," 421.

28. The covenant does not mention a sign, which may be due to the unilateral nature of the covenant.

29. The land is understood as both Canaan and a place for Yahweh to dwell; the people are Israel; and the blessing are both material and spiritual.

30. McKnight, "Covenant," 142.

In Gen 17:1–22 the term covenant occurs thirteen times. Here God changes Abram's name to Abraham and gives circumcision as the sign of the covenant (as the rainbow had been the identifying marker of Noah's covenant). Both of these covenants contained promissory elements that sound unconditional: in the first, God will not again flood the earth; in the second, he will make Abraham exceedingly fruitful, which is three times labeled "an everlasting covenant" (Gen 17:7, 13, 19). But unlike the earlier universal covenant, Abraham's relationship with God clearly contains stipulations (walk before me and be blameless, 17:1; cf. 17:9–14).

Arnold argues that Abraham's covenant was at once deeper and narrower than Noah's, meaning more was revealed to fewer. The universal scope was replaced with the individual concerns of a wandering nomad. But the ancestral covenant of Gen 12–50 also foreshadows and prepares for the third covenant mentioned in the Bible, the Mosaic covenant, where the scope becomes national (Exodus-Deuteronomy). While the progression from Noah to Abraham was a narrowing process, that from Abraham to Moses is a broadening one. The principles of the ancestral family covenant are now applied to the nation Israel. These covenants (ancestral and Sinaitic) are more organically bound together than either was to the universal covenant of Noah (Exod 2:24; 3:6, 15).[31]

The Mosaic covenant is primarily concerned with maintaining the unique relationship between Yahweh and Israel, and thus contains some means of sustaining communion between a holy God and a sinful people. This relationship between Yahweh and Israel is a confirmation and, in a sense, a fulfillment of the promises to Abraham. Having redeemed Israel from slavery, God reveals more of his nature to them, establishes a unique relationship with them, and promises to fulfill the land promise (Exod 2:24–24; 3:7–8; 6:6–8; 13:5, 11). According to Williamson, nowhere in the Mosaic covenant is the actual inheritance of the promised Land placed in any doubt. The focus is not on what Abraham's descendants must do in order to inherit the land (this had been granted unconditionally in Gen 15), but rather on how they must conduct themselves within the land as the special kind of nation God intended them to be (Exod 19:5–6).[32]

It is clear from the conditional framework of this text that the covenant involved bilateral obligations (If you obey . . . then). For his part, God would make Israel unique among the nations; they would be his special treasure, a priestly kingdom, and a holy nation. However, to be these things Israel must keep Yahweh's commandments (Exod 20:1–7) and the ordinances of

31. Arnold, *1 and 2 Samuel*, Loc. 9823.
32. Williamson, "Covenant," 424.

the Book of the Covenant (Exod 21–23). These components of the covenant had a revelatory purpose. Just as ancient laws codes generally made a statement about the king who created them, the covenant obligations revealed at Sinai reveal some of the nature and character of God. Being in a special relationship with Yahweh involved more than privilege; it also entailed responsibility.

Williamson concludes that "only by maintaining the ethical distinctiveness enshrined in God's instructions to Abraham could Israel, the patriarch's promised descendants, enjoy the proper relationship anticipated in Gen 17. For Yahweh to be their God, Israel had to be like him. Like their ancestor, Israel must walk before God and be blameless (Gen 17:1). Thus, the primary concern of the Mosaic covenant was the way in which the divine-human relationship between Yahweh and the great nation descended from Abraham should be maintained."[33]

We now return to the Davidic covenant of 2 Sam 7 to offer a few words on how this covenant fits into the progression of revelation from Yahweh. Arnold finds that

> we see a narrowing from the national covenant of Moses to the royal family. God descends again to Israel, this time in light of the new sociopolitical context of monarchy. In the Mosaic covenant, Yahweh was portrayed as the sovereign suzerain, the overlord of the vassal nation, Israel. Now with the reality of a king, royal court, and standing army, God deepens and furthers his promises to Abraham as confirmed by the Mosaic covenant. Only this time the concept of a kingdom is dominant, implying that God will guarantee the continuance of the new kingdom by assuming responsibility for it. God seems to say that he will take David's throne for himself and make it his own to ensure its permanence (2 Sam. 7:16).[34]

Some scholars draw a sharp contrast between the Davidic and Mosaic covenants. But this approach merely repeats the mistake of many Israelites living at the time of Jeremiah—namely, that of allowing one covenant to supersede another. Arnold finds that if we elevate the promises to David over the stipulations of Moses, we have a skewed understanding of how God sought to relate to the Israelites. We need to learn to read the idiosyncratic features of each covenant in light of the new situation each addresses. From

33. Ibid. For our purposes we are subsuming the covenant in Deuteronomy as a renewal of the Mosaic covenant for a new generation. This is, of course, a simplification, as the covenant in Deuteronomy reaffirms obligations laid out in both the covenant of circumcision (Gen 17 and Deut 30:6–10) and anticipates the new covenant to come.

34. Arnold, *1 and 2 Samuel*, Loc. 9781.

prehistoric flood plains to ancestral individuals, from national legislation to royal charters, God sought to reveal himself to Israel and through that revelation to establish relationship. We must read the differences in the covenants in light of the historical developments, all the while recognizing a basic organic unity to the program of revelation God has established. Part of our problem (and one that can stand in the way of building a bridge from this text to our culture) is a misconception of "covenant" as an abstract, changeless idea. But this brief survey has demonstrated that the concept has assumed forms that are at one and the same moment different but similar.[35]

Essentially, the Bible seems to relate the Davidic covenant to others in the Old Testament in an organically unified way while recognizing their genuine differences, which are due largely to historical and functional reasons. These are differences of degree rather than of kind. Jon Levenson writes, "the voice of Sinai is heard on Zion," so that David depends on, builds on, and complements Moses and Abraham.[36] He adds: "The traditions correct each other. Each is fulfilled only in the presence of the other. The whole is greater than the sum of its parts."[37]

The final covenant in the Old Testament is disclosed in Jer 31:31–34 and unpacked in the context of other prophetic texts including Jer 30–33; Ezek 34; 36–37; and Isa 40–66.

> "Behold, the days are coming," declares the LORD, "when I will make a new covenant with the house of Israel and the house of Judah, not like the covenant that I made with their fathers on the day when I took them by the hand to bring them out of the land of Egypt, my covenant that they broke, though I was their husband," declares the LORD. "For this is the covenant that I will make with the house of Israel after those days," declares the LORD: "I will put my law within them, and I will write it on their hearts. And I will be their God, and they shall be my people. And no longer shall each one teach his neighbor and each his brother, saying, 'Know the LORD,' for they shall all know me, from the least of them to the greatest," declares the LORD. "For I will forgive their iniquity, and I will remember their sin no more."

This new covenant is understood on multiple levels. First, the new covenant will be both national and international. Both Jeremiah and Ezekiel primarily describe a national view against the historical context of the

---

35. Ibid, Loc. 9848.

36. Levenson, *Sinai and Zion*, 209.

37. Ibid.

Babylonian exile (Jer 33:6–16; Ezek 36:24–38; 37:11–28). This fits well with the Davidic covenant of a reunified Israel, renovated land, and a coming Davidic king. However, the scope of the new covenant clearly transcends national and territorial boarders. Isaiah picks up on this international priority (extending the Abrahamic covenant) where the scope of the covenant will extend to the ends of the earth and ultimately encompass all nations (Isa 42:6; 49:6; 55:3–5; 56:4–8; 66:18–24).

Second, the new covenant will involve both continuity and discontinuity. Palmer Robertson outlines several features that underline the new covenant's continuity with previous divine covenants, including its emphasis on divine Torah, its focus on Abraham's lineage, and its use of covenantal language like "I will be their God and they will be my people."[38] Therefore, the new covenant may be understood through the lens of God's prior revelation. However, the newness of the covenant should not be minimized. Williamson highlights that the new covenant completely removes sin from its language, transformation is now internal and based in the heart, and the relationship with God is now intimate. "Significantly, all these aspects of the new covenant emphasize the most important of its novel elements: its indestructibility. Unlike previous covenants, the new covenant cannot be broken unilaterally."[39]

Third, the new covenant will be both climactic and eternal. In many ways, the prior covenants culminate in the provisions of the new covenant. Some of the key aspects of earlier promises include physical inheritance, renewed relationship, blessing on a national and international scale, and an everlasting dynasty. Therefore, it is evident that the new covenant is climactic in promise and eternal in scope.

Initially, the Israelites identified the new covenant promises of Jeremiah with the hope of the return from exile and the second temple era.[40] When the promises of the covenant were not satisfied in the generations after the return from exile, the people grew anxious for a messiah who would fulfill the promises. It is into this era that Jesus arrived, preaching a new message from God.

38. Robertson, *The Christ of Covenants*, 281.

39. Williamson, "Covenant," 427.

40. See chapter 14, "Exile and Hope"; and chapter 15, "Renewed Community," for a detailed discussion of this topic.

IMPLICATIONS FOR READING THE NEW TESTAMENT

One final question remains as part of our exploration of covenants: How does this Davidic covenant relate to the New Testament? Second Samuel 7:14 contains an especially important promise in this regard, when Yahweh says of David's offspring: "I will be his father, and he will be my son." Though opinions differ, Arnold argues that "this expression, which is parallel to the covenant phrase "I will be your God" (Gen 17:7; Exod 6:7, etc.), denotes adoption rather than begetting. Henceforth, Israelite kings (or, more specifically, Judahite kings) will be thought of as sons of Yahweh (Pss 2:7; 89:26). For Christian readers, God's father-son relationship with the Son of David reverberates throughout the gospel story, beginning with the baptism of Jesus (Matt 3:17). This text is clearly programmatic for New Testament authors when defining Jesus as the Son of David (or, relying on 2 Sam 7:14a, as the Son of God, see Heb 1:5)."[41]

The New Testament's messianic use of our text is possible not simply because of the predictive, forward-looking nature of the chapter but also because of how other Old Testament texts build on the themes. Arnold goes on to argue that the messianic tradition during the Second Temple finds a messianic link. "Indeed, building on the powerful Jerusalem/Zion concepts of the previous chapters, 2 Sam 7 constitutes an 'ideological summit' for the Old Testament as a whole. To continue the summit metaphor, from this peak we are able to look back and reflect on great themes leading up to this height while at the same time turning to look forward to the culmination of these promises. When future Davidic kings failed to serve Yahweh as David had done, the conviction grew in ancient Israel that another Son of David could be expected who would deliver the nation (Isa 11:1; Mic 5:2)."[42] Gordon adds that "we shall not be exaggerating the importance of the Nathan oracle, therefore, if we see it as the matrix of biblical messianism."[43]

Turning briefly to explore the other Old Testament covenants and their fulfillment in the New Testament, we find that Jesus is the climax of the Old Testament covenantal promises. While the new covenant is only mentioned by Jesus at the Last Supper, the Gospels make the connection evident by discussing the fulfillment of specific covenantal promises. Through Jesus the promises made to Abraham find their ultimate fulfillment (Matt 1:1, 17; 3:9; 8:11–12; Luke 1:55, 72–73). Jesus is the one anticipated in the Pentateuch, and Jesus is the one in whom the obligations of the Mosaic covenant

---

41. Arnold, *1 and 2 Samuel*, Loc. 9863.

42. Ibid, Loc 9868.

43. Gordon, *1 and 2 Samuel*, 235.

have been both fulfilled and transcended (Matt 3:15; 5:17–48; 9:16–17; 11:28–30). Jesus is the royal son of David (Matt 3:17; 4:15–16; 15:22; 16:16; 22:41–45; Luke 1:69–70) who will shepherd the people of God (Matt 2:6; 15:29–39; John 10:1–16). Finally, Jesus is portrayed as the remnant of the true Israel through whom salvation will come to all nations (Matt 2:15; 4:1–11; 5:13–16; 8:11; 12:18–21; 25:31–34; 28:19; Luke 2:14, 32) and in whom the new covenant blessings of forgiveness are expressed (Matt 1:21; 8:1–4, 17; 9:1–8; 11:2–5).[44]

The Pauline epistles mention the term covenant nine times. Paul's use in Romans and Ephesians relates that God's covenantal promises to Israel will indeed be fulfilled, but only in the genuine heirs of the covenant, Abraham's spiritual descendants (Rom 9–11; Eph 2:11–22). In his letters to the Corinthians Paul distinguishes between the new and old covenants (1 Cor 11:25; 2 Cor 3:6). In Galatians he establishes the distinctions between the Abrahamic covenant over the Mosaic. For Paul, the crucial point is that Abraham's genuine heirs are not simply those who can claim biological descent from the patriarch, but rather those who believe (Gal 3:7).

Perhaps the most developed discussion for the New Testament fulfillment of Old Testament covenants is found in the book of Hebrews. The author twice quotes the new covenant passage of Jeremiah (Heb 8:8–12; 10:16–17) and spends significant effort exploring the covenants (7:22; 8:6–10:31; 12:18–24; 13:20). Hebrews contrasts the old and new covenants by emphasizing the superiority of the promises, sacrifice, mediator, blessing and inheritance involved in the latter. While the necessity of the new covenant demonstrates that the old was in some sense deficient; however, the fault was not in the covenant itself but in those who failed to keep them. Not surprisingly, therefore, it is the intrinsic inadequacy that is rectified by the Spirit in the new covenant, a fact which the writer is keen to underline (8:10–12; 10:16–17). Thus, the contrast in Hebrews between the covenants is similar to that of Paul; it is not between something evil and something good, but between something good and something better.[45]

As we mentioned in the beginning of this study, God's use of covenant demonstrates both his unifying theological message and use of progressive revelation. We also find that an understanding of covenants is essential to the understanding of the Bible's metanarrative.

We now turn to explore how an awareness of God's use of covenants might be used within the modern church.

---

44. Williamson, "Covenant," 427.

45. Ibid., 429.

IMPLICATIONS FOR AND IDENTITY WITH
THE MODERN CHRISTIAN CHURCH

If God's essential act is one of covenant making, then his people's task is fundamentally to lead others into that covenant relationship and to live faithfully in terms of his covenant. Fulfillment of God's covenant allows mankind to occupy the proper place they deserve in God's creation: they are made in the male-female image of God, but they are fallen. In his grace, however, God has provided the path to restoration through a covenant relationship. If God's fundamental relationship to mankind can be described as covenantal, then the task of his people is to lead others into that covenant and to live faithfully.

Covenant thinking not only defines our relationship with God, it also summons God's people through that covenant to a life of faithfulness. If the covenant with Abraham fails to address the human need for moral direction, God began to clarify his plan through the covenant with Moses (Exod 19–24).

When the Mosaic covenant failed to remedy the moral condition of mankind, God provided hope through the covenant with David. As David's heirs quickly failed to follow Yahweh's leadership, God reached out again through his prophet Jeremiah. McKnight concludes that the hope and expectation delivered in Jer 31:31–34 becomes reality in the death and resurrection of Jesus Christ. This event, in connection with Pentecost and the creation of the church as a new-covenant community, establishes that covenant morality is only effective through the blood of the eternal Son and the internalization of the covenant through the Spirit.[46]

McKnight continues, stating that "covenant enables us to see that the end of history is a glimpse of God's intent from the beginning of history. The end of history finds humans bowing before Jesus Christ (Phil 2:5–11) and offering God their praises of the worthiness of his Son (Rev 5). That is the climax of the covenant relationship. It means that from the beginning the telos (goal) of God has been to lead all humans to bow before him in eternal worship and praise. That praise finds its motivation in the blood-stained Lamb, who is the conquering Lion of Judah."[47]

---

46. McKnight, "Covenant," 143.

47. Ibid.

QUESTIONS FOR FURTHER STUDY

1) Why do you think God made covenants with mankind?

2) In your opinion, what is the role of God's covenants in the metanarrative of history?

3) What is mankind's responsibility regarding God's covenant? What are the consequences if mankind does not fulfill its responsibility?

4) Read 2 Sam 7 carefully. Do you believe the covenant that God made with David is conditional or unconditional? Why?

5) Jeremiah 31:34 states that "No longer will they teach their neighbor, or say to one another, 'Know the LORD,' because they will all know me, from the least of them to the greatest." What do you think this means?

BIBLIOGRAPHY AND RECOMMENDED READING

Anderson, A. A. *2 Samuel*. WBC 11. Waco: Word, 1989.

Arnold, Bill T. *1 and 2 Samuel*. NIVAC. Grand Rapids: Zondervan, 2003. Kindle edition.

Blaising, Craig A. "Dispensations in Biblical Theology." In *Progressive Dispensationalism*, by Craig A. Blaising and Darrel L. Bock, 106–27. Grand Rapids: Baker Academic, 2000.

————. "The Extent and Varieties of Dispensationalism." In *Progressive Dispensationalism*, by Craig A. Blaising and Darrel L. Bock, 9–56. Grand Rapids: Baker Academic, 2000.

Block, Daniel I. *The Book of Ezekiel Chapters 25–48*. NICOT. Grand Rapids: Eerdmans, 1998.

Brueggemann, Walter. *A Commentary on Jeremiah: Exile and Homecoming*. Grand Rapids: Eerdman, 1998.

Dearman, J. Andrew. *Jeremiah and Lamentations*. NIVAC. Grand Rapids: Zondervan, 2002.

Duguid, Iain M. *Ezekiel*. NIVAC. Grand Rapids: Zondervan, 1999.

Feinberg, John. *Continuity and Discontinuity: Perspectives on the Relationship between the Old and New Testaments*. Wheaton, IL: Crossway, 1988.

Gentry, Peter J., and Stephen J. Wellum. *Kingdom through Covenant: A Biblical Theological Understanding of the Covenant*. Wheaton, IL: Crossway, 2012. Kindle edition.

Gordon, Robert P. *I and II Samuel: A Commentary*. Grand Rapids: Zondervan, 1986.

Hess, Richard S. *The Old Testament: A Historical, Theological, and Critical Introduction*. Grand Rapids: Baker Academic, 2016.

Horton, Michael S. *God of Promise: Introducing Covenant Theology*. Grand Rapids: Baker, 2006.

Hugenberger, Gordon. *Marriage as a Covenant: A Study of Biblical Law and Ethics Governing Marriage Developed from the Perspective of Malachi*. VTSup 52. Leiden: Brill, 1994.

Kitchen, Kenneth A. "Egypt, Ugarit, Qatna and Covenant." *UF* 11 (1979) 453–64.

Lane, Daniel C. "The Meaning and Use of the Old Testament Term for 'Covenant' (*berît*): With Some Implications for Dispensationalism and Covenant Theology." PhD diss., Trinity International University, 2000.

Levenson, Jon. *Sinai and Zion: An Entry into the Jewish Bible.* New York: HarperCollins, 1985.

Martens, Elmer A. *God's Design: A Focus on Old Testament Theology.* Grand Rapids: Baker, 1981.

McKnight, Scot. "Covenant." In *Dictionary for Theological Interpretation of the Bible,* edited by Kevin J. Vanhoozer, 141–43. Grand Rapids: Baker Academic, 2005.

Poythress, Vern S. *Understanding Dispensationalists.* Phillipsburg, NJ: P&R, 1993.

Rendtorff, Rolf. *The Covenant Formula: An Exegetical and Theological Investigation.* Translated by Margaret Kohl. Old Testament Studies. Edinburgh: T. & T. Clark, 1998.

Robertson, O. Palmer. *The Christ of Covenants.* Phillipsburg, NJ: P & R, 1981.

Taylor, John B. *Ezekiel: An Introduction and Commentary.* TOTC 22. Downers Grove, IL: InterVarsity, 2009.

Williamson, Paul R. *Sealed with an Oath: Covenant in God's Unfolding Purpose.* NSBT 23. Downers Grove, IL: InterVarsity, 2007.

5

LIBERATION AND DELIVERANCE

JAMES SPENCER

INTRODUCTION

Necessitated by sin, required in a fallen world, and often forgotten by those whom it benefited most, God's liberation demonstrates his unfailing love for creation and his commitment to restoring a world distorted by human rebellion. Entailing far more than physical safety or political freedom, the liberation of God offers humanity the renewed opportunity to remember God faithfully within a world order empowered by the theological reality of God's faithfulness.

As a term within Old Testament theology, "liberation" has most often been associated with a particular species of theology, namely liberation theology. Gustavo Gutiérrez's 1971 work titled *A Theology of Liberation* has become one of the most recognized, foundational works of liberation theology, particularly within the Latin American tradition. As described by Gutiérrez, liberation theology "is an expression of the right of the poor to think out their own faith."[1] The emphasis on the poor in Gutiérrez's work serves the broader purpose of critically assessing the church's responsibility

1. Gutiérrez, *Theology of Liberation*, xxi.

vis-à-vis the poor and the oppressed.[2] The Israelite's Exodus from Israel and God's salvation as a whole are central to Gutiérrez's formulation of liberation theology. He asserts "a close link between creation and salvation," which is "based on the historical and liberating experience of the Exodus."[3] He goes on to identify creation as God's original act of salvation that is "regarded in terms of the Exodus, a historical-salvific fact which structures the faith of Israel."[4]

Not all theologians have embraced Gutiérrez's approach. Nunez, while ultimately sympathetic to Gutiérrez's concerns, critiques Gutiérrez's approach in which "liberating historical praxis determines the meaning of theology."[5] Pannenberg argues that Gutiérrez's conception of liberation theology and others like it require a theory of justice noting, "The problem is that the aspirations of social classes and of nations who think of themselves as oppressed are not necessarily justified. Whether they are or whether their claims are excessive can be determined only by standards of justice."[6]

Gutiérrez's work is not representative of all theologies that might fall into the liberation theology camp. Liberation theology encompasses works While there is not space to do justice to the unique aspects of each instance of liberation theology, Rowland offers some helpful characteristics of liberation theology more broadly. He notes that liberation theologies are "rooted in ordinary people's everyday experience of poverty" and that those experiences are "closely related" to the interpretation of Scripture, as well as the affinity of liberation theologies for biblical books that are "often ignored or despised" by other Christian communities. Rowland also underscores the deep connection between liberation theology and the life of the church, particularly in rural and urban settings. Liberation theology, according to Rowland, is "explored not just in the tutorial or seminar but engages the whole person in the midst of a life of struggle and deprivation. It is a theology which, above all, often starts from the insights of those men and women who have found themselves caught up in the midst of that struggle, rather

2. Ibid., 102. Note also De La Torre's treatment concerning structural sin and its significance for theological reflection to Hispanic American religion in De La Torre, *Hispanic American Religious Cultures*. Similar themes are echoed in the work of Boff, Chittister, Segundo, and Sobrino. See Boff, *Church, Charism and Power*; Chittister, *Fire in These Ashes*; and Segundo, *Liberation of Theology*. While each of these scholars make unique contributions to the overall movement of liberation theology, the underlying presuppositions of these theologians places them into a broader category with Gutiérrez.

3. Gutiérrez, *Theology of Liberation*, 86.

4. Ibid., 89.

5. Nunez, *Liberation Theology*.

6. Pannenberg, *Christian Spirituality*, 65.

than being evolved and handed down to them by ecclesiastical or theological experts."[7]

Though liberation theologians are certainly right to identify instances of systemic evil and to call the church to extend its theological activity beyond personal piety, the Old Testament's witness to liberation, particularly as it is described in Israel's exodus from Egypt, has a decidedly theological purpose from which justice and mercy derive. Liberation provides God's people with the theological context in which God can be remembered and faithful living empowered.

LIBERATION AND THE GOSPEL

While the gospel is often, and rightly, understood as the message that God sent Jesus to die for sinners and conquer sin and death so that all who believe in Him may have eternal life, those who place their faith in Christ also inherit a shared history, a collective memory, of God and his acts. The people of God remember Christ's death and resurrection, His faithfulness to Israel, the exodus from Egypt, and a host of other acts through which God revealed himself to the faithful and unfaithful alike. This remembrance is not simply an act of recall or a bringing to mind the past action of God. Instead, remembering the actions of God entails a new way of life re-ordered by the ongoing acknowledgement of God's wisdom, presence, and power.

The liberating message of the gospel offers those who accept the opportunity to develop the sort of character commensurate with the Kingdom of God. The gospel provides the context for a life of peace, gentleness, humility, and gratitude that cannot be cultivated by a world ordered by human wisdom. Christian character is only possible in a world in which God acts, rules, and empowers those faithful to him. It is only possible in a world in which women and men have been liberated by the message of the gospel. In the end, the proclamation of the gospel is not only a matter of evangelism, but of the embodied witness of those who have been liberated from sin to live for righteousness.

7. Rowland, "Introduction: The Theology of Liberation," 2.

ANALYSIS OF KEY TEXTS

The Exodus as a Clash of World Orders

The first two chapters of Exodus portray God's continued care for the nation of Israel despite the malicious activities of Pharaoh. Pharaoh is portrayed as a powerful, obstinate leader whose concern for national security requires the development of an oppressive regime characterized by forced labor and genocide. As Gordon McConville states, "here rule is in the hands of an all-powerful figure, whose concern for order . . . is characterized by fear and the readiness for domination by force. In Pharaoh's mind, the world threatens his order with war and sedition, and this leads inexorably to a policy of repression and cruelty."[8]

With the growth of the Israelite population, the Pharaoh "who knew not Joseph" (Exod 1:8) sets in motion a series of attempts to curtail Israelite growth for fear that the Israelites will turn against Egypt and side with Egypt's enemies should an enemy decide to attack (v. 10). It would appear that Pharaoh's motivation is not simply fear in the Israelite's collective might though he does recognize that the Israelites have become a threat (v. 9). He is also concerned with their departure (v. 10). Pharaoh has built an empire on the backs of the bruised, which is threatened by potential military action and uprisings, as well as the departure of the slave labor that is allowing Egypt to prosper.

In an effort to minimize the Israelite threat, Pharaoh opposes Israel's mandate, which was originally given in Gen 1:28. The connection of the Creation Mandate with Israel is underscored by the use of certain terminology in Exod 1:7. The use of "fruitful," "multiplied," and "filled" recalls the employment of these same terms in the proclamation of the creation mandate in Genesis further strengthening the connection between Genesis and Exodus.[9] Andrew Schmutzer describes the mandate to "be fruitful and multiply" as "God's functional blessing, a vitality of relationship, status, and capability for both propagation and governance."[10] Though originally

8. McConville, *God and Earthly Power*, 52.

9. Though Yahweh is not the stated source behind the fruitfulness and multiplication of Israel, the connections between Exod 1:7 and other passages in the Pentateuch suggests divine empowerment. The repetition of one or more of these verbs in connection to the divine blessing of God's covenant people are repeated at several points in the Pentateuch (Gen 1:28; 9:1, 7; 17:6, 20; 26:22; 28:3; 35:11; 47:27; 48:4; Exod 23:30; Lev 26:9). See Schmutzer's treatment of this theme as it relates to Genesis 1–11. Schmutzer, *Be Fruitful and Multiply*. Note also the discussion in Cohen, "*Be Fertile and Increase, Fill the Earth and Master It.*"

10. Schmutzer, *Be Fruitful and Multiply*, 226.

given to all humankind in Gen 1:28, Israel would now embody the mandate as a nation "whose covenant and legislation were retrospectively grounded in the theological language of the Creation Mandate that called for fertility, dominion, and the imposition of world order."[11]

Understanding Exod 1:7 as a manifestation of Yahweh's blessing rooted in the Abrahamic covenant and the pronouncement of human destiny in Gen 1:28, highlights Pharaoh's opposition to the purposes of a God whom he does not know (5:2). Pharaoh understands the growth of the Israelites as a threat to the nation's security (Exod 1:9–10) and imposes a system of hard labor and oppression in an attempt to control the Israelites. When the Israelites continue to multiply despite their labor, Pharaoh changes his strategy to one of more direct population control through the elimination of all newborn Israelite males.

Pharaoh first attempts to implement his program of genocide by enlisting the "Hebrew midwives" (1:15–21). Though it is often assumed that the midwives are actually Hebrew by ethnicity, the Hebrew text does not require such a reading. It may be that the midwives were Egyptian and simply assigned to work with the Hebrews. Pharaoh addresses the command for forced labor and for the drowning of the Hebrew males in the Nile to the Egyptians using the phrase "all his people" (1:9, 22). Though not conclusive, the Egyptian audience of the other two commands suggests that the midwives are also part of Pharaoh's people and should be identified as Egyptian. In this reading, even Pharaoh's subjects exhibit the fear of the Lord refusing to assist Pharaoh in his attempt to limit the Israelite threat. God shows favor to the midwives and "the people increased and became even more numerous." Once again, Pharaoh's attempts to oppose God's creation mandate fail.

After his failed attempt to enlist the midwives in his plans, Pharaoh commands "all his people" to "cast into the Nile" every newborn son. While this plan appears to have been carried out, Moses, whom God will use as he delivers Israel, is drawn out of the Nile and adopted by Pharaoh's daughter. The liberation of Moses foreshadows the coming liberation of Israel, though as the ensuing narrative makes clear, Moses himself is not Israel's deliverer. When Moses kills an Egyptian taskmaster who is mistreating a Hebrew man, not even the Hebrews recognize his right to do so (Exod 2:14). Pharaoh chases Moses out of Egypt highlighting Moses' inability to oppose the Pharaoh's will.

Whereas Pharaoh is unsuccessful in his destruction of the Hebrews, Moses is unsuccessful in delivering the Hebrews. Both men react to what they perceive to be emergent situations, yet neither is able to change the

11. Ibid.

state of things through their reactions. It is this dynamic that makes Exod 1–2 pivotal for understanding the significance of God's liberation in the rest of the exodus narrative. God's liberation is not simply political. It is covenantal. The goal of such liberation is not the liberation of the oppressed as such, but the liberation of God's oppressed covenant people whose worship and service to him is being stifled. God's liberation in this instance, while benefiting the people of Israel, has as its end the fulfillment of the covenant that God made with Abraham, Isaac, and Jacob and the glorification of God.

This goal could not have been achieved by Moses or through an Israelite revolution. Shifting power from one human government to the next lead by one would-be-savior after another, isn't liberation. . . it's a change of scenery. There is a fundamental difference between a regime change and God's liberation, namely that God's liberation comes with the theological empowerment to live unencumbered by concerns related to security and abundance. For instance, God's liberation brings manna and water in the desert (Exod 16:35; 17:6; Num 11:9; Deut 8:15), protection from enemies (Deut 7:1–2; 23:14), and future security (Deut 12:10–11). As such, God's people may worship and serve him alone without reserve or regret. The uniqueness of God's liberation is well illustrated in the command to keep Sabbath to which we will now turn.

The Sabbath Connection

It is difficult to overestimate the importance of the exodus to the formation of Israel's theology. Describing the significance of the exodus, Gerhard Von Rad asserts, "wherever it occurs, the phrase 'Yahweh delivered his people from Egypt' is confession in character. Indeed, so frequent is it in the Old Testament, meeting us not only in every age (down to Dan IX 15), but also in the most varied contexts, that it has in fact been designated as Israel's original confession."[12] The significance of the exodus is not only evident in Israel's confession, but also in the prescription of practices that keep the exodus fresh in the minds of the Israelites. One such prescription is that of the weekly Sabbath rest.

The command to practice Sabbath occurs in Exod 20:8–11 and Deuteronomy 5:12–15. The exodus from Egypt is not mentioned explicitly in Exod 20:8–11 with the rationale for the Sabbath command being identified as the seven day pattern of creation being found in 20:11. Because God created the world in six days and rested on the seventh, the people of Israel are to work for six days and rest on the seventh. Whereas the Sabbath command

---

12. Von Rad, *Old Testament Theology*, 175–76

in Exodus identifies God's creative activity as the reason for Israel's Sabbath, the command in Deuteronomy omits any explicit rationale for Sabbath practice. Instead, the command in Deuteronomy focuses on the result of Sabbath keeping, which is the remembrance of God's liberationn the Exodus from Egypt.

The connection between Sabbath and exodus raises the question of why Sabbath would remind the Israelites of their former slavery and liberation from Egypt. Sabbath has often been viewed as being motivated by concerns related to social justice, particularly in Deuteronomy. As Miller notes, "the primary impetus to social justice in Deuteronomic theology is the command to keep the sabbath."[13] Von Rad distinguishes between the reference to creation in Exodus, which he identifies as a theological element, and the more humanitarian nature of Deuteronomy.[14] Such understandings may be influenced by the omission of any reference to creation and by the final purpose clause in Deut 5:14 ("so that your male servant and your female servant may rest as well as you"). Walter Harrelson seems to have been influenced in this manner focusing almost exclusively on the social-ethical aspect of the command in Deuteronomy noting,

> Human beings need rest, and especially do servants need rest
> . . . the slaves or servants of human beings, at least one day in
> seven, must know that God does not condemn human beings to
> slavery forever . . . Deuteronomy underscores the social-ethical
> need for human beings to have rest from grinding labor. The
> human being is not just an instrument, a tool, and labor is not
> all that human beings are made for.[15]

Pinchas Kahn follows a similar line of thought suggesting, "The Deuteronomy version relates reasons for the Sabbath to God's Almightiness, to Israel's redemption from Egypt and ensuing freedom from slavery. The sanctification of the Sabbath is now primarily described as a sociological scheme protecting slaves and workers."[16] While the Sabbath certainly has implications for the "least of these" in society, it is not primarily a social-ethical command, but a theological one.[17]

13. Miller, "Human Sabbath," 82.

14. Rad, *Deuteronomy*, 58.

15. Harrelson, *Ten Commandments and Human Rights*, 80. This purpose is explicitly stated in Exod 23:12 and is listed as an effect of God's ceasing from his labor in 31:17; however, other purposes are listed in 31:14–16 (cf. also Lev 16:31).

16. Kahn, "Expanding Perspectives of the Sabbath," 240.

17. Note, for instance, that the Sabbath serves as a "sign" between God and Israel that is linked to God's identity as the sanctifier of Israel. See Timmer for a fuller discussion

The social-ethical implications of the command identified by Harrelson and others are driven less by humanitarian concerns than by concerns related to right theological expression. God's liberation and subsequent rule differs from that of Pharaoh in that endless labor is not required to sustain a national economy. Given that the Sabbath is meant to remind the Israelites of their slavery and liberation from Egypt, the practice of Sabbath and the provision of rest to those who serve the Israelites should be viewed in contrast to the treatment of the Israelites in Egypt in order to underscore the theological reality in which God's people now live their lives.

Israel was not delivered from Egypt so that they could rebuild the Egyptian system under Israelite rule. Liberation was not intended to bring about a reversal of power relations, but a fundamental change in the system of governance. Pharaoh's economy required labor and precluded the worship of the Lord. Once they were delivered, however, Israel was brought under the rule of the Lord. This new Sovereign is capable of providing for his people without their work. The call to practice complete rest on the Sabbath recalls that the power behind the Israelite economy is not found in the amount of labor accomplished, but in the provision of God. Labor done on the Sabbath, even that done by servants and animals, conveys wrong theology and undercuts God's faithfulness to those who keep his commandments.

The continued remembrance of Israel's slavery and subsequent liberation solidifies the distinction between Israel and other nations. The practice of Sabbath, like various other practices in Israel, stands in contrast to the governing systems of other nations. In the case of Sabbath, God's liberation allows Israel to enter a world unlike that of the nations which must depend upon slave labor and tyranny for survival. Such dependence, as illustrated by the Egyptian regime under Pharaoh and the subsequent exodus, denies loyalty to Yahweh and produces a society in which the worship of Yahweh must be made subordinate to the labor deemed necessary to sustain that society. Walter Brueggemann notes that Israel's work stoppage "attests that it does not belong to and is not defined by the production pressures and schedules and quotas of the world . . . Work stoppage is not only a great act of trust in YHWH, but it is a daring act of refusal. Israel refuses because to be defined by production (and consumption) entails the loss of the very freedom given in the Exodus."[18]

Israel's Sabbath is more than a humanitarian activity. It is an ongoing practice that is made possible by God's liberation and continually reminds Israel that they no longer live under the regime of Pharaoh, but under the

---

of the connection between God and sanctifier and Sabbath. Timmer, *Creation*.

18. See Brueggemann, *Deuteronomy*, 74.

benevolent hand of the Lord. The liberation of Israel from Egypt serves as the defining event to which the Israelites look to understand themselves as a nation. In the practice of Sabbath, Israel enacts a new way of life made possible by God's liberation of the Israelite people from Egypt. God's liberation brings with it new possibilities for living within the world. Sabbath, as one such possibility, proclaims the far-reaching nature of God's liberation, which was not simply freedom from slavery, but freedom to live according to God's Law. Horst Preuss summarizes the implications of the exodus well noting, "Israel's way of life, including, for example, its orientation to kingship, to luxury and urban existence, to the cult, and to other nations, is grounded in and illuminated by the exodus event."[19]

UNITY OF THE THEME IN THE OLD TESTAMENT

The exodus serves as the founding event of the nation of Israel and defines God's identity in relation to Israel. Even before he has rescued the Israelites from Egypt, he had begun to introduce himself to them as the one who "will bring you out from under the burdens of the Egyptians" (Exod 6:6–7). Similar statements are found throughout Scripture (Exod 13:9; 16:6, 32; 18:1; Lev 19:36; 25:38; Num 23:22; Deut 6:12; 16:1; Josh 24:6; 1 Kgs 8:21, 53; 2 Chr 7:22; Jer 7:22; 11:4; 34:13; Dan 9:15). The identification of God as the one who brought the Israelites out of Egypt is employed in different ways throughout the Old Testament. In the Pentateuch, when God identifies himself as the one who brought the Israelites out of Egypt, it is often intended to authorize the Lord's commands (Exod 20:2; Lev 19:36; 22:33; 25:38; Num 15:41; Deut 5:6) or to provide the reason for those commands (Lev 25:42, 55; cf. Deut 13:10). The celebration of the Passover (Exod 23:15; 34:18; Deut 16:1–6), consecration of the tent of meeting (Exod 29:43–46) and the festival of booths (Lev 23:42–43) are also motivated by a desire for the Israelites to know that God is the one who delivered them from Egypt. So central is the identity of God as deliverer that the Israelites are called not to forget him when they are brought into the Promised Land (Deut 6:12; 8:14), but to teach their children that the Lord brought the Israelites out of slavery (6:21).

God's identity as the God of the exodus is not forgotten outside of the Pentateuch. Joshua uses it to bolster the confidence of the Israelites when they are about to enter the Promised Land (Josh 2:10). In Judges, the Israelites do not simply forsake the Lord through their worship of foreign idols. Instead, they forsake "the Lord, the God of their fathers, who had brought

---

19. Preuss, *Old Testament Theology*, 47.

them out of the land of Egypt" (Judg 2:12). The exodus is also utilized to request God's favor (Judg 6:13; 1 Kgs 8:51, 53; Dan 9:15). Perhaps most significant is the use of the exodus in prophetic calls to repentance. Jeremiah begins his critique of Israel with a reference to the exodus from Egypt (2:6) noting that despite the Lord's liberation and provision, the Israelites continued to worship idols. Hosea 11:1 makes a similar point. Despite the liberation of the Lord, the Israelites have refused to remain faithful. Though it does not call the people of Israel to repent, Isa 51:9–10 recalls the exodus to emphasize God's capacity to save the Israelites.

The Old Testament, particularly the book of Isaiah, also speaks of a new exodus, which will surpass the previous exodus from Egypt (Isa 35:10; 43:16–21; 51:9–10; 51:1; 52:7–12).[20] The portrayal of the coming restoration of God in terms of the original exodus from Egypt is significant. Von Rad notes, "A remarkable aspect of Deutero-Isaiah's message is that on the one hand he so depicts the departure of the exiles from Babylon as to recall the first exodus from Egypt and the miracles which accompanied it; yet he is also aware that Yahweh's new revelation is something which cannot possibly be represented."[21]

CONTINUITY WITHIN THE NEW TESTAMENT

References to the exodus are relatively infrequent within the New Testament. Stephen recounts the events of the exodus in Acts 7:17–36 as part of his broader recitation of Israel's history. The Pharaoh of the exodus is referenced in Rom 9:17 as an example of the manner in which God uses humanity to display his glory. Hebrews highlights the faith of Moses in denying the riches of Egypt, leaving Egypt, keeping the Passover, and leading the Israelites through the Red Sea (11:24–29).

In addition to the more explicit allusions to the exodus, the New Testament develops the new exodus motif, which was introduced by the Old Testament prophets. Each of the gospels utilizes similar mechanisms to employ the new exodus motif. Rikki Watts has argued that several portions of the Gospel of Mark echo the language describing the new exodus in Isaiah.[22] David Pao's study identifies similar uses of Isaiah in Luke-Acts

---

20. Block also identifies the new exodus motif at numerous points in Ezekiel (11:17; 20:34–35; 20:41–42; 28:25; 29:13; 34:13; 36:24; 37:12, 21; 39:27). See Block, *Book of Ezekiel*, 353.

21. Rad, *Message of the Prophets*, 214.

22. Watts, *Isaiah's New Exodus in Mark*.

to develop a new exodus motif.[23] In addition to the specific textual allusions, such as those sited by Watts and Pao, there is a broader thematic use of the new exodus motif apparent within the New Testament. Pao notes, ". . .in the development of the identity of the early Christian movement, the appropriation of ancient Israel's foundation story provides grounds for a claim by the early Christian community to be the true people of God in the face of other competing voices."[24] This understanding of the role of the new exodus motif underscores both the continuity between Israel and the community of believer's in the New Testament and discontinuity as this new community participates in and benefits from its own exodus.

IMPLICATIONS FOR THE MODERN CHURCH

God's liberation more generally, and the exodus in particular, continue to remain relevant to the modern church. First, the exodus and the subsequent new exodus shape the identity of the Church. God's people have been rescued from "all that oppresses human life and well-being and opposes God."[25] Just as the Israelites were given the opportunity to live life outside of the present world order, to govern their society in a way different than Pharaoh, so the Church has been given the opportunity to live outside the normal boundaries of the world.

The Church does not need to reason by the logic of the world, yet it often does. Commenting on the manner in which the Church and individual Christians think about justice, Stanley Hauerwas notes, "Christians have lacked the power that would enable themselves and others to perceive and interpret the kind of society in which we live. Christians have rightly thought that they have a proper investment in making this, and other societies, more nearly just, but have forgotten that genuine justice depends on more profound moral convictions than our secular polity can politically acknowledge."[26] Hauerwas's point is that believers sometimes forget that justice is not the fruit of secular society. Instead, justice, in its fullest sense, is most truly manifested through the atoning work of Christ on the cross and through the believing community that is empowered to live in accordance with that sacrifice. Learning to reason theologically stands at the heart of the Church's identity as it is seeks to live faithfully in the midst of a hostile world.

23. Pao, *Acts and the Isaianic New Exodus.*
24. Ibid., 5.
25. Wright, *Mission of God*, 278.
26. Hauerwas, *Community of Character*, 74.

Second, God's liberation requires more than a change in societal power relations. It requires more than changes in legislation or societal practice. The church cannot seek to deliver the oppressed through political or humanitarian means alone. Instead, the church must seek to participate with God in his efforts to deliver those who are still oppressed. The church should not only demonstrate the manner of its new life in God, but should also strive to move with God as he acts within society. To suggest that the church should move with God rather than act of its own accord should prompt the church to theologically informed action that is bathed in prayer and refined by practice.

God's liberation, as it has been experienced by the church, offers a radical shift in thought and life. The extreme nature of the shift precludes the possibility that this liberation comes through human action. The Church must recognize that its role is not to act as an agent of liberation, but to follow God to fulfill the Great Commission. The church must take strides to ensure that its actions in the world are not its actions alone, but that the church is participating with God. Prayer, fasting, worship, the performance of sacraments, and the continued obedience of the believing community remain central to the practices of the believing community, yet the church must also remain pliable to the movement of God so that its inability to move does not preclude their participation in God's activity.

QUESTIONS FOR DISCUSSION

1. How are God's liberation and law giving related in the history of Israel?

2. In what manner do our various Christian practices today (like Sabbath) reflect God's character?

3. While we may not live under a pharaoh, the world continues to combat God and seek to minimize those who follow him. How do you see this happening in the world?

BIBLIOGRAPHY AND RECOMMENDED READING

Block, Daniel I. *The Book of Ezekiel, Chapters 1–24*. NICOT. Grand Rapids: Eerdmans, 1997.

Boff, Leonardo. *Church, Charism and Power: Liberation Theology and the Institutional Church*. Translated by John W. Diercksmeier. 1985. Reprint, Eugene, OR: Wipf & Stock, 2012.

Brueggemann, Walter. *Deuteronomy*. AOTC. Nashville: Abingdon, 2001.

Chittister, Sister Joan. *The Fire in These Ashes: A Spirituality of Contemporary Religious Life*. Franklin, WI: Sheed & Ward, 1999.

De La Torre, Miguel A. *Hispanic American Religious Cultures*. Santa Barbara: ABC-CLIO, 2009.

Gutiérrez, Gustavo. *A Theology of Liberation*. Translated by Sister Caridad Inda and John Eagleson. Maryknoll, NY: Orbis, 1988.

Harrelson, Walter J. *The Ten Commandments and Human Rights*. Macon, GA: Mercer University Press, 1997.

Hauerwas, Stanley. *A Community of Character: Toward a Constructive Christian Social Ethic*. Notre Dame: University of Notre Dame Press, 1991.

Kahn, Pinchas. "The Expanding Perspectives of the Sabbath." *JBQ* 32 (2004) 239.

McConville, J. G. *God and Earthly Power: An Old Testament Political Theology*. New York: T. & T. Clark, 2006.

Miller, Patrick D., Jr. "The Human Sabbath: A Study in Deuteronomic Theology." *PTSB* 6 (1985) 81–97.

Nuñez, Emilio A. *Liberation Theology*. Chicago: Moody, 1985.

Pannenberg, Wolfhart. *Christian Spirituality*. Louisville: Westminster John Knox, 1983.

Pao, David W. *Acts and the Isaianic New Exodus*. Eugene, OR: Wipf & Stock, 2016.

Preuss, Horst Dietrich. *Old Testament Theology*. Louisville: Westminster John Knox, 1996.

Rad, Gehard von. *Deuteronomy: A Commentary*. Translated by Dorothea Barton. OTL. Philadelphia: Westminster, 1966.

———. *The Message of the Prophets*. Translated by D. M. G. Stalker. New York: Harper & Row, 1972.

———. *Old Testament Theology*. Translated by D. M. G. Stalker. New Introduction by Walter Brueggemann. 2 vols. OTL. Louisville: Westminster John Knox, 2001.

Rowland, Christopher, ed. *The Cambridge Companion to Liberation Theology*. Cambridge Companions to Religion. Cambridge: Cambridge University Press, 1999.

Schmutzer, Andrew J. *Be Fruitful and Multiply: A Crux of Thematic Repetition in Genesis 1–11*. Eugene, OR: Wipf & Stock, 2009.

Segundo, Juan L. *The Liberation of Theology*. Translated by John Drury. 1976. Reprint, Eugene, OR: Wipf & Stock, 2002.

———. *Theology and the Church: A Response to Cardinal Ratzinger and a Warning to the Whole Church*. Translated by John W. Diercksmeier. Edinburh: T. & T. Clark, 1987.

Sobrino, Jon. *Christology at the Crossroads: A Latin American Approach*. Translated by John Drury. Maryknoll, NY: Orbis, 1978.

Timmer, Daniel C. *Creation, Tabernacle, and Sabbath: The Sabbath Frame of Exodus 31:12–17; 35:1–3 in Exegetical and Theological Perspective*. Forschungen zur Religion und Literatur des Alten und Neuen Testaments 227. Göttingen: Vandenhoeck & Ruprecht, 2009.

Watts, Rikki E. *Isaiah's New Exodus in Mark*. Grand Rapids: Baker, 1997.

Wright, Christopher J. H. *The Mission of God: Unlocking the Bible's Grand Narrative*. Downers Grove, IL: InterVarsity, 2006.

6

TORAH

RUSSELL L. MEEK

INTRODUCTION

Though few among us would deny the importance of the Law, or Torah, in the Old Testament, there remains significant confusion over what exactly Torah is and its function in the life of the New Testament believer. "Torah" is a Hebrew word that is typically translated "law" in English Bibles. Its New Testament counterpart, *nomos*,[1] also means "law" and likely accounts for the popular English translation of its use in the Old Testament. However, Torah means much more than law. In translating it with the English term "law," Christians have lost much of the breadth and depth communicated by the Hebrew term. Instead of "law," keeping with its broader meaning in Hebrew, we understand Torah to mean "instruction";[2] more specifically, Torah is instruction in living as the redeemed people of God.[3]

---

1. On Paul's use of *nomos*, see Moo, "'Law,'" 73–100.

2. Dyrness, *Themes in Old Testament Theology*, 129; Sweeney, "Book of Isaiah," 51.

3. Vogt, *Interpreting the Pentateuch*, 26–28.

Torah is also the term used to describe the first five books of the Old Testament,[4] also known as the Pentateuch, or the books of Moses. These five books dovetail into each other, thus forming one successive narrative with legal material (i.e., "law") interwoven throughout it.[5] However, the legal material forms only part of the narrative, and it is within the narrative that the legal material must be interpreted. God did not reveal his Torah as a list of "dos and don'ts" but rather in the context of the story of redemption. As we think through Torah, then, we must not confine it simply to the concept of law but rather see it as part of the larger picture of God's working in the world. As Gary Schnittjer explains, the Torah is "the beginning of a larger story that explains the meaning of the human situation and the hope for salvation. Torah is life."[6]

As we discuss Torah, we must of course consider the legal implications of Genesis–Deuteronomy and its role in governing the life of the people of Israel. However, we must also consider its role as the story of God's interaction with and redemption of his people. Ultimately, the entire Old Testament can be discussed in relationship to Torah.

We will see in the following pages that keeping Torah was paramount for the Israelites' relationship with Yahweh. Each of the three Jewish divisions of the Old Testament (Torah, Prophets, and Writings) is primarily concerned with Torah. The Pentateuch outlines the God's instructions ("Torah") for living in relationship with him. It tells the people of Israel how, now that Yahweh has redeemed them, they must live in order to maintain that special relationship. The prophets enter the story of God's work in the world long after the Torah has been revealed. They censure the people for a lack of obedience to Torah. They call for repentance and a return to faithful obedience to God's revealed Word—the Torah. When the people continue to rebel and refuse to keep Torah, we see their ultimate exile from the land of Israel. Wisdom literature extols Torah and highlights the importance of obedience to God's instruction.

TORAH AND THE GOSPEL

Biblical scholars have spent significant time and energy wrestling with the basic question of how the gospel of Jesus Christ changes the way Christians

---

4. We have chosen the term "Old Testament" over "Hebrew Bible" because this text is intended explicitly as a Christian theology of the Old Testament.

5. Schnittjer, *Torah Story*, 34.

6. Ibid., 39.

view and interact with Torah.[7] First, Torah is not entirely different from New Testament teaching. Its purpose was to teach the Israelites how to live in relationship with God; keeping Torah was never a way of *earning* righteousness but rather a response to an already existing relationship.[8] Obedience to Torah was to flow out of a heart devoted to and already in relationship with Yahweh. Furthermore, to use New Testament terms, the Israelites' relationship with God was based on his grace, which was exhibited in the covenant with Israel that he instituted apart from Israel's merit—God chose them from among all the peoples of the world in order to have a special relationship with them (Deut 7:6–8). Finally, their relationship with Yahweh was for the purpose of their being a light that would draw the nations to him. Each of these aspects of Torah remain true for the New Testament believer: God has revealed that we must be obedient to him (2 Tim 3:16); our obedience does not earn salvation (Rom 3:22); our obedience flows out of a loving relationship with him (Jas 2:14–26); that relationship is based on grace, not works (Eph 2:8–9); and we are to be a light to the nations (Matt 28:18–20). Furthermore, in Matt 5:17 Christ states that he came not to abolish Torah but to fulfill it.

Despite the continuity between Torah and the gospel, the gospel does indeed bring about significant change to Torah. Most importantly, as Jeremiah prophesied, God himself writes the gospel on the believer's heart in a way that enables him to live in right relationship with God (Jer 31:33; see also Ezek 36:26–28).[9] In contrast, the Torah was to be written on the heart by the believer, not God himself (Deut 6:6–9). Moreover, Christ himself is the arbiter of the new covenant that Jeremiah foresaw.[10] It is he who now makes restitution for sins once for all, as opposed to the imperfect sacrifices outlined in the Torah (Heb 10:1–18). Before examining in full how the New Testament relates to Torah, let us turn to key texts within the Old Testament that shape our understanding of the theological significance of Torah.

7. For a presentation and analysis of several popular views, see Gundry, ed., *Five Views*.

8. Skeel and Longman, "Criminal and Civil Law in the Torah," 81.

9. See Kaiser, *Toward an Old Testament Theology*, 233.

10. Dyrness, *Themes*, 141.

ANALYSIS OF KEY BIBLICAL TEXTS

Deuteronomy: The Importance of Keeping Torah

Space limitations preclude a full discussion of the giving of Torah found in the Old Testament, therefore this section will focus on the significance that Deuteronomy places on keeping Torah. Several key texts in Deuteronomy teach that God will bless those who are faithfully obedient to Torah, while he will curse those who are disobedient to Torah (see, e.g. Deut 6:1–25; 7:11–15; 24:17–22; 28:1–68). Taken together, these passages teach three important concepts related to Torah.[11]

First, Israel's relationship to Yahweh is not based on keeping Torah; instead, it flows out of Yahweh's gracious choice of Israel. The book repeatedly reminds the people that because Yahweh rescued them from slavery in Egypt, they should respond with obedience to him. Therefore, while obedience to Torah is a stipulation of Israel's relationship with Yahweh, it was never a condition of entering into that relationship.[12] Second, Israel must obey Torah from the heart (see Deut 6:1–25). That is, empty obedience is not sufficient to keep the commands of the Lord; rather, their obedience must come from a deep love and fear of Yahweh. The people are to love Yahweh with their entire heart, strength, and innermost being (Deut 6:5). As a result of this love, the people must keep Torah on their hearts continually and faithfully pass it along to their children. Third, Israel's response to Torah—whether obedience or disobedience—played a crucial role in the quality of life they would experience. Keeping the covenant handed down by Yahweh would result in such blessings as children, good health, long life, abundant crops and herds, and overall stability in the land of Israel (see especially Deut 7:11–15). Failing to keep Torah would result in the opposite: the people lives would be cut short, they would be expelled from the land, and they would experience dire consequences for their refusal to live in faithful obedience to Yahweh (see especially Deut 28:15–68).

---

11. The idea that obedience results in blessing and disobedience results in cursing is commonly called "retribution theology." On this concept, see, among others, Gammie, "Theology of Retribution," 1–12; van Leeuwen, "Wealth and Poverty," 25–36.

12. See Routledge, *Old Testament Theology*, 173.

Isaiah and Jeremiah:
Torah for All People and Torah for the Heart[13]

Torah figures prominently in each of the Major Prophets as well as the Book of the Twelve (the Minor Prophets). The book of Isaiah begins with a statement "denouncing economic and social oppression," issues with which Torah dealt specifically.[14] In this first message, the prophet pleads with the people to "give ear to the Torah of God" (Isa 1:10). The prophet goes on to state that there will be a time when "all the nations" will travel to Zion in order to learn from Yahweh, "for from Zion Torah goes forth and the word of Yahweh from Jerusalem" (Isa 2:3). Marvin Sweeney points out that this passage (Isa 2:2–4) is "generally understood as the prophet's vision of eschatological peace and co-existence among the nations of the world, and thereby constitutes a vision of a new world order in which YHWH's sovereignty is recognized by all the earth."[15]

These first two passages that mention Torah in Isaiah indicate at least two important concepts for our understanding of the prophetic view of Torah. First, the prophet calls the people of Israel to listen to Yahweh's Torah, or instruction, in order that they may once again be reconciled to Yahweh (see Isa 1:18–20). Second, Isaiah foretells a future time in which *all people*, not only the people of Israel, will submit to the instruction of Yahweh. As Charles Halton points out, then, "while the book of Isaiah, along with most other OT texts, presents *tôrâ* as a divine gift to Israel, it does not picture *tôrâ* as Israel's exclusive possession."[16] In sum, Isaiah sees all nations, not only Israel, as benefiting from and responsible to Yahweh's Torah, thus indicating that even in the Old Testament the people of God—albeit in a different manner—were responsible for engaging the nations "evangelistically" (see also Isa 51:4).[17]

The prophet Jeremiah, along with Ezekiel (Ezek 11:19; 36:22–38), speaks of a time when Yahweh will make a covenant with Israel and Judah in which he himself will write his Torah on their hearts. As noted above, Deut 6 teaches that the people themselves were to place God's instruction

13. Though much of critical scholarship has now moved away from the position that the prophetic literature predates Torah, this author presupposes that the prophetic literature came after and relies upon the Torah. This was the predominant view until the work of Julius Wellhausen in the nineteenth century (see Meek, "On the Development of Historical Criticism," 130–47).

14. Halton, "Law," 494.

15. Sweeney, "Book of Isaiah," 50.

16. Halton, "Law," 495.

17. Ibid. On the role of Israel in God's mission, see Wright, *Mission of God*.

on their hearts. Jeremiah, on the other hand, prophesies of a time when Yahweh will place his Torah on the heart of his people. Because of Yahweh's role in the new covenant, the people of God will finally be able to succeed in maintaining faithful obedience to him. The transition to the new covenant does not abolish Torah; rather, it highlights the importance of Yahweh's role in enabling the people to keep his statutes through him.

Summary

These passages teach that a theology of Torah must account for the supreme role of Yahweh as both the giver of Torah and the one who enables its keeping. Furthermore, keeping Torah was never meant to be a means of earning a relationship with God; rather, obedience is required by those already in relationship with God through his grace. Finally, Torah was not meant for the people of Israel only, but Israel was intended to be faithfully obedient to Yahweh in a way that caused other nations to seek him also.

UNITY OF TORAH WITHIN THE OLD TESTAMENT

Torah is a theme that runs throughout the entirety of the Old Testament. The Pentateuch records the giving of Torah, the requirements it places on the people of God, and the benefits and consequences of keeping or not keeping those requirements. The prophetic books decry the people's refusal to keep Torah and outline the consequences—already described in the Pentateuch—for their disobedience to Yahweh. Finally, the wisdom literature further explicates the impetus to keep Torah, along with dealing with the thorny issue of the suffering of the obedient.

Presentation of Torah

The Pentateuch recounts the story of Israel from the creation of the cosmos up until the people are on the edge of Canaan, about to enter and take possession of the land promised to their forefathers. Most important for our purposes is the giving of Torah at Sinai and the recounting of the Torah at Mount Horeb.

Exodus 1–12 tells of Yahweh's miraculous delivery of Israel from slavery in Egypt, and at the end of Exodus 12 (vv. 43–51) Yahweh institutes the Passover feast that is to stand as a reminder of Yahweh's faithfulness to the descendants of Abraham, Isaac, and Jacob. Shortly thereafter the people cross the Red Sea, after which Yahweh feeds Israel with bread from heaven. Even here, in Exod 16, we can see that the people struggle with keeping Yahweh's instruction, for many of them disobey by either taking too much manna or looking for it on the Sabbath. Nevertheless, Yahweh continues to be faithful to Israel, providing them with water from a rock and military victory of Amalek. Then the people come to Mount Sinai, where Yahweh presents them with his requirements (Exod 19). The remainder of Exodus through Numbers outlines the various laws that the people were required to keep, with narrative interspersed throughout the giving of these laws. Deuteronomy then summarizes the history of God's faithfulness of Israel's disobedience during the wilderness years and reissues the Torah for the new generation of Israelites who are about to enter Canaan.

In the giving of Torah and the narrative that surrounds it a few themes emerge. First, Israel's relationship with Yahweh is based solely on Yahweh's covenant commitment to her fathers Abraham, Isaac, and Jacob and the consequent rescue of Israel from Egypt. Second, although Israel's relationship with Yahweh was based solely on his grace, he nevertheless required obedience to his statutes. Relationship preceded obedience, and obedience was a natural outworking of the already established relationship. Obedience was not a pre-condition of Israel's relationship with Yahweh. However, the people's obedience or disobedience to Torah in large part determined the quality of life they could expect; to oversimplify, obedience would result in blessing while disobedience would result in cursing.

Third, Yahweh's instructions cover all aspects of life, indicating that God was concerned not simply with how Israel worshiped him but with everything they did, down to the type of clothing they wore (Lev 19:19; Deut 22:11). They are not merely commands regarding how to worship and interact with Yahweh—though they are at least that. Israel's relationship with God was all-encompassing, thus the instruction covers all aspects of life, including how the people are to worship, interact with others, and treat the land God had given them.

Most of all, Yahweh expects allegiance to him alone: "You shall not have other gods before me" (Exod 20:13). This first command brings us back to the first principle of the giving of Torah: Israel's relationship with God is based on his grace. In turn, he expects them to worship him and him alone. The prophets are most concerned with disobedience to this most basic command, from which stems the rest of their complaints against Israel and Judah. Once they refused to worship only Yahweh, their treatment of fellow humans plummeted well below the standard that Yahweh exhibited when he brought Israel out of Egypt and that he commanded throughout the Pentateuch.

Breaking Torah

Whereas the Pentateuch records the giving of Torah, the Prophets speak against the people's disobedience to Torah, calling them to repentance and warning against the coming judgment that was promised in the Pentateuch. J. Scott Duvall and J. Daniel Hays have summed up the overall message of the prophetic books in a way that captures the importance of Torah in them:

1. You have broken the covenant; you had better repent.

2. No repentance? Then judgment!

3. Yet, there is hope beyond the judgment for a glorious, future restoration.[18]

Duvall and Hays also point out the three primary ways in which the people have broken Torah: religious ritualism, idolatry, and social injustice.[19] Each of these issues is addressed clearly and repeatedly in Yahweh's instruction to Israel, so the people had no excuse for their disobedience. Because of their continued disobedience to Torah despite the prophetic call to repentance, God's people ultimately suffered exile, first the Israelites at the hands of the Assyrians then the Judahites at the hands of Babylon.

Despite the judgment that ultimately came upon the people of God because of their disobedience to Torah, the final aspect of the prophetic message—hope for a future—declares in no uncertain terms that Yahweh would restore his people.[20] Furthermore Jeremiah and Ezekiel spoke of a time when obedience would be possible because God himself would write Torah on the hearts of his people, thus enabling to be faithful to him. Therefore, while the prophetic relationship to Torah is largely a condemnatory call to repentance and return to obedience, it concludes on a hopeful note that speaks of a time when God's people would follow God's instruction.

Keeping Torah

The wisdom literature[21] of the Old Testament presents a conundrum for those who attempt to demonstrate its relationship to the rest of the Old

18. Duvall and Hays, *Grasping God's Word*, 403.

19. Ibid., 403–6.

20. Note that Yahweh's restoration is still not strictly dependent upon the people's obedience to Torah. They must demonstrate repentance and return to Yahweh, but the ultimate cause of their restoration is that Yahweh keeps his promises to Abraham and David. See Levenson, *Sinai and Zion*.

21. Though not technically wisdom literature, Psalms is treated under the broad

Testament.[22] Despite this, it is clear that Old Testament wisdom literature is concerned with teaching its audience the importance of keeping Torah.[23]

There are three psalms that are widely considered "Torah Psalms": Pss 1, 19, and 119.[24] Each of these psalms extols Yahweh's instruction in various ways. Psalm 1 details the life of abundance that can be expected by the one who keeps Torah; Ps 19 praises Torah for its perfection and ability to renew one's life; Ps 119, the most famous Torah Psalm, spends 176 verses describing the wonder of Yahweh's instruction and its many benefits. Additionally, scholars have noted that the five-book division of the Psalter intentionally relates it to the Pentateuch.[25]

Proverbs likewise places a high value of keeping Torah through righteous living. Essentially, Proverbs can be read as an elaboration on Torah that uses vivid word pictures to provide readers with examples of Torah applied. Furthermore, Proverbs highlights what was already seen in the Pentateuch: "A righteous life includes . . . more than strict adherence to the law."[26]

Ecclesiastes and Job also deserve mention here, though the traces of Torah in these books are less explicit. Both books struggle with the fundamental principle of Torah keeping outlined in Deuteronomy and illustrated in the Prophets, namely that obedience will lead to blessing and disobedience will lead to cursing. Job, the clearest example of the righteous sufferer, ultimately finds solace not in his own obedience to Torah but in God's self-revelation. Ecclesiastes struggles with various situations in which the wicked receive the rewards of righteousness and the righteous receive the consequences of wickedness (e.g. Eccl 3:16–17; 4:1–3; 5:8–9). However, rather than cast away Torah, the book argues that the appropriate response of humans in light of unpredictability of life is to enjoy the gifts God has given (e.g. Eccl 2:24–26; 3:10–15, 16–22; 5:18–20 [17–19]; 8:10–15; 9:7–10; 11:7–10) and to "fear God and keep his commands" (Eccl 12:13).

---

category of wisdom literature.

22. See Meek, "Wisdom Literature," 63–77.

23. As with the prophetic corpus, the present discussion presupposes that the Pentateuch predates wisdom literature, which was the predominant view until the rise of historical criticism (see n12 above). For the view that the law arose out of wisdom literature, see Jackson, *Wisdom-Laws*, 45–59.

24. See Wells and Magdalene, "Law," 420.

25. E.g., Wilson, "Shape of the Book of Psalms," 129–42.

26. Ibid., 421. Wells and Magdalene are arguing that Proverbs adds wisdom to the "formula" for attaining blessing from Yahweh. However, even in the Pentateuch one can see that righteousness is much more than "mere obedience" to the law but rather includes the proper heart toward Yahweh and his instruction (see above).

PRESENCE OF TORAH IN THE NEW TESTAMENT

Torah is a formative theme that runs throughout the Old Testament. The same can be said of the New Testament. The following discussion will argue that there is no tension in the New Testament in regards to the relationship between followers of Christ and the Torah. As in the Old Testament, for Christians today obedience to God's instruction flows out of the already established relationship based on God's gracious gift. Here we will look briefly at Jesus's fulfillment of Torah.

Jesus as Fulfillment of the Law

Jesus states in Matt 5:17 that he has not come to do away with the Law and Prophets but rather to fulfill them.[27] Jesus continues: "until heaven and earth pass away, not an iota, not a dot, will pass from the Law until it is accomplished. Therefore, whoever relaxes one of the least of these commandments and teaches others to do the same will be called least in the kingdom of heaven, but whoever does them and teaches them will be called great in the kingdom of heaven" (Matt 5:18 ESV). Is Christ teaching that each part of the Torah must be kept in its entirety? Not necessarily, for as Schreiner points out, Jesus's statements about the fulfillment of the Law must be interpreted in light of the entirety of Matthew's Gospel.[28]

In looking at the rest of Matthew, it seems that "Matthew's point is probably that the ministry of Jesus fulfils the true intention in giving the law, and one cannot understand the Old Testament without identifying the one to whom it pointed."[29] This becomes clearer in Jesus's Sermon on the Mount, in which he demonstrates that true obedience to Torah is not simply the outward keeping of commands. It is insufficient simply not to commit the physical act of adultery; rather, one should maintain a standard of purity that eschews lustful thoughts (Matt 5:28).

This understanding of Jesus's demonstration of the true intention of Torah also explains why aspects of Torah such as circumcision and dietary restrictions are no longer binding on Christians (Mark 7:19; Acts 10:1—11:18; 15:1–29). As Schreiner argues, these two aspects of Torah were physical indicators of the separation between Jew and Gentile that are no longer necessary now that Christ has come.[30] True circumcision is circumcision

---

27. For a full discussion on this text, see Schreiner, *Law and Its Fulfillment*, 234–40.

28. Ibid., 235.

29. Ibid., 240.

30. Ibid., 228–29.

of the heart (Rom 2:29), and what comes out of a person's mouth, not what goes into it, is what makes one unclean (Matt 15:18).

Finally, whereas Jesus's life and ministry clearly demonstrated the true intent of Torah, his death and resurrection made it possible for humans to have unhindered communion with God. As prophesied by Ezekiel and Jeremiah, when Christ died the veil in the temple was torn (Matt 27:51), thus demonstrating the inauguration of the new covenant in which God writes his Torah on the hearts of his people. Schnittjer is correct: "The meaning of Leviticus 18:5 is true for all to whom it applies: the one who obeys the law will live by it. The Five Books of Moses and Romans agree that it is true in principle, but a fictional or hypothetical category in the context of sinful humankind. No one obeys. The Torah damns sinners."[31] This is where the beauty of the gospel is most evident, for whereas every human since Adam had failed to keep Torah in its totality, Jesus completely fulfilled its demands by living a sinless life. All who place faith in him receive the righteousness that could never be attained through their own efforts. This sacrificial death, and giving of life through grace, is the fulfillment of Torah.

In sum, it can be said that there is significant continuity between the Torah as presented in the Old Testament and the type of obedience that God requires in the New Testament. Torah's intent was *not* to provide a means of salvation for the people of God. Instead, obedience to Torah was the proper outworking of an already established relationship that was based solely on the gracious gift of Yahweh. He rescued Israel; as a result, they were to obey him. In the same way Christians are called to loving obedience to the Father based on the gracious establishment of a relationship with him. No one can earn a right relationship with God through obedience to him. The right relationship has already been established through Christ's atoning death on the cross. Obedience to his Word, then, must flow out of love for God based on what he has already done on the cross.

Despite the similarities in what God requires of his people, Torah and gospel are indeed different. In one sense Torah speaks death.[32] The laws outlined in the Pentateuch cannot be kept by mere humans. They show the way to faithful obedience to the Father, but the narrative surrounding them shows that humans are a sinful and rebellious lot. In this the Old and New Testaments are in complete agreement: the Law brought death because people were made aware of God's instruction and yet remained in disobedience.

In another sense, though, Torah speaks life in that it shows the deep human need for a savior. It is "the beginning of the story that reaches its

31. Schnittjer, *Torah Story*, 534.
32. Ibid.

height in the death and resurrection of the Messiah. The Torah story is the beginning of the gospel story . . . The gospel does not remove the need for Torah, it enlarges it. The story that the Torah began finds its completion and goal in the gospel."[33] Torah shows us that Yahweh places upon us certain demands that we are unable to keep, which highlights our constant need of grace. The gospel is the good news that God has demonstrated his grace by reconciling sinners to himself through Jesus Christ. What humanity could not do, Christ has done.

TORAH AND CHRISTIANS TODAY

What, then, is the relationship between Torah and Christians today? How are Christians to understand Torah? Since it is clear that the Old Testament was supremely concerned with Torah, and Jesus Christ states that he is the fulfillment of Torah, we cannot simply cast it aside. An important concept for the church to grasp is that Jesus has both completed Torah's demands on behalf of those who place faith in him and has demonstrated its true intent. Yahweh's instruction is, and always was, meant to show people how to live in right relationship with him based on grace. The question remains, though, whether Christians are to obey Torah, or if they are to cast aside one of the most prominent themes in the Bible. We contend, along with Paul, that "All Scripture is inspired by God and is profitable for teaching, for rebuking, for correcting, for training in righteousness, so that the man of God may be complete, equipped for every good work" (2 Tim 3:16–17 ESV). Consequently, we must also determine how Christians are to apply Torah.

Perhaps the most common approach in evangelical circles to applying Torah is to divide the commands into the categories of moral, civil, and ceremonial. Civil laws apply specifically to the theocratic state of ancient Israel while ceremonial laws are no longer applicable because Christ has provided the ultimate sacrifice. Moral laws remain because they address how the people of God are to live in the world.

This approach is very helpful for determining which laws apply to Christians today. However, it is problematic because such divisions are foreign to the biblical text. Moral laws appear in the same context as civil and ceremonial laws (e.g., Lev 20 contains laws regarding sexual purity and dietary restrictions). Furthermore, the original Israelite audience did not distinguish between secular and religious the way that modern Western Christians do. As Vogt points out, "For the original audience of the legal material of the Pentateuch, issues relating to 'civil' life were considered to

---

33. Ibid., 534–35.

bear as much religious significance as moral or ceremonial issues, because all of life was lived in the presence of Yahweh. It is hard, then, to draw distinctions that would have been foreign to the mind of the original author and audience of the laws."[34] Finally, there is a grave danger that dividing the laws into these categories might cause the reader to miss rich theological truth that remains applicable even when the particular law itself does not.[35] For example, the principle behind prohibiting the mixing of fabrics in clothing is that Yahweh himself is holy.[36] By wearing only clothes made from one type of fabric, the people of Israel were daily reminded of the purity and holiness of Yahweh.

Therefore, instead ignoring the texts that seem inapplicable, we should seek to interpret and apply *all* of Torah in a way that draws out its theological significance.[37] To do this, we must remember that Christ showed that the true intent of Torah was not only to prevent certain physical activities (e.g. adultery, murder), but rather to address the heart issue that lay beneath those outward expressions. Therefore, when reading Torah, we should seek to understand what gave rise to a particular command. Once the underlying principle, that is, its theological significance, is determined, we can apply the command to our modern-day context. This is precisely what Jesus did in the Sermon on the Mount. For example, the issue that lay behind the prohibition against adultery was the sanctity of marriage that God established in the garden of Eden. In order to protect the marriage relationship, adultery is forbidden. The heart issue that ultimately leads to adultery is lust; therefore, maintaining a pure thought life also staves off adultery.[38] Of course, this principle is much more difficult to keep than is the command not to commit adultery, which further highlights the Christian's need for Christ.

By reading Torah with the intent of understanding and applying its underlying theological principles, we are able to recover a significant portion of the Bible for modern-day Christians. In the process we will re-discover the deep theological significance of a portion of the Bible that has too often been neglected because of its ostensible inapplicability to the Christian life.

---

34. Vogt, *Interpreting the Pentateuch*, 44.

35. Note that this is merely a danger, not a foregone conclusion, inherent in this approach.

36. Ibid.

37. Duvall and Hays (*Grasping God's Word*, 355–72) describe an excellent method for doing this, which is summarized here.

38. For discussion of how Christians are to interpret and apply Old Testament texts, see Vogt, *Interpreting the Pentateuch*, 32–46.

QUESTIONS FOR DISCUSSION

1. Why has Torah been neglected by modern-day Christians? What is lost by this neglect? What can be gained by returning to study Torah?

2. Describe the theological significance of Torah according to the prophetic literature. In what ways would Christians today be indicted by the prophets in regards to our obedience to God's instruction?

3. What is the significance of using the term "Torah" instead of the term "Law"? How does this change the way you read and interpret the Law?

4. Read Deuteronomy 22:8. What is the theological significance of this command? How can it be applied in a modern context?

BIBLIOGRAPHY AND RECOMMENDED READING

Duvall, J. Scott, and J. Daniel Hays. *Grasping God's Word: A Hands-On Approach to Reading, Interpreting, and Applying the Bible.* 3rd ed. Grand Rapids: Zondervan, 2012.

Dyrness, William A. *Themes in Old Testament Theology.* Downers Grove, IL: IVP Academic, 1977.

Gammie, John G. "The Theology of Retribution in the Book of Deuteronomy." *CBQ* 32 (1970) 1–12.

Gundry, Stanly N., ed. *Five Views on Law and Gospel.* Grand Rapids: Zondervan, 1999.

Halton, J. Charles. "Law." In *Dictionary of the Old Testament: Prophets,* edited by Mark J. Boda and J. Gordon McConville, 493–501. Downers Grove, IL: InterVarsity, 2012.

Jackson, B. S. *Wisdom-Laws: A Study of the Mishpatim of Exodus 21:1—22:16.* Oxford: Oxford University Press, 2006.

Kaiser, Walter C., Jr. *Toward an Old Testament Theology.* Grand Rapids: Zondervan, 1978.

Van Leeuwen, Raymond C. "Wealth and Poverty: System and Contradiction in Proverbs." *HS* 33 (1992) 25–36.

Levenson, Jon D. *Sinai and Zion: An Entry into the Jewish Bible.* New York: HarperOne, 1987.

Meek, Russell L. "On the Development of Historical Criticism." *Midwestern Journal of Theology* 13 (2014) 130–47.

———. "Wisdom Literature and the Center of the Old Testament." *CTR* 11.2 (2014) 63–77.

Moo, Douglas J. "'Law,' 'Works of the Law,' and Legalism in Paul." *WTJ* 43 (1983) 73–100.

Routledge, Robin. *Old Testament Theology: A Thematic Approach.* Downers Gove, IL: IVP Academic, 2008.

Schnittjer, Gary. *The Torah Story: An Apprenticeship on the Pentateuch.* Grand Rapids: Zondervan, 2006.

Schreiner, Thomas R. *The Law and Its Fulfillment: A Pauline Theology of Law.* Grand Rapids: Baker, 1993.

Skeel, David, and Tremper Longman III. "Criminal and Civil Law in the Torah: The Mosaic Law in Christian Perspective." In *Law and the Bible: Justice, Mercy, and Legal Institutions*, edited by Robert F. Cochran Jr. and David van Drunen, 80–100. Downers Grove, IL: IVP Academic, 2013.

Sweeney, Marvin. "The Book of Isaiah as Prophetic Torah." In *New Visions of Isaiah*, edited by Roy F. Melugin and Marvin A. Sweeney, 50–67. JSOTSup 214. Sheffield: Sheffield Academic, 1996.

Vogt, Peter. *Interpreting the Pentateuch: An Exegetical Handbook*. Handbooks for Old Testament Exegesis. Grand Rapids: Kregel Academic, 2009.

Wells, B. and F. R. Magdalene. "Law." In *Dictionary of the Old Testament: Wisdom, Poetry, and Writings*, edited by Tremper Longman III and Peter Enns, 420–27. Downers Grove, IL: InterVarsity, 2008.

Wilson, Gerald H. "The Shape of the Book of Psalms." *Int* 46 (1992) 129–42.

Wright, Christopher J. H. *The Mission of God: Unlocking the Bible's Grand Narrative*. Downers Grove, IL: IVP Academic, 2006.

7

THE MESSIAH WITHIN
THE PSALTER

Bryan C. Babcock

INTRODUCTION

Psalms is a collection of poetry that has, for centuries, refreshed the hearts of its readers. We read about the jubilant celebration of mankind rejoicing with their God. We also read about the sorrows and pain caused by sin and share in the comfort of forgiveness. These psalms touch our sole and bring us closer to God.

But are the psalms speaking only within an historical context at the time of writing? Or might these poetic passages also contain a prophetic component that will later be revealed? This chapter explores how some royal psalms include both an original historical context and a prophetic component that is only realized through the death and resurrection of Christ.

For this chapter we will examine Ps 110, which begins with "A Psalm of David. The Lord (*Yahweh in the original Hebrew*) says to my lord: 'Sit at my right hand, until I make your enemies your footstool.'" But who is this second "lord" who is invited to sit at God's right hand—is it Jesus, David, or Solomon? The words are a bit ambiguous, making the identification difficult.

The essence of the question is whether the original author acted as a prophet and wrote the psalm with a full understanding of the coming Messiah or whether the author wrote based upon a contemporary historical context. If the latter, then the original writing contained both a contemporary historical context *and* an as yet unrecognized meaning pointing to the Messiah.

Psalm 110 continues in v. 4 with "the LORD has sworn and will not change his mind, 'You are a priest forever after the order of Melchizedek.'" This second important verse tells us that the "lord" from v. 1 is both a king and a priest—something unusual and perplexing for Israel. These two passages (vv. 1 and 4) are among the most referenced Old Testament texts by New Testament authors. The New Testament authors reference these two passages over thirty times, and many of these quotations and allusions hold dramatic theological significance.

The key questions to explore when studying Psalm 110 are: 1) who is the "my lord" referenced in the psalm (v. 1)? Is it David, Jesus, or someone else? 2) How can this figure be exalted to sit on a glorified throne next to God? And 3), in v. 4, who is the "priest" who will be in the order of Melchizedek?

A reading of the psalm highlights the inherent ambiguity, as the referent for several pronouns is unspecified. Depending upon your interpretation, the pronouns in the passage might imply various meanings. Below is a translation of the psalm outlining some possibilities for the referent of the pronouns:

> The LORD [*God*] says to my Lord [*God, Messiah, the king, or the king's son Solomon*]: "Sit at my [*God's*] right hand, until I [*God*] make your [*Messiah's, king's, or king's son's*] enemies your footstool."
>
> The LORD [*God*] sends forth from Zion your [*Messiah's, king's or king's son's*] mighty scepter. Rule in the midst of your [*Messiah's, king's or king's son's*] enemies!
>
> Your [*Messiah's, king's or king's son's*] people will offer themselves freely on the day of your [*Messiah's, king's or king's son's*] power, in holy garments; from the womb of the morning, the dew of your [*Messiah's, king's or king's son's*] youth will be yours [*Messiah's, king's or king's son's*].
>
> The LORD [*God*] has sworn and will not change his [*God's*] mind, "You [*Messiah, king or king's son*] are a priest forever after the order of Melchizedek."
>
> The Lord [*God, Messiah, or the king*] is at your [*God, Messiah, king or the king's son*] right hand; he [*God, Messiah, king or*

the king's son] will shatter kings on the day of his [*God, Messiah, king or the king's son*] wrath.

He [*God, Messiah, king or the king's son*] will execute judgment among the nations, filling them with corpses; he [*God, Messiah, king or the king's son*] will shatter chiefs over the wide earth.

He [*God, Messiah, king or the king's son*] will drink from the brook by the way; therefore he [*God, Messiah, king or the king's son*] will lift up his [*God, Messiah, king or the king's son*] head. (Ps 110:1–7)[1]

This chapter employs an historical-contextual methodology to study the original context and structural unity of the psalm at the time of authorship. Further, we will discuss the essential coherence between an Old Testament understanding and the ultimate meaning in Christ. As you can see from the pronoun interpretations above, there is great room for ambiguity in the passage. Therefore, careful attention to details in the language is essential to understanding the meaning. When all the data is brought together, we hope to better understand the intention of the original author. Further, we will offer applications for the modern church.

THEME: MESSIAH IN THE PSALMS

Judaism and Christianity share the view that many of the psalms point toward a coming Messiah. The authors of the New Testament identify roughly fifteen psalms as falling into this category. These passages give us a theological understanding of the coming Christ. This section will explore several of the shared features of the messianic psalms and provide a glimpse into their theological understanding.

Beginning in Ps 2 we find the prominent feature of the *anointed king who will accomplish great things*. This kingly figure, assisted by God, overthrows the foreign kings and powers of the entire earth (Ps 2:2–5). In addition, God gives the kings of the other nations as his inheritance and the ends of the earth as his possession (v. 8). The king is "anointed," using the term *māšîaḥ*, or Messiah/Christ. While the initial context for this language was likely a Davidic king's coronation. The superlative language points to a fulfillment far in excess to the life of King David (or other Davidic kings)—pointing to a fulfillment as some later date.

---

1. Unless otherwise noted, Scripture quotations in this chapter are the author's translation.

Psalm 45 expands on this king who will rule the world. In the context of a wedding song, the writer alludes to a *divine king whose reign will last forever* (Ps 45:6). Verses 6–7 read "Your throne, O God, will last for ever and ever; a scepter of justice will be the scepter of your kingdom. You love righteousness and hate wickedness; therefore God, your God, has set you above your companions by anointing you with the oil of joy." Twice in this verse the psalter calls the king "God." The author of Hebrews clarifies that the intended referent of the Psalm was Jesus (Heb 1:8). In the same chapter, Hebrews links Ps 97:7 and Ps 102:25–27 with a divine anointed king worthy of being called God.

The first chapter of Hebrews also draws a connection between Pss 2 and 89 and the Messiah. The passages discuss the king as the *Son of God and heir to the entire earth.* Psalm 89:27 indicates that God "will appoint him (the king) my first born, the most exalted of the kings of the earth." The psalm goes on to note that this messianic king's reign will endure as long the heavens and that God will maintain his covenant with the king forever. While this is a clear echo back to the Davidic covenant, it also points forward to a son who is to come. This message of the messianic king as son is also supported in Ps 2:7, where God decrees that the king has become God's son.

Several other characteristics of the coming messianic king are found in the psalms. These traits include a *suffering servant* (Pss 69:17; 86:2, 4, 16), the *stone that builders rejected* (Ps 118:22), and *the son of man* (Ps 8:4). Each of these characteristics is confirmed as applying to Christ through New Testament authorship. Armed with an overview of messianic characteristics, we now turn to an in-depth exploration of Ps 110.

ANALYSIS OF A KEY TEXT: PSALM 110

Psalm 110 includes seven verses divided into 3 sections:

- Verses 1–3: God establishes the king
- Verse 4: God establishes a priest-king
- Verses 5–7: God secures the king's rule

The first section of the psalm begins with the heading "A Psalm of David." This designation is found in multiple psalms including 101, 108–10, 122, 124, 131, 133, and 138–45. The Hebrew (*lĕdāwid*) includes a preposition that can be translated *to* David, *for* David, *by* David, *of* David, or *about* David. The authorship of the psalm is often attributed to David. However, we may (at a minimum) support the notion that the psalm concerns David or a direct descendent of David.

Verse one continues "The LORD says to my Lord." The psalm begins with a special phrase reserved to indicate a prophetic utterance (*nĕ'um Yahweh*), "from the LORD." This prophetic formula is often identified with the prophets Isaiah, Jeremiah, Ezekiel, and Amos before they speak God's words. However, the term is applied once to David in 2 Sam 23:1 as David speaks a prophetic utterance form God before he dies. Therefore, we know that the psalm is a prophetic statement from the LORD (Yahweh). The speaker of this prophecy may be a prophet; however, one cannot rule out a prophetic statement from David himself. If the utterance from God is spoken by a prophet, then the focus of the psalm is upon God's word to the king. If, however, the utterance is spoken by David, then the focus of the psalm is either upon a future exalted individual who is to come (the Messiah) or upon David's son (possibly Solomon) who will soon sit on the throne. Perhaps the best clue to the meaning of the passage is found in the choice of the Hebrew form for the word "lord." When an author desires to write "my Lord" (referring to God) the typical pointing is *ădōnāy*. However, in this passage the author writes *ădōnî* which is most often used to describe *any* person of higher authority (e.g., the king). While the pointing does not rule out God as the referent, it more likely points to David or Solomon.

The utterance of God begins in v. 1, reading, "Sit at my right hand, until I make your enemies your footstool." From ancient times, to the right hand of authority is a place of honor and power. The addressee in the passage is metaphorically invited to sit in a place of prestige (cf. Ps 80:17 [18]). The intertwining of God's throne with the king's throne is supported in 1 Chr 28:5, where Solomon is invited to sit on the throne of the kingdom of God forever (cf. 29:23; 1 Chr 9:8). In addition, God not only honors the individual but uses God's own power to act on behalf of the individual to overwhelm and dominate the addressee's enemies. The imagery of enemies bent over as a footstool is prominent in Egyptian iconography (also present in Assyrian iconography). The king was often depicted as sitting on a throne with his feet resting on the backs of a defeated enemy.

Depending upon who is voice in the passage, this verse may be interpreted in several ways. First, the statement may be a prophetic statement that a future messianic king will rise and be seated at God's right hand while God subdues the future messiah's enemies. Second, the prophecy may apply to David where an idealized David is glorified and supported by God. The language of the Davidic covenant supports this interpretation. The context would also fit a coronation renewal ceremony for David, who is serving as the chosen king by God. In this case, David is seated at his throne next to the throne of God in God's temple. Therefore, the image is both literal and metaphorical. Third, the statement may apply to a son of David (Solomon). If this third option is correct, the context of the passage would fit the coronation ceremony in which David is passing his authority to the future king. Similar language of sitting at the right hand is found 1 Kgs 2:19 regarding Bathsheba, who sat at Solomon's right hand. At this point in the analysis, each of the options reads as possible. In order to settle on the best historical context, we must see if each fits the context of the remaining verses.

Verse 2 continues the utterance of God, reading, "The LORD sends forth from Zion your mighty scepter. Rule in the midst of your enemies!" This passage both supports and further explains the oracle in v. 1. Interpretation of the verse is not without challenges. In verse one, the LORD is speaking in the first person, whereas in v. 2 the verbs change from first person to third person. The options are either that the oracle has ended and the speaker is explaining the meaning of the oracle or, more likely, that God is referring to himself in the passage. The metaphor changes as the subject of the oracle is no longer sitting at the right hand of God. Instead, the king or Messiah is now acting (through the power of God) to rule over the enemies in battle. The location of Zion is used as a metonymy to locate the kingdom at Jerusalem and the "mighty scepter" to represent the powerful king, commissioned by the LORD, leading the Israelites into battle. The author specifically chooses a Hebrew verb for "rule," clarifying that the rule mentioned is to subdue and dominate by force (*rādâ*).

This section comes to a close with v. 3: "Your people will offer themselves freely on the day of your power, in holy garments; from the womb of the morning, the dew of your youth will be yours." The passage continues the theme that the subject of the passage will be victorious in battle. The people will joyously follow the king/Messiah into battle at the time of the subject's powerful anointing by God. Two keys support this interpretation. First, the verb for "offer themselves" is most often associated with a voluntary offering for the temple. Second, those volunteering for military service are in holy garments. An alternate translation reads "holy splendor," which supports the notion that the people of Israel are acting with God's support. The second half of the verse is more difficult to understand. "From the womb of the morning" is not found elsewhere in the Bible. However, a similar phrase is found in Isa 14:12 with the meaning of a rapid rise (or fall). Therefore, this phrase may imply that the king/Messiah will rise quickly with the help of the Israelites to defeat their enemies. The passage may alternatively mean the morning. The meaning of the final clause is also challenging. It is possible that the "dew of your youth" refers to the youth of the warriors—implying that the success of the young and untrained army lies with God. Or, following Ps 133:3, that the dew refreshes the king. A third option is found in 2 Sam 17:12, where the warriors will fall like dew upon the enemy. Despite the possible understanding of the metaphor, it seems clear that God's oracle is one of support, protection, and domination over the addressee's enemies.

The psalm moves to a second oracle in v. 4. "The LORD has sworn and will not change his mind, 'You are a priest forever after the order of Melchizedek.'" This second word from God (continuing in the third person) is intensified, as it is not only an oracle but also a solemn oath from the LORD. The first message from God involves placing and supporting the king on the throne. The impression of the prior statement is one of military power. Now God states that the king is also a priest. Melchizedek was first mentioned in Gen 14:18 encountering Abraham after a battle with neighboring kings. The Bible depicts Melchizedek as a priest-king of Salem (Jerusalem) who worships the God Most High (*El Elyon*). While many neighboring nations around Israel combined the office of the priesthood and the role of king, the biblical laws distinguish clearly between the offices of king, prophet, and priest. Despite this distinction, David and Solomon are both exceptions to this practice, as both are addressed in multiple theocratic roles. As an example, 2 Sam 6:14 depicts David dancing in a priestly robe (linen ephod). In addition, David performs functions as a priest in 2 Sam 6:17–18—giving a blessing and in charge of sacrifices. Each are functions reserved only for the priests. Similarly, Solomon gives a priestly blessing, performs offerings, and extends his authority over the high priest (1 Kgs 2:27, 35; 8:14, 55, 62–64). As these passages suggest, it seems that God elevates David (and his heirs) giving him charge over the true worship of the LORD.

We now turn to the third section of the psalm with God securing the king's rule. Verse 5 reads, "The Lord is at your right hand; he will shatter kings on the day of his wrath." This passage continues with some interesting interpretational issues. First, in v. 1 we find "The LORD says to my Lord," where the second "Lord" in v. 1 likely refers to a human king (due to the use of the Hebrew *ădōnî*; see above). Now the Hebrew form points to the identification of God as Lord (using *ădōnāy*). Because the author has now utilized two distinct forms of the same word it becomes clear that the "lord" most likely refers to God. In addition, the evidence supports the conclusion that the first use of "lord" (*ădōnî*) was intentional to specify a non-divine lord—i.e., the king. Based upon this conclusion, we will now position the king as referent in the psalm.

A second interpretive point is that the message continues in the third person. While God is speaking an oracle to the king, God refers to himself as "God" and "he." Also, the king is no longer at God's right hand. Now

God is at the king's right hand. To be positioned at the right hand is found elsewhere as a position of protection and support (Pss 16:8; 109:31; 121:5). The metaphor has once again switched positions between the king and God. In v. 1 God is conducting the action on behalf of the king. Verses 2–3 shift to the king accomplishing the action with the support of God. No in v. 5 God again takes on the action, destroying enemies and shattering foreign kings. The choice of the verb "to shatter" is found in a similar context in Ps 18:38 [39] where God supports the king in battle. The king will benefit as God moves forward to secure the king's kingdom. The verse also references a day of God's wrath. Two items are remarkable about the presence of this phrase. First, v. 5 is tied to v. 3 through the use of parallelism as v. 3 mentions the king's day of power and now in v. 5 we find God's day of wrath. Second, the term for wrath is the ordinary word for anger (*'ap*) and not the word for divine wrath (*hemah*). The implication is that when the king fights fiercely, it is due to his anger (providing a source of energy).

The oracle continues in v. 6: "he will execute judgment among the nations, filling them with corpses; he will shatter chiefs over the wide earth." The message moves from a statement of ongoing protection and military support to a future aspect of judgment. Nations that resist Israel and the will of God will be judged. The concept of God's judgment upon the nations is common among both prophetic texts (e.g., Jer 25:31; Ezek 5:8, 15; 36:19; 39:21; Joel 3:2, 12) and psalms (e.g. Pss 2:9; 7:8; 9:8; 76:9). The oracle continues with strong language that this judgment will include the death of armies (corpses) and the destruction of leaders. The message concludes with hyperbolic language that the reach of God's judgment will stretch over the entire earth.

The psalm concludes with a final statement: "he will drink from the brook by the way; therefore he will lift up his head." The subject of this passage is ambiguous and difficult to discern. In v. 6 the third-person personal pronoun refers to God. If God continues as the subject of this passage, then after the judgment God pauses to drink from a brook and lifts up God's own head. If so, then perhaps God is refreshing (purifying?) himself after judgment. While possible, this understanding seems unlikely. The more likely option is that the oracle has ended and the king drinks from a brook and the "lifting up his head" idiom refers to the king being refreshed after God has completed God's protection and judgment. In other words, the king is able to live in peace while standing in confidence and triumph.

What Is the Setting for the Psalm?

The setting for the psalm is likely a coronation event. The speaker appears as a court prophet or priest speaking to David giving three oracles to the king—"The Lord (God) says to my lord (David), 'sit at my right hand . . .'" (Ps 110:1). If this setting is correct, then the speaker is viewing David as the ideal king. He is glorified to sit at God's right hand as God punishes all of Israel's enemies and subduing them under David's feet. This idealized metaphor fits the time of David through the prophetic covenant in 2 Sam 7 as well as the court writings of surrounding nations—especially Egyptian texts and iconography.

The oracle in the psalm continues with God acting on behalf of the king to rule over surrounding nations. The writer uses a metaphor of the king's scepter coming from Zion for the king's control of nations like Edom and Moab. This again fits David's historical context. However, the writing is idealized; David did not control all nations. The psalm concludes with more poetic imagery of David leading an enthusiastic army in victory over Israel's foe.

The psalmist next speaks to David, declaring him both king and priest. This claim is supported by relating David to Melchizedek, who ruled as a priest king of Jerusalem in the time of Abraham. The psalmist also identifies David as adopted into the priesthood, just as Melchizedek was adopted into being a High Priest of Yahweh (God). As discussed above, both David and Solomon are viewed as conducting various functions reserved for the priest. Therefore, the passage supports an historical understanding for David.

Finally, a third oracle continues the theme of an idealized victory for King David over his enemies. God is viewed at the king's right hand delivering victory over Israel's enemies. God will overturn kingdoms, crush foreign rulers, and deliver judgment upon all the earth. The initial hearers would have understood the statement as an idealized metaphor for the support of Israel and David by God. While David did substantially expand the kingdom of Israel, he did not rule the entire earth. This form of idealized metaphor for divine support of the king is quite common in ancient Near Eastern texts of the period. Kings were viewed in hyperbolic language as exterminating an entire nation and ruling to "four corners of the earth."

Each of these components matches the historic context for the time of King David. Further, the writings of proximate ancient Near Eastern nations supports both the content and style for the psalm. Finally, the language of psalm fits with the language of a coronation of the king—spoken to the king by a priest or prophet conducting the ceremony. Therefore, we conclude the text held a contemporary historical context at the time of David before the full prophetic understanding of the oracles is made clear in the New Testament.

UNITY OF THE THEME IN THE OLD TESTAMENT

There is messianic development arising from Ps 110 as this text is interpreted by later communities. However, to understand fully this development it is important to take a step back and discuss the foundation of messianic thought. Central to the idea of a Messiah is the idea of progressive revelation, the notion that Scripture was both written by individuals and guided by the Holy Spirit. As such, the original author may have had one understanding when writing. However, a fuller understanding (intended originally by the Holy Spirit) becomes clear in later scriptural interpretation.

The concept of a messianic figure is grounded in the Davidic covenant: a king with an eternal house (2 Sam 7:16), anointed with God's spirit to rule justly with righteousness (Ps 21:9ff) as the people's source of strength and life (Lam 4:20; 2 Sam 21:7; Hos 3:4–5). David is viewed as the ideal king who performs God's will and, as a result, is granted an eternal reign. The nation viewed this language as literal (not hyperbolic) and expected an heir of David to rule over a united Israel for all time.

This notion is challenged within two generations as the kingdom is ripped in two after Solomon's reign. Additionally, both kingdoms are lost to Assyria and then Babylon. Therefore, because the promises of God seem to go unfulfilled, the Israelites begin to look to the Scripture as pointing toward a "new" David who will restore the godly kingdom of Israel.

The royal psalms not only discuss a current king (often David and Solomon) but also point to an ideal future king. The anointed king rules to the ends of the earth (Ps 2:7–8) as long as the sun endures (72:5) and sits at the right hand of God (110:1). Many of the psalms foreshadow suffering and rising in glory. This matches both the immediate context where David will be successful and his heirs will suffer—only to be restored in later generations—and messianic expectation in the New Testament.

The prophets demonstrate that a future David-like king would rule Israel. When Ahaz abused the people, Isaiah (Isa 7:14) says a future son of David would reign. Later, Isaiah includes the Suffering Servant passages (42:1–7; 49:1–6; 50:4–11; 52:13–53:12). Micah 5:2–6 announces a king to come from Bethlehem. The prophets view the loss of the Davidic dynasty as a punishment upon the nation for sinful behavior. These prophets then call for revival and repentance, after which the nation and dynasty will be restored. Zechariah and Haggai foreshadow the rise of Zerubbabel (a son of

David) and Joshua (high priest), and when they failed the hope shifted to a future messiah. (Some of this shift in interpretation is seen in the Greek translation in the Septuagint/LXX.)

The death of the postexilic prophets (Haggai, Zechariah, and Malachi) signaled the end of the prophetic voice in Israel. The levitical singers compensated for this void in the Second Temple period by bringing an eschatologically oriented message of hope and consolation to the postexilic community (1 Chr 16:7–36; 25:1–31; 2 Chr 20:18–30). This was increasingly applied to the royal psalms that pointed to judgment and vindication. Theologically, the focus on David shifted to an ongoing Davidic promise through the Davidic covenant—with fulfillment in a messianic reign.

During the Second Temple period the idea of a Messiah intensified (e.g., 1 Enoch, Syriac Apocalypse, Baruch, Apocalypse of Abraham, 4 Ezra/2 Edras). 1 Enoch discusses the son of man (46:1–3) as the chosen one—a heavenly figure with God from the beginning of time and the judge of the world. The Syriac Apocalypse discusses "my Anointed" (29:3; 39:7; 40:1; 70:9; 72:2) as a royal figure who ushers in a period of bliss (74:2). The Messiah will reign over God's remnant (40:2–3). In 4 Ezra a divine figure ushers in a new eon of incorruptibility after his death (7:30–44). *Testament of Levi* (4:4; 5:2; 10; 14–15), while edited in the Christian era, discuss priesthood and kingship. The Book of Jubilees features Jacobs blessing of Levi and Judah (31:13–20). A descendent of Judah will rule, pointing to both David and a future king. In the Qumran texts the Teacher of Righteousness writes about a new era with a duly appointed high priest and a Davidic prince (the high priest was more important). The Dead Sea scrolls demonstrate a Qumran community expectation of two Messiahs, one political and one priestly. David was now considered a prophet (see 11QPsa): "All these he uttered through prophecy which was given him from before the Most High."[2] The early Greek translation of the Psalms (called the Septuagint or LXX) shows this changing view in its nuanced translation of passages like Ps 1:5, which is changed from "will not stand" to "will not rise," leading to an eschatological idea of rising from the dead. Finally, the message of the Psalms of Solomon anticipates God's deliverance through a Davidic king (17:5–6, 21; 8:5, 7, 11).

Turning specifically to Ps 110, there are no specific references to the psalm in the rest of the Old Testament. It is possible that Isaiah uses the exaltation theme in Isa 52:13 during the exaltation of the Suffering Servant (understood by the Targum messianically). The notion of being "high and lifted up" is usually reserved by Isaiah only for God (e.g., 6:1; 14:13–14; 33:10). A second possible adoption of the exaltation theme from Ps 110 may

2. 11QPsa.

be found in Dan 7:13, where the Son of Man is given the glory and honor reserved only for God.

There are, however, several Second Temple period writings that find messianic connections with Ps 110. The Dead Sea Scrolls envision Melchizedek as a messianic figure. He will preside over Israel's new-exodus liberation at the end of days (11Q13, II, 4; cf. Isa 61:1). Further, he makes atonement for the sins of the people (II, 6–8), effects God's judgment (II, 13), and is exalted into God's presence (II, 9–11). A final reference occurs in 4Q491c 1, 11, where a messianic figure wins an eschatological battle, vindicates the priestly community, and rises to be enthroned with God. Each case is connected to Ps 110 through similar themes, similar language, and the mention of Melchizedek (cf. *b. Sukkah* 52b where Melchizedek returns in the messianic age).

Following the idea of a messianic figure who is a priest, several pseudepigraphal texts interpret themes also found in Ps 110. The *Testament of Levi* describes a new priest who will rise into God's chamber like a king (18:2–3; cf. Ps 110:3). In addition, this messianic figure will be the final in the line succession (18:8; cf. Ps 110:4) and will grant authority to destroy wicked spirits (18:12; cf. Ps 110:1). The *Testament of Job* (33:3) relates that a suffering Job points to a second throne at the right hand of God as his source of vindication, stating that his "throne is in the upper world." While not messianic, *Mekilta Exodus* 15:7–8 relates God destroying various enemies using a quote from Ps 110:1–4.

In the first century AD the rabbinic literature depicts David as an eschatological figure sitting on a throne with God. The similitudes of *1 Enoch* 37–71, uses similar language to Isaiah's Suffering Servant and Danial's Son of Man to identify David as the chosen one sitting upon God's throne at the end of days. Rabbi Akiba argues a similar position when reading Dan 7:9 (*b. Hag.* 14a; *b. Sanh.* 28b). Akiba finds two thrones (one for God and one for David; cf. Ps 110 1–2); however, in his interpretation David is given a radiant crown and throne of fire. The Targum of Ps 110 interprets the psalm eschatologically, with David appointed as the leader of the age to come because of his meritorious righteousness (Ps 110:4). In an echo of both Ps 110 and Gen 14, God will rise to defeat the foreign kings. However, in many texts Abraham (and not David) sits that the right hand of God (*b. Sanh.* 108b.; *Midr. Ps.* 110:4; *Tanh.* Gen 3:17; 4:3).

Based upon the available references and allusions to Ps 110 in later discussion, what can we conclude? A historical review would argue that later Jewish interpretation built upon the Davidic covenant in 2 Sam 7, finding that David was a type of ideal king and that God's promises to David were literal. Because the promises to David, through the time of the exile and return, had not been fully realized, God must have a future "Davidic king" in mind. In searching the Scriptures, the rabbis linked David, the Suffering Servant, and the Son of Man as a future eschatological king. In addition, these rabbis found a future messianic priest who would come in power (Qumran interpretation). By the first century, many were looking to Ps 110 and Melchizedek as the unifying link. Therefore, these two individuals—a Davidic king and a powerful priest—were not two different individuals. Rather the two were one messianic figure, a priest-king in the order of Melchizedek *and* a divine king in the line of David. This evolving understanding (progressive revelation) was adopted by the New Testament authors.

IMPLICATIONS FOR READING THE NEW TESTAMENT

As you can see from the section above, the New Testament authors are joining a long history of Old Testament interpretation. A historical-contextual review argues that a trajectory set in 2 Sam 7 with the Davidic covenant already existed. Further, this understanding was interpreted through the lens of the divided monarchy, the exile, and the Second Temple period. The contemporary (first century AD) interpretation understood the earlier Scripture as pointing toward a singular messianic priest-king. Authors of the New Testament built upon the earlier interpretations and added a progressive understanding. These New Testament authors used Ps 110 in three ways to support the association of the psalm with the Messiah: eschatological typology, rhetorical typological, and realized typology.[3] This section of our study will unpack each of these uses by various New Testament authors.

Eschatological Typology:
Partial Fulfillment Now and Partial Fulfillment Later

In the Synoptic Gospels Jesus uses Ps 110 typologically and eschatologically to support the messianic claim in Matt 26:64; Mark 14:62; and Luke 22:69. We define the term typological as something mentioned in an Old Testament passage (a person, action, event, or some other item) that is viewed through the New Testament lens as a prefiguration or type of something in the future in which the subject is developed in a fuller and richer way. Essentially, the New Testament author reveals a relationship between the Old

---

3. These categories were created following discussions with Kathy Maxwell. I truly appreciate her allowing me to adopt and revise her work.

Testament person/action/event that was heretofore unknown but is made clear in the New Testament. The interpretation here also has an eschatological component as the New Testament revelation is as yet unfulfilled and points to a later time when the literal understanding will be realized.

These three parallel passages (Matt 26:64; Mark 14:62; and Luke 22:69) relate the questioning of Jesus before the Sanhedrin. The high priest asks if Jesus believes himself to be the Messiah. Jesus's response relies upon an eschatological messianic typological interpretation of Dan 7:9–13 and Ps 110: 1–3. In his reply Jesus says, "But I tell you, from now on you will see the Son of Man seated at the right hand of Power and coming on the clouds of heaven." In this passage Jesus associates himself with the Son of Man from Dan 7:13 who is prophesied to arrive on the clouds and the Lord who sits at the right hand of God in Ps 110:1. The high priest understands this statement as messianic and responds by tearing his clothes and calling the association blasphemy. Thus Jesus, who is still very much in human form, is pointing to a future where he will return on the clouds. This future scene is eschatological in nature, as Jesus will be revealed as the Messiah at a still future time. Everyone will know who Jesus is when he is seated at the right hand of God (as in Ps 110), returning on the clouds using God's might to judge the world.

Therefore, Jesus is building upon the progressive understanding of the Second Temple period in which Ps 110 is viewed through a messianic lens. The New Testament understating was that being seated at the right hand of God conveyed a royal (and perhaps messianic) status. Jesus connects Ps 110 with Dan 7, demonstrating a typological connection between the Old and New Testaments. Based upon Jesus's revelation, we now understand that Ps 110 is not just relating to a royal individual metaphorically seated at the right hand of God. Instead the "Lord" seated with God in Ps 110:1 is the Messiah. Further, Jesus clarifies that he is, in fact, this Messiah. While making a typological connection, Jesus still points to a future eschatological fulfillment when humanity will fully understand this claim, namely when Jesus first sits at God's right hand and then returns on the clouds at the end of the age.

A second example of an eschatological-typological use of Ps 110 occurs in Heb 5:6. The author of Hebrews uses Ps 2 and Ps 110 to demonstrate that Jesus (as the Son of God) is the Messiah. Earlier in the book of Hebrews (Heb 1:5—2:18) the author narrates that Jesus was higher than the angels. The author relies upon Ps 2:7 in relation to 2 Sam 7:14 to argue that the Son (Jesus) is superior by virtue of his unique relationship to the Father, a uniqueness demonstrated by his enthronement as God's Messiah. In the current passage (Heb 5:5–6) the author of Hebrews relates that Jesus, as the Son, is also the High Priest entrusted to atone for sins in the earthly sacrificial system. Relying upon Ps 2:7 and Ps 110:4, the author uses an eschatological typology to specify that God chose Jesus to be the High Priest for humanity. As Jesus was not a Levite (as expected of a high priest), the author of Hebrews finds that Jesus was "a priest forever, after the order of Melchizedek" (from Ps 110:4), therefore appointing Jesus to serve as High Priest. The typological association involves a fuller understanding that the subject of Ps 110 is Jesus as Messiah, and not the earlier understanding of a Davidic king. The eschatological component arises from the understanding that Jesus serves in this role "forever." Thus, the writer of Hebrews understands the verse to be typological prophecy about Jesus's appointment to a unique form of priesthood, fulfilled perhaps at the Messiah's resurrection and exaltation to the right hand of God.

Rhetorical Typology:
Correcting Contemporary Messianic Assumptions

Again, in the Synoptic Gospels, Jesus uses typological interpretation of Ps 110 to support a messianic claim (Matt 22:44; Mark 12:36; and Luke 20:42–43). However, in these passages Jesus uses the psalm to correct the current messianic understanding. In these accounts the Pharisees gather together to test Jesus. During the course of the questions, Jesus turns the tables by asking the Pharisees what will be the ancestry of the Messiah (Matt 22:42a). They respond that the Messiah will be a descendant of King David. Jesus replies in Matt 22:43–45, stating "How is it then that David, in the Spirit, calls him Lord, saying 'The Lord said to my Lord, Sit at my right hand, until I put your enemies under your feet.' If then David calls him Lord, how is he his son?" The essence of the question revolves around the notion of respect. If David is the speaker in Ps 110:1 ("The Lord says to my Lord"), then David is speaking to two people of higher position. The first "Lord" is God, but the second "Lord" could not be David's son (Solomon) because Solomon is of a lower rank than David. Therefore, the rhetorical argument is that if David calls this messianic figure lord, how can it be a son of David? Jesus is not denying that the Messiah holds a Davidic ancestry. However, Jesus is correcting the contemporary understanding by arguing that the Messiah cannot be merely a human descendent of King David. Therefore, the suggested conclusion is that the Messiah is not *only* the son of David but *also* the son of God.

Peter adopts a similar rhetorical-typological argument in Acts 2:34–35. Immediately following the Pentecost, Peter begins to preach. His goal is to explain the significance of the Spirit pouring forth onto the crowd and the identity of Jesus as the Messiah. At the end of the message Peter turns to Ps 110 for rhetorical support that Jesus is the Messiah and to correct the errant contemporary belief that David may be the Messiah. Peter begins his argument in 2:29 by stating "Brothers, I may say to you with confidence about the patriarch David that he both died and was buried, and his tomb is with us to this day." Peter goes on by stating that,

> Being therefore a prophet, and knowing that God had sworn with an oath to him that he would set one of his descendants on his throne, he foresaw and spoke about the resurrection of the Christ, that he was not abandoned to Hades, nor did his flesh see corruption. This Jesus God raised up, and of that we all are witnesses. Being therefore exalted at the right hand of God, and having received from the Father the promise of the Holy Spirit, he has poured out this that you yourselves are seeing and hearing. For David did not ascend into the heavens, but he himself says, "The Lord said to my Lord, Sit at my right hand, until I make your enemies your footstool." Let all the house of Israel therefore know for certain that God has made him both Lord and Christ, this Jesus whom you crucified." (Acts 2:30–36)

Using Ps 110:1 as a rhetorical-typological text, Peter is arguing that before David died, he knew that another would come who would not die and would rise to a position of royal authority at the right hand of God. David dies and was buried, and yet Jesus rose into heaven, therefore Jesus is the Messiah. A similar rhetorical-typological argument is found in Heb 1:13, where only a divine messiah would sit above the angels at God's right hand.

Realized Typology:
The Mentioned Typological Connection Is Already Complete

Several passages within the Pauline corpus, general epistles, and the book of Acts relate a third typological understanding of the psalms. The writers of these passages reveal a literal understanding of Ps 110 with aspects of the psalm having already been completed (or realized). As such, Jesus is shown to be the Messiah because the messianic aspects to the psalm have already occurred. Passages such as Acts 7:55; 1 Cor 15:25; Eph 1:20; Col 3:1; and 1 Pet 3:22 each contain this form of typology.

In Acts 7 we find the testimony and stoning of Stephen. Just prior to Stephen's execution, Luke writes that Stephen "gazed into heaven and saw the glory of God, and Jesus standing at the right hand of God. And he said,

'Behold, I see the heavens opened, and the Son of Man standing at the right hand of God.'" In this passage Stephen is combining the messianic components of Dan 7 with a realized view of Ps 110:1. The passage is unprecedented. Perhaps Stephen is finding a parallel to his comments in Act 7:2 where the glory of God appears to Abraham. Additionally, the passage is unique as Jesus is not seated at the right hand of God (as in Ps 110:1) but rather standing. One possible explanation is that some action is anticipated by the Messiah—resulting in a new posture. Conceivably, a better answer is a combination of the seated Messiah in Ps 110:1 with the avenging Messiah in v. 5. Thus the passage brings an awareness of the entire psalm into view.

Paul uses the same realized typology on several occasions to support his arguments. In 1 Cor 15:25 Paul quotes from Ps 110:1 to support the claim that Jesus, as the Messiah, has conquered death. Paul writes, "For he must reign until he has put all his enemies under his feet. The last enemy to be destroyed is death" (1 Cor 15:25–26). Paul changes the original context of the psalm to relate that Jesus's victory over death is one of the "enemies" brought under Jesus's feet. Paul expands this idea in his letter to the Ephesians in discussing God's power, "which he exerted in Christ when he raised him from the dead and seated him at his right hand in the heavenly realms, far above all rule and authority, power and dominion, and every title that can be given, not only in the present age but also in the one to come. And God placed all things under his feet and appointed him to be head over everything for the church, which is his body, the fullness of him who fills everything in every way" (Eph 1:20–23). Here Paul is supporting his argument that Jesus is the Messiah because the prophecy in Ps 110:1 has already been realized—Jesus is exalted, sitting at the right hand of God, exercising God's eternal power. Paul uses a final reference to Ps 110 in Col 3:1. The letter to the church at Colossae includes an instruction by Paul to live a holy life. Paul argues that "if then you have been raised with Christ, seek the things that are above, where Christ is, seated at the right hand of God" (Col 3:1). Paul uses Ps 110:1 as a realized statement that mankind should live in holiness—seeking Christ because he was exalted to be in heaven at the right hand of God. Each of these Pauline arguments is based upon a realized-typological understanding of the Ps 110.

A final use of the psalm in a realized form occurs in 1 Pet 3:22. In this passage Peter is discussing the power of the resurrection for Jesus. Pater concludes his argument in v. 22 by stating that Jesus "has gone into heaven and is at the right hand of God, with angels, authorities, and powers having been subjected to him." The passage attributes Ps 110:1 to the Jesus as the Messiah. Additionally, the fulfillment of the prophecy is completed and utilized to demonstrate the Messiah's authenticity.

IMPLICATIONS FOR AND IDENTITY WITH
THE MODERN CHRISTIAN CHURCH

Now that we have explored how New Testament authors used Ps 110, it is time to ask so what? What is the contemporary use of this information to the modern church? I think we can use this information in four significant ways. First, we can better understand the historical context of the psalms at the time of David. Second, the analysis informs how God utilized progressive revelation to disclose God's message. Third, we can better discern how the Messiah was understood by Jews in the first century (at the time of Jesus). And fourth, we might better appreciate the hermeneutical process utilized by New Testament authors when interpreting Old Testament passages.

By examining Ps 110 we discover that the original author included several elements that are, at first glance, unclear. When viewing the psalm considering other contemporary ancient Near Eastern texts, it seems most likely that the psalm is a coronation text with three oracles read at David's coronation. These oracles may have also been re-read at later coronation ceremonies. Due to the ambiguity in the text, there are other possible historical contexts that fit psalm.

How is this important? As a Christian reading the Old Testament we need to look first at an Old Testament passage through the lens of the original reader. This often means searching surrounding texts for clues and reading documents from contemporary neighbors of Israel that included similar material. Only then can we explore the relationship of the Old Testament passage to the New Testament. This methodology for analysis yields a deeper understanding for Christian study and use in ministry.

Second, by examining each reference to Ps 110 in the Bible we are able to view progressive revelation in practice. It is evident that Ps 110 was written with a specific historical context in view. However, it is equally clear that God inspired the original author to record the event with some ambiguous language. This intentional ambiguity (inspired by the Holy Spirit) was clarified by later authors as also pointing to Jesus as the Messiah. It is essential to understand the passage hermeneutically by first exploring the original historical context, then to study the unfolding of God's intended meaning as interpreted by later inspired biblical authors. The present chapter provides a basic framework for such an analysis.

Third, an examination of Ps 110 provides an excellent example for the development of messianic thought through time. As we discussed above, the messianic expectation is founded in the Davidic covenant of 2 Sam 7. God guarantees David that the ultimate king will come from his line. This Davidic king will rule in an idealized way—victory over all enemies, a

kingdom enduring forever, a secure place for Israel, and a father-son relationship with God. Each of these idealized elements finds some fulfillment
in David and Solomon; however, the complete set is not fulfilled in the
united monarchy. These aspects remain unfulfilled with increasing tension
as Israel moves through the period of the divided monarchy and into exile.
Psalm 110 matches the idealized language of 2 Sam 7, even capturing the
father-son relationship with God. The prophecies of 2 Sam 7 and Ps 110 are
later enhanced by the prophecies in Daniel and interpreted by Jewish scholars as pointing to a Davidic messiah. This messianic figure would restore the
nation and fulfill the prophecies. The New Testament authors add the final
piece to the puzzle to demonstrate that Jesus is the expected Messiah. This
study establishes a framework that may be utilized in an exploration of messianic thought. We have touched upon many of the significant messianic
Old Testament biblical passages. Further, we have provided a framework for
study of Second Temple period writings.

Finally, fourth, this short analysis of Ps 110 provides a framework for
a study of Old Testament passages utilized in the New Testament. When
a student of the Bible finds a reference in the New Testament to an earlier
Old Testament passage, how should we explore the meaning? In the study
above we offered a few hermeneutical clues that might be employed in biblical exegesis. Once various candidates are discovered, we can go back to the
psalm and begin a bottom-up analysis. First, we would conduct an in-depth
exegetical analysis of the psalm (linguistic, textual, historical-contextual,
cross-cultural, and theological). This analysis would explore prior biblical
works upon which the author might have relied.

Second, we would explore the surrounding psalms for any additional
contextual clues. One topic to explore is whether the placement of the psalm
within a book impacts our interpretation. This would include the study of
both the context of the surrounding psalms and possible date of authorship.
Third, we would look for any interpretational clues as to how later authors
used the psalm. Fourth, we might explore ties to any inter-testamental literature and the development of messianic components.

Finally, we would move back, considering the completed analysis, to
reevaluate the New Testament passages that rely upon the psalm. Key questions might include:

- Is the translation exact (to the BHS or LXX), or were subtle changes
  made to emphasize a point? If not an exact quote, is it an echo?

- What is the implied meaning of the New Testament text?

- What is the context of the New Testament passage within its book?

- What hermeneutical steps is the author taking or assuming in their use of the psalm?

- If there are multiple references, quotes, or echoes, how do these create a broader understanding of both the Psalm and New Testament passages?

This methodology helps us to ensure that our hermeneutical process explores the historical context of an Old Testament passage. The methodology also ensures that our New Testament understanding is informed by a full understanding of Scripture.

CONCLUSION

This study set out to accomplish two primary goals: first, to present an historical-contextual analysis of Ps 110 in light of the psalm's use in the New Testament; second to outline (by example) a hermeneutical method that might be employed by others for the examination of Old Testament texts used by the New Testament. We found that the psalmist of Ps 110 included King David as the primary referent. The voice of the psalm is most likely a court prophet who gives an oracle to David including elements similar to (and consistent with) the Davidic covenant of 2 Sam 7. New Testament authors, inspired by the Holy Spirit, utilized the text to demonstrate that Jesus is the Messiah. We argued that the New Testament authors used Ps 110 in three ways: eschatological typology, rhetorical typology, and realized typology. We defined typology as a New Testament revelation of an Old Testament passage revealing a new understanding in light of progressive revelation. In this case that the Old Testament passage referring to King David in an immediate prophetic context is ultimately fulfilled in Jesus as the Messiah. After we determined the existence of a typological relationship between Ps 110 and later New Testament passages, we examined the form of relationship. The study concluded that some New Testament authors referenced Ps 110 as partially fulfilled in the first century AD while looking to the second coming of Christ for ultimate fulfillment (eschatological typology). Other passages used Ps 110 as an argument for Jesus as the Messiah to correct a contemporary misunderstanding (rhetorical typology). Finally, some New Testament authors used Ps 110 as already fulfilled prophecy in Christ (realized typology).

Ultimately we argued that students of the Bible should not attempt to conduct a typological analysis of Old Testament passages that are not specified in the New Testament. However, we can utilize a hermeneutical study of passages identified in the New Testament that quote or allude to Old Testament passage. As such, this study offered a historical-contextual hermeneutical method for the study of the New Testament's use of Old Testament passages.

QUESTIONS FOR DISCUSSION

Discussion Questions

1) Read Pss 2 and 110. Do you think that the original author had the Messiah in mind? Why/why not?

2) What makes a psalm messianic?

3) Read Ps 22 and Passion Narratives in the Synoptic Gospels. How is the psalm used by Jesus and the author of the Gospels?

Assignments

1) Prepare an outline of the key passages in the Old Testament that point to a coming Messiah. What role does the psalms play in this understanding?

2) Read Pss 2, 22, 45, and 110. List all the characteristics of the coming Messiah.

BIBLIOGRAPHY AND RECOMMENDED READING

The following works will be helpful in conducting a historical-contextual study of the psalms.

Psalms Material

Alter, Robert. *The Book of Psalms: A Translation with Commentary*. New York: Norton, 2008.

Bartholomew, Craig G., and Ryan P. O'Dowd. *Old Testament Wisdom Literature: A Theological Introduction*. Downers Grove, IL: IVP Academic, 2011.

Bauckham, Richard. *Jesus and the God of Israel: God Crucified and Other Studies on the New Testament's Christology of Divine Identity*. Grand Rapids: Eerdmans, 2008.

Brueggemann, Walter, and William H. Bellinger Jr. *Psalms*. NCBC. Cambridge: Cambridge Univeristy, 2014.

Goldingay, John. *Psalms*. Vol. 1, *Psalms 1–41*. Grand Rapids: Baker Academic, 2006.

————. *Psalms*. Vol. 2, *Psalms 42–89*. Grand Rapids: Baker Academic, 2007.

————. *Psalms*. Vol. 3, *Psalms 90–150*. Grand Rapids: Baker Academic, 2008.

Hilber, John W. *Cultic Prophecy in the Psalms*. BZAW 352. Berlin: de Gruyter, 2005.

————. "Psalm CX in the Light of Assyrian Prophecies." *VT* 53 (2003) 253–66.

Kidner, Derek. *Psalms 1–72*. TOTC. Downers Grove, IL: InterVarsity, 2008.

————. *Psalms 73–150*. TOTC. Downers Grove, IL: InterVarsity, 2008.

Lucas, Ernest C. *Exploring the Old Testament: A Guide to the Psalms and Wisdom Literature*. Exploring the Old Testament 3. Downers Grove, IL: InterVarsity, 2003.

Ross, Allen P. *A Commentary on the Psalms*. Vol. 1, *1–41*. KEL. Grand Rapids: Kregel Academic, 2011.

VanGemeren, Willem A. *Psalms*. Rev. ed. Expositor's Bible Commentary 5. Grand Rapids: Zondervan, 2008.

Waltke, Bruce K., and James M. Houston. *The Psalms as Christian Worship: A Historical Commentary*. Grand Rapids: Eerdmans, 2010.

Watts, J. W. "Psalm 2 in the Context of Biblical Theology." *HBT* 12 (1990) 73–97.

Watts, Rikk E. "Mark." In *Commentary on the New Testament Use of the Old Testament*, edited by G. K. Beale and D. A. Carson, 111–250. Grand Rapids: Baker Academic, 2007.

Wright, N. T. *The New Testament and the People of God*. Christian Origins and the Question of God 1. Minneapolis: Fortress, 1992.

METHODOLOGICAL READING

Baker, David L. *Two Testaments, One Bible: A Study of the Theological Relationship Between the Old and New Testaments*. Rev. ed. Downers Grove, IL: InterVarsity, 1991.

Goppelt, Leonhard. *Typos: The Typological Interpretation of the Old Testament in the New*. Grand Rapids: Eerdmans, 1982.

Hays, Richard B. *Echoes of Scripture in the Letters of Paul*. New Haven: Yale University Press, 1989.

Longenecker, Richard N. *Biblical Exegesis in the Apostolic Period*. 2nd ed. Grand Rapids: Eerdmans, 1999.

Wright, Christopher J. H. *Knowing Jesus through the Old Testament*. Downers Grove, IL: InterVarsity, 1992.

8

GOD'S DWELLING PLACE

Bryan C. Babcock

With these words God commands Moses to build a structure where God may dwell among his chosen people:

> Then the Lord spoke to Moses, saying, "Tell the Israelites to raise a contribution for Me; from every man whose heart moves him you shall raise My contribution. This is the contribution which you are to raise from them: gold, silver and bronze, blue, purple and scarlet material, fine linen, goat hair, rams' skins dyed red, porpoise skins, acacia wood, oil for lighting, spices for the anointing oil and for the fragrant incense, onyx stones and setting stones for the ephod and for the breastpiece. Let them construct a sanctuary for Me, that I may dwell among them. According to all that I am going to show you, as the pattern of the tabernacle and the pattern of all its furniture, just so you shall construct it." Exod 25:1–9 (NASB)[1]

---

1. Unless otherwise noted, Scripture quotations in this chapter are the author's translation

115

INTRODUCTION

Where is God? Is he immanent—being always present with his creation? Or, is he transcendent—somehow removed from the presence of humans? During the time at Mt. Sinai, God commands Moses to build a structure, a sanctuary where he may dwell among the people of Israel. The theological significance of this sanctuary, called the tabernacle, is quite important. We identify three theological points that are unpacked in this chapter.

First, the notion of a sanctuary highlights the presence and consequence of sin. God is holy and therefore unable to be in the presence of sin. Humanity is sinful and therefore unable to be in the presence of God. Because God desires to be present with his creation, he commands the building of the tabernacle. The tabernacle is a holy space where God may dwell and offers a sacrificial space where the priests may make atonement for the sins of the Israelites. In this way, Moses and the priests may enter the holy space and physically meet with God. Theologically, this highlights the theme that humanity (after the fall) is separated from God. However, God has provided a way to bridge the chasm created by sin and restore a relationship with humans.[2]

Second, the tabernacle includes high fabric walls and an internal holy of holies where God dwells. This physical manifestation of God's separateness points to God's transcendent nature. The description of God's sanctuary includes several references to a menacing cloud above the structure that indicates God's mighty presence above and within the tent. The outer courtyard keeps prying eyes from peering into God's sacred space. Finally, the holy of holies houses God's sacred objects only accessible by the holiest of the priests.

Third, God instructs Moses to erect the tabernacle within the Israelite camp using a portable design. In this way, God reveals his immanence in that he desires to be among his people (i.e., inside the camp). Further, wherever the people go, God desires to stay among them. Theologically, this indicates that God's presence is what constitutes a holy space—God's sacred space of the tabernacle travels with the Israelites.

Each of these theological points is unpacked as we explore the design, construction, and furnishings of God's sanctuary. In addition, we will examine how the initial tent of meeting changes into the tabernacle and ultimately into the temple in Jerusalem. Then we will explore how these Old Testament expressions of God's presence, holiness, and restoration are viewed through the lens of the New Testament.

2. For more information on ritual, see Babcock, *Sacred Ritual*, 12–48; Babcock, "Sacred Time," 1–23.

THEME OF GOD'S TABERNACLE

The theme of God's tabernacle finds a close connection to the creation account in Genesis 1–3. Gordon Wenham finds three points of similarity after first arguing that the garden of Eden represents the ultimate sacred space (or temple) as it is the location where God is present with his creation. In the garden God walks, talks, and relates to Adam and Eve as the model for the ideal interaction between God and humans. Therefore, according to Wenham, the tabernacle represents an ideal sacred space where God and humans may be in fellowship. First, Wenham argues that the entrances to the garden and the holy of holies are protected by cherubim. In Gen 3:24 God places cherubim at the eastern entrance to the garden. The entrance to both the tabernacle and the garden face eastward (Gen 3:24; Exod 27:13–16). Further, two cherubim sit atop the ark of the covenant with the partial purpose of protecting the ark that is placed in the most holy area of the tabernacle (Exod 25:17–24). In addition, a cherubim design is present on the curtains separating the holy space within the tabernacle (Exod 26:31). As such, the cherubim play a vital role in protecting God's sacred space from other space considered profane.

Second, Wenham concludes that both the garden and the tabernacle include sacred symbols of a tree. The garden includes a tree of life central to both the narrative and location (Gen 2:9; 3:24). Similarly, the tabernacle locates a lamp stand, fashioned after a tree, in the middle of the holy space to give it light (Exod 25:31–40).

Third, God uses the same terminology to describe work in both the garden and the tabernacle. Genesis 2:15 relates that "Then Yahweh God took the man and put him into the garden of Eden to cultivate it and keep it." The key Hebrew verbs describing the responsibilities of the man are to cultivate and to keep the garden. Similarly, God uses these same Hebrew roots (in noun form) when prescribing the duties and service of the priesthood and the Levites within the tabernacle (Num 1:53; 3:7–8; 8:26; 18:5–6).

Another example comparing the creation account of Genesis 1–3 and the tabernacle text comes from Samuel Balentine. He argues that Exod 25–40 recreates the pattern of creation (Exod 25–31), fall (Exod 32–34), and recreation (Exod 35–40) found in Gen 1–2; 3–6; and 6–9.[3] The similarity is further tied to the term ark found in both accounts. Balentine argues that Noah's ark is a symbolic floating box-like structure (similar to the ark of the covenant) and that both are places of safety/holiness in the midst of chaos/profanity.

---

3. Balentine, *Torah's Vision of Worship*, 140–41.

Philip Jenson explores the tabernacle through the lens of holiness in *Graded Holiness: A Key to the Priestly Conception of the World*. He finds, that a gradient of holiness is present in the sacred spaces found in Exod 25–31 and 35–40. The tabernacle and the camp define several distinct zones of sacred space outlining boundaries for a holiness gradient. These zones include differing amounts of physical space and each does not correspond to an exact degree of holiness. Despite this limitation, Jenson argues that "it is possible to correlate the holiness word group with the spatial dimension through the terms applied to the various zones."[4] He delineates five zones within the gradient as follows:

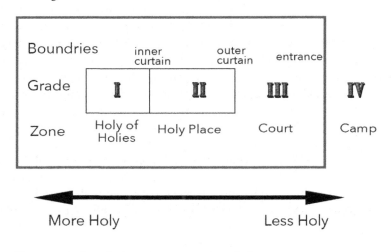

Zone	Description	References
I	Holy of Holies	Exod 26:33; Num 4:4, 19
II	The Holy Place	Exod 26:33; 29:30; Lev 6:30; Num 3:28; 28:7
III	The Court	Exod 27:9-19; Num 4:26, 32
III-A	A Holy Place	Exod 29:31; Lev 6:16, 26-27; 7:6; 10:13; 24:9
III-B	Entrance of the Tent of Meeting	Exod 29:4, 32, 42; Lev 1:3; 3:2; 12:6; 16:7
III-C	The Sanctuary	Exod 25:8; Lev 12:4; 19:30; 20:3; Num 3:28
IV	A clean place	Lev 4:12; 6:11; 10:14; Num 19:9
V	An unclean place	Lev 14:40-41,45

Jenson argues that the tabernacle expresses a holiness gradient that is evident in several ways. First, the model expresses a gradient for people in relationship to the tabernacle. The non-Israelites outside the camp are

4. Jenson, *Graded Holiness*, 90.

considered profane and unclean. The Israelites, as people of God, are clean, but not holy. The Levites, who can enter the tabernacle, are clean and generally considered holy. However, the high priest, chosen by God is considered most holy and able to access the holy of holies.

Second, the holiness gradient is evident in the materials used to construct the tabernacle and items within the sacred space. According to Jenson, the costliness of an item is proportional to its closeness to God (e.g., gold, then silver, then copper). The most holy areas tend to use solid gold and occasionally pure gold formed over wood. Less holy spaces use pure gold formed over wood and less often solid pure gold. Clean areas that were not particularly holy use copper.

Third, Jenson argues for a gradient exhibited through the type and design of woven materials used in the tabernacle. The most holy locations describe the highest-grade thread, including blue, purple, and scarlet weave of twisted linen. In addition, the fabric was formed into a veil and included images of cherubim. Other less holy locations included a patterned weave made of plain wool and linen. These materials were formed into screens and curtains. The lowest level of holiness, courtyard and fence areas included simple woven curtains. This same gradient applied to garments ranging from the most holy ephod with an elaborate breastplate, to an ephod rob and sash, and finally to a simple tunic.

Jon Levenson also explores the tabernacle as a microcosm with a continuum. In this model the tabernacle represents a miniature cosmos. "The sanctuary is a world, this is, an ordered, supportive, and obedient environment," corresponding to the depiction of the creation in Gen 1.[5] As such, God's presence fills the sanctuary in a similar way that God's glory fills the entire world (Isa 6:3). Because people are allowed to participate in the building of the tabernacle, Levenson argues that mankind is able to participate in the "divine ordering of the world."[6] Mankind is then able to approach God and beseech his intervention in their lives.

The theme of the God's sanctuary is also examined through the literary description of the tabernacle text. One examples is Robert Longacre's exploration of Exod 25–31 finding that the account falls into seven major sections divided by the phrase "The Lord spoke to Moses" (Exod 25:1; 30:11, 17, 22, 34; 31:1, 12).[7] Rolf Knierim adds that the phrase designates that the

---

5. Levenson, *Creation and the Persistence of Evil*, 91.

6. Ibid. See also Gorman, *Ideology of Ritual Space*, 230.

7. Longacre, "Building for the Worship of God," 21–49.

origination of the tabernacle and its design were both a holy command of God and not a human endeavor.[8]

Finally, the tabernacle may be viewed in light of other ancient Near Eastern textual and archaeological evidence. Victor Hurowitz compares the description of the construction of the tabernacle with other ancient Near Eastern temples, finding five points of similarity: (1) divine authorization for building the sanctuary (Exod 25:1–9); (2) conveyance of a divine commission to the builders (Exod 34:29–35:19); (3) collection of materials for building and call for artisan builders (Exod 25:20–36:7); (4) chronicle of the building process and furnishings (Exod 36:8–39:43); and (5) concluding notes and dedication (Exod 40:1–38).[9]

KEY BIBLICAL TEXT: EXODUS 25–40

The tabernacle sanctuary of Exod 25–40 was God's sacred dwelling space in the midst of Israel's camp as the nation progressed from Mt. Sinai to the banks of the Jordan River and into the promised land of Canaan. The tabernacle continued as Yahweh's sanctuary through the time of the Judges until the united monarchy when David and Solomon built the temple (2 Sam 7:6; 1 Kgs 8:4; 2 Chr 1:3–6).[10] The account of the tabernacle is divided into three sections. The first section is a direct discourse from Yahweh to Moses prescribing the specific elements, dimensions, and furnishings of the sanctuary (Exod 25–31). This discourse is interrupted by an act of rebellion within the camp—resulting in the creation of the golden calf (Exod 32–34). After Moses restores order, Exod 35–40 relates the yearlong construction of the tent sanctuary while the Israelites are camped at Sinai. The account repeats much of the earlier text, often word for word, emphasizing upon the reader the importance of the material. Once complete, the glory of Yahweh

8. Knierim, "Conceptual Aspects in Exodus 25:1–9," 113–23.

9. Hurowitz, "Form and Fate of the Tabernacle," 127–51; Hurowitz, "Priestly Account of Building the Tabernacle," 21–30. Hess, following the prior work of Kenneth Kitchen and Daniel Fleming, finds a similarity between the dimensions of the Egyptian royal war tent of Ramesses II (c. 1275 BC) and the tabernacle. He goes on to note that these structural dimensions were discontinued by the Egyptians after 1200 BC. Hess, *Israelite Religions*, 202–5. See also Kitchen, "Desert Tabernacle," 14–21; Kitchen, "Tabernacle," 119–29. Fleming argues that texts from the thirteenth-century-BC Ugarit and eighteenth-century-BC Mari describe dimensions and structures similar to the biblical tabernacle. Fleming, "Mari's Large Public Tent," 484–98.

10. First Samuel 7:1–16 makes clear that the temple is David's idea and does not originate with God. God allows the construction of a temple to replace the tabernacle, but relates that he has moved from place to place among the Israelites and never asked for a permanent temple (1 Sam 7:7).

occupied the sacred space and, while not guaranteed (Ezek 10), Yahweh's presence continually manifested itself in the tabernacle throughout the balance of the Pentateuch (Exod 40:34–35). Yahweh's presence was known because wherever the Israelites traveled, the cloud of God's presence could be seen during the day and a fire of God's presence at night (Exod 40:36–38; Num 9:15–23; 10:11–12, 33–34).

Three primary terms in Exod 25–40 describe God's tent. The first term is found in Exod 25:9 and is usually translated "tabernacle" (literally *dwelling place*). The verbal root of the word points to the immanence of God as he "dwells" among the people. The second word found in the narrative for the tabernacle is translated "sanctuary." The term sanctuary is the most common word used for the tabernacle complex, deriving its form from the root for holy. This holy aspect of the root highlights the holiness and separateness of God. The transcendent implication of the term "sanctuary" is contrasted with the immanence of the term "tabernacle" to create a theological tension which we will explore later in our discussion. The third word found denoting the tabernacle complex is translated "tent of meeting." This term seems to emphasize the movable aspect of the tabernacle and is derived from the verbal root meaning to assemble, gather, or meet in the niphal.

We now turn our attention to the function of the tabernacle in relation to Yahweh and the Israelites. The sacred space of God's sanctuary served three distinct functions. First, it served as God's royal office with all the trappings of a moving royal palace. Second, the tabernacle was a holy space where God could dwell on earth. And third, the sanctuary was a meeting space where God and mankind could dwell together. The balance of this section will unpack how the tabernacle could function, simultaneously, as each of these three types of space.

Tent as Royal Space

With the Israelites safely out of Egypt and camped at the base of Mt. Sinai, God makes his covenant with Moses. The Israelites will be God's people and he their only God. In addition, Yahweh will protect, lead, and rule over his people. It is easy to view Moses as the leader, or king, of the chosen people. However, the text of Exodus makes it clear that God is king. In Exod 25–31 God commands Moses to build a tent sanctuary so God, as king, may have a royal space to communicate with and dwell among his people.

Both the Israelites and Yahweh live in a tented space. However, it is clear from the beginning of the dialogue that God's tented space is distinct from his peoples' space—a royal tent. First, just a couple verses after Yahweh calls to Moses, God commands that the Israelites should contribute: gold, silver, and bronze metals; blue, purple, and scarlet material; fine linen, and goat hair (Exod 25:3–5). These are the construction materials for a royal palace, not the simple adornments of a commoner. In addition, the Israelites will compile spices and anointing oils usually used for a royal coronation and precious gems suitable for a king (Exod 25:6–7). Not only does the type of material used point to a royal tent but also the amount of precious metal. Alexander notes that the chronicle of the construction of the tabernacle records the use of approximately two thousand pounds of gold, eight thousand pounds of silver, and five thousand pounds of bronze in the construction of the tabernacle and furnishings (Exod 38:21–31).[11]

Second, the construction of the tabernacle and the orientation of rooms points to a royal space (Exod 26:1–37). The use of blue, purple, and scarlet fabrics along with gold clasps with cherubim impressions points to the royal nature of the tented space. The materials are used to create an outer-walled royal fence and a two-roomed building. This two-roomed building symbolizes a living chamber and throne room for the king. In addition, the rectangular outer-walled structure with a divided two-room inner structure is similar to the royal tent Ramesses II used when traveling outside of Egypt.[12] In this way, the space is designed as the royal living and ruling quarters of a traveling king—perhaps modeled after the Pharaoh's tent.

Third, the furnishings within the tabernacle indicate the area is a royal space. Exodus 25:10–22 outlines the specifications of an acacia wood chest overlaid with pure gold—inside and out. The chest is then adorned with an atonement cover including two cherubim facing each other with outstretched wings (25:17–22). While the chest is designed to hold the Testimony that God will soon give Moses, it also serves as the footstool of Yahweh's throne. Psalm 99:1 is one example depicting Yahweh as king enthroned above the ark: "The LORD reigns, let the peoples tremble; he is enthroned *above* the cherubim, let the earth shake" (see also 1 Sam 4:4; 2 Sam 6:2; 2 Kgs 19:15; 1 Chr 28:2; Pss 80:1; 99: 5; 132:7). The location of the chest (throne) in the smaller room is consistent with the ancient Near Eastern precedent of a tented throne room for the king when traveling in a foreign land.

The text designates a second piece of furniture in the tabernacle—a wooden table overlaid with pure gold and a solid gold trim (Exod 25:23–30). The table is adorned with solid gold plates, dishes, pitchers, and bowls. The

11. Alexander, *From Paradise to the Promised Land*, 226.

12. Hess, *Israelite Religions*, 204. Hess notes the depiction at Abu Simbel. The same scene is visible at the Ramesseum near Luxor.

table is to be ready with the bread of Presence at all times. The presence of a dining area that is ready for the king at all times clearly has royal overtones. The description of the furnishings within the tabernacle concludes with the inclusion of solid-gold lamp stand. The lamp is to be fashioned after a tree with seven lamps, each patterned after a branch and having flowerlike cups. Three branches are to one side and three to the other (25:31–40). No explanation is given for the lamp; the lamp may represent the tree of life (Gen 3:22) or it may represent the lamp stand of a king in his royal chambers.

After reviewing the language in Exod 25, it is clear that the tabernacle is a special space—befitting a king. As such, Yahweh commands Moses to make him a portable royal palace. The tented royal space is likely patterned after a model the Israelites had seen before—the royal tent of Pharaoh in Egypt. Therefore, Moses is creating a royal space for Yahweh, their king, to dwell among and rule over his people.

Tent as Holy Space

While the tabernacle is a royal space, it is also much more. The space functions as the dwelling of God and is, therefore, a sacred space. The tabernacle complex is rectangular and oriented along an east-west axis with the opening facing eastward. This orientation is similar to other sacred temples throughout the ancient Near East. The complex includes an outer barrier, courtyard with offering altar, and a two-roomed holy place and holy of holies, features also common in ancient Near Eastern temples. The outer fence separates the Israelites (who are not holy) from God's presence. Exodus often reiterates that inadvertent contact between the two would result in the death of the Israelite. Therefore, just like the boundary established by Moses around Mt. Sinai (Exod 19:12–13, 21–24), the courtyard fence prevents the Israelites from coming into Yahweh's divine presence.[13] The courtyard is significant to the holy space as it creates a transitional space between the camp (a clean space) and the holy space of the tabernacle rooms. This transitional space includes an offering altar where priest may make atonement for the people and move between a state of cleanliness and holiness.[14]

This orientation is similar to the temple orientation in Egypt, where the sanctuaries of the gods were rectangular, included a courtyard, a most

13. Alexander, *From Paradise to the Promised Land*, 229.

14. As discussed above, Jenson views the tabernacle complex in light of the larger Israel camp finding that the area outside the Israelite camp is profane, the camp itself is clean (but not holy), and the tabernacle complex represents varying degrees of holiness climaxing in the holy of holies.

holy chamber, and the temple opening faced east. This direction was important in Egypt as the rising sun (a god) was thought to bring renewed life each morning. Thus the morning sunlight spread its first rays through the entrance of the temple.

A second aspect of the tabernacle as holy space is the clothing attributed to the priests who tended to the needs of Yahweh. Because the tabernacle complex is holy ground, the priest must become holy in order to work within the courtyard and sanctuary. The holiness of the priest is partially demonstrated through his clothing. The priests are to wear sacred garments made from gold, colored yarn and fine linen (Exod 28:1–5). These sacred objects were fashioned into robes, tunics, sashes, caps, turbans, a breastplate, and an ephod. Each item of clothing designated varying degrees of holiness and was cleaned and anointed to the special service of the priests and Yahweh.[15]

A final indicator that the tabernacle is a holy space revolves around the rites and offerings made to God. Exodus 29 and 30 prescribe the consecration rites of the priests and atonement sacrifices. First, after assembling the material for the later offerings, Moses is commanded to wash, clothe, and pour oil upon the priests (Exod 29:1–9). Moses begins by anointing his brother, Aaron, who will serve as high priest. Once the high priest is ordained, Moses anoints the other priests. After all the priests are consecrated, they lay their hands upon the head of the bull and slaughter it at the entrance to the tent of meeting. A portion of the blood from the bull is placed upon horns of the altar (purifying the altar) with the rest poured at its base (cf. Lev 4:3–12). The entire bull is consumed by fire—part on the altar and part as a sin offering outside the camp (Exod 29:10–14). A similar process is repeated with two rams. After laying their hands upon the ram's head and slaughtering the rams, the first is burned as a whole burnt offering to Yahweh—atoning for the sins of the priests and a present reminder of the consequence of sin (Exod 29:5–18; cf. Lev 1:10–13). The blood of the second is used to further anoint the priests, the altar, and the priestly garments. Once completed, the second ram, an offering of bread, and an offering of oil are combined and consumed by fire as a burnt offering. Unlike the first ram, the breast of the second ram will be a wave offering consumed by the priests. Similarly, the thigh of the second ram will be a presentation offering consumed by the priests (similar to the fellowship offerings in Lev 3:6–11; 7:12–15). The process is repeated each day for seven days, using a bull and two lambs to complete the purification process (Exod 25: 35–46).

15. For a detailed review of the priestly clothing, see Dam, "Priestly Clothing," 643–46; Kaiser, *Exodus*, 525–32.

The design of the tabernacle complex, the priestly garments, and the rites of atonement and fellowship serve as ever present reminders that the tabernacle is a sacred space. God is holy and requires holiness from his people. The tabernacle is a holy space and God creates a means by which his priest may move into a state of holiness and fellowship with Yahweh.

Tent as Meeting Space

Exodus 33:7–11 relates that Moses would talk to Yahweh from a tent erected outside the camp. When anyone had a question of God, they would go near the tent of meeting and Moses (on their behalf) would enter into the tent. Once inside, God would descend (as a pillar of cloud) and remain at the entrance to the tent. Moses would speak to God "face to face, as a man speaks with his friend" (Exod 33:11). This passage emphasizes two points. First, Moses and God have a direct and personal relationship facilitated by the tent of meeting. Second, the tent of meeting is "outside" the camp. The location highlights the transcendent nature of God as needing to be separate and apart from the Israelites.

The construction of the tabernacle, which replaces the tent of meeting in Exod 33, makes a dramatic shift in this theological orientation. Now the tent is located within the Israelite camp. In addition, Moses and the priests will meet directly with Yahweh. Exodus 29:43–44 states that Yahweh "will meet there with the sons of Israel, and it shall be consecrated by my [Yahweh's] glory. I [Yahweh] will consecrate the tent of meeting and the altar; I [Yahweh] will also consecrate Aaron and his sons to minister as priests to me [Yahweh]." God no longer needs to descend when Moses enters the tent, as all were able to see his presence in the tent of meeting due to the cloud (during the day) and fire (at night). Theologically, the tabernacle as tent of meeting continues to express God's desire to have a direct relationship with his creation. However, the new location inside the camp brings God's immanent nature to light. God still remains separate from the Israelites due to the outer curtain/fence (transcendence); however, the tent is now among his people and no longer external to their lives—expressing his immanence.

A final point about the tent as meeting space is appropriate. As discussed above, the tent of meeting may symbolize the garden of Eden, which was a place where God and humans were able to live together. So too, the tent of meeting is designed as a meeting space where Yahweh may dwell among his people. Now, because of the rituals, the altar, and the wash basin a sinful humanity may make atonement for sin. Therefore, a sinful humanity may once again commune with a holy God.

UNITY OF THEME WITHIN THE OLD TESTAMENT

The tabernacle and later the temple were central to Israel's view of God's character, worship, and holiness. God chooses to set his divine presence in the middle of the Israelite camp. his holiness is attested in the rites, rituals, and celebrations conducted at the entrance of the tabernacle. When they go to war, God is present in his tabernacle, guiding the armies to victory. As the Israelites move, Yahweh's presence moves with them. Finally, when the Israelites settle in the promised land, God relocates from his tented sanctuary to a permanent location. We now turn to explore the role of the tabernacle throughout the Old Testament and how it informs our understanding of God.

Holy Community

The artisans complete the construction of the tabernacle at the end of the book of Exodus (ch. 40) as Israel camps at the base of Mt. Sinai. The last verses of the chapter describe how the glory of God, as a cloud, descends upon the tented sanctuary. God is now among the Israelites and will guide them as they journey toward the promised land.

The account of Moses continues into the book of Leviticus, in which Yahweh speaks to Moses from the opening of the tent of meeting. Moses, acting as intermediary, is to teach the Israelites what it means to be holy and how to worship God. The first several chapters of Leviticus prescribe how the Israelites will ritually atone for sin, provide offerings, and celebrate their relationship with God. The tabernacle stands out as the central location where all Israelites must go to provide offerings. One representative example comes from Lev 4. If the entire community sins, they must present a sin offering once they become aware of the sin. God commands that . . .

> the assembly shall offer a bull of the herd for a sin offering and bring it before the tent of meeting. Then the elders of the congregation shall lay their hands on the head of the bull before the Lord, and the bull shall be slain before the Lord. Then the anointed priest is to bring some of the blood of the bull to the tent of meeting; and the priest shall dip his finger in the blood and sprinkle *it* seven times before the Lord, in front of the veil. He shall put some of the blood on the horns of the altar which is before the Lord in the tent of meeting; and all the blood he shall pour out at the base of the altar of burnt offering which is at the doorway of the tent of meeting. (Lev 4:13–19)

This passage highlights the importance of the tabernacle in several ways. First, it is a central public location where those seeking atonement or worshiping Yahweh must do so in public. No one seeks forgiveness in private. Second, the worshiper presents themselves to God at the entrance to the tent—with the emphasis on the tent as meeting space. Third, the worshipers place their hands upon the head of the offering so that the sacrifice acts through substitutionary atonement for their sins. And finally, fourth, the blood of the sacrifice is used throughout the tabernacle complex to cleanse and purify the altar, the doorway, the priests, and ultimately the worshiper. In this way the ritual system revolves around the sacred space of the tabernacle with the intent to maintain the holiness and purity of the community.

War Camp and Safe Space

Moving into the book of Numbers focuses our attention on the tabernacle as a portable war headquarters. Yahweh is seen in Num 1–10 ordering a census of eligible warriors from the confines of his tabernacle. In addition, Moses is commanded to orient the tribes in a circular defensive position around the tent sanctuary. In this way each tribe—with identifying standard—takes a military posture with the tabernacle as command post (Num 2). The section ends with a retelling of the commemoration of the tabernacle as the Israelites prepare for war. This theme continues into Joshua as Yahweh commands his generals in final preparation for the invasion of Canaan. Joshua 18–19 further supports this conclusion in relating the division of the land after the conquest. The victorious tent of meeting is erected at Shiloh and the entire assembly appears before Yahweh, their king and general, to allocate the territory. These references highlight the importance of the tent of meeting as the mobile military command post where Yahweh directs his military actions (cf. Pss 60:6; 68:17–36).

As we move from the time of Joshua to the time of the united monarchy, the tabernacle is seen in Psalms as a place of refuge. In Ps 27 David says "Yahweh is my light and my salvation; whom shall I fear? Yahweh is the defense of my life; whom shall I dread? . . . For in the day of trouble he will conceal me in his tabernacle; In the secret place of his tent he will hide me; he will lift me up on a rock" (Ps 27:1, 5). In this psalm David reveals that the tabernacle is not just a place for a king at war but also a safe place where those in danger may find shelter. This theme is echoed in Ps 20: "May Yahweh answer you in the day of trouble, may the name of the God of Jacob set you on high. May he send you help from the sanctuary and support you from Zion" (Ps 20:1–2). Therefore, the tabernacle is both the headquarters for the military king and a protected space where the righteous may find safety.

Presence of God

The presence of Yahweh among the Israelites has been addressed above and we will only briefly discuss it here. Wenham explores the theme of presence beginning in the garden of Eden (Gen 1–3). The tabernacle uses similar symbolism to highlight that one goal of the tent of meeting is to allow God a place to be among his people. Once complete, God caused his presence to dwell continuously in the tabernacle until the completion of the temple of David during the united monarchy.[16] The tented sanctuary allowed God to dwell in the middle of the Israelites. In addition, the portable nature of the tent allowed God to remain among his people as they moved through the desert and into the promised land—both exhibiting his immanence. The glory of God displayed through a fiery cloud and the distance required between the inner tented sanctuary and the outer curtain fence both reveal God's transcendent nature. These two features of God's character are held in tension throughout the remainder of the Pentateuch and into the united monarchy.

Yahweh then resided continuously in the temple until the people had sufficiently defiled themselves and the sanctuary such that God's glory withdrew (Ezek 8:4; 10:3–4, 18–19; 11:22–25). Despite the desertion of Yahweh's glory from the temple, there was the promise of God's return to a new and permanent sanctuary. In Ezek 43:1–9 the prophet sees the glory of God coming from the east and once again filling the temple with the hope of a continued and intimate presence.

From Tabernacle to Temple

The account of King David's reign demonstrates his love for God and God's blessing upon David. In 2 Sam 7:2 David looked upon his new palace and told Nathan, "See now, I dwell in a house of cedar, but the ark of God dwells within tent curtains." While Yahweh has not requested a permanent sanctuary, he does authorize David to plan for the construction of the temple and places his blessing upon David so that: (1) David's name will be great among the nations; (2) Israel will have a permanent and peaceful home;

---

16. Kutsko, *Between Heaven and Earth*, 79–87.

(3) David's heirs will continue to rule the nation. The new sanctuary begun under David's reign is completed by Solomon, David's son (1 Kgs 5–9; Jer 33:14–16). The design of the temple will mirror the tabernacle with the same furnishings, altar, courtyard, and two-chambered holy place. Once complete, the priests carry the ark of the covenant into the temple and God's glory descends in a cloud upon the sanctuary (1 Kgs 8:10). Solomon gives a prayer of dedication and Yahweh responds with a conditional acceptance:

> I have heard your prayer and your supplication, which you have made before Me. I have consecrated this house which you have built by putting My name there forever, and My eyes and My heart will be there perpetually. As for you, if you will walk before Me as your father David walked, in integrity of heart and uprightness, doing according to all that I have commanded you *and* will keep My statutes and My ordinances, then I will establish the throne of your kingdom over Israel forever, just as I promised to your father David, saying, "You shall not lack a man on the throne of Israel." But if you or your sons indeed turn away from following Me, and do not keep My commandments and My statutes which I have set before you, and go and serve other gods and worship them, then I will cut off Israel from the land which I have given them, and the house which I have consecrated for My name, I will cast out of My sight . . . And this house will become a heap of ruins; everyone who passes by will be astonished and hiss and say, "Why has Yahweh done thus to this land and to this house?" And they will say, "Because they forsook Yahweh their God, who brought their fathers out of the land of Egypt, and adopted other gods and worshiped them and served them, therefore Yahweh has brought all this adversity on them. (1 Kgs 9:2–9)

God's response to Solomon confirms that God will dwell in the temple. However, Yahweh's presence is now conditional upon the actions of the Israelites. If they fail to keep God's statues and ordinances, then God will withdraw his presence and allow the destruction of the temple—leaving the community separate and apart from God.

The Israelites were constantly within sight of the tabernacle when they lived in the desert. Now that the nation has spread throughout a large area, the people must travel to Jerusalem to visit the temple and experience God's presence. These annual pilgrimages to the temple are viewed as occasions of great joy and the psalmist equates a single day in the temple as better than a thousand years elsewhere (Isa 30:29; 35:10; Pss 42:4; 43:3–4; 63:2–5; 65:1–4; 84:1–10; 122:1–9; 137:6).

The presence of Yahweh in the tabernacle and temple was central to Jewish theology. The hope of a new temple and the restoration of God's presence becomes the essential eschatological hope after the temple was destroyed in 587/6 BC (Ezek 9:3; 10:1–22; 11:23). The tension is eased slightly when God promises that he will be a sanctuary in the foreign nations during the exile and that his presence is across the heavens and the entire earth (Ps 139:7–12; Ezek 11:16). Ultimately, the people would return from exile and make a new temple and a new beginning for God's presence (Jer 31:31–34; Ezek 20:40–44; 33:14–16; 4:1–16); however, their hope is only partially fulfilled with the construction of a new temple. While the new sanctuary is more beautiful than the last (Hag 2:9; Zech 14:10–21), the dedication does not conclude with the glory of Yahweh descending upon the holy of holies as it had in the past (Ezra 6:13–18). God is shown to dwell in the temple. However, there is the expectation in Isaiah of a new interpretation of God's presence and the hope of a new "temple" (Isa 44:28; 56; 60; 66).

IMPLICATIONS FOR READING THE NEW TESTAMENT

The New Testament refocuses our view of the temple/tabernacle in Jerusalem in favor of another temple: within the individual believer, as the church community, and as a future eschatological holy sanctuary. Mark records the coming destruction of the temple (Mark 13:1–2) with the focus on Jesus as the new temple. This is exemplified when the curtain separating the holy of holies from the holy place is torn at Jesus's death (Mark 27:51). Jesus has removed the barrier between Yahweh and his creation (Heb 9:1–10:18). One of the primary roles of the tabernacle was a sacred space where humanity could atone for their sins and move into fellowship with their God. Jesus's death made obsolete these sacrifices of lambs, goats, and bulls. This relationship of Christ as the once-and-for-all atonement sacrifice is highlighted in Hebrews:

> When Christ came as high priest of the good things that are already here, he went through the greater and more perfect tabernacle that is not man-made, that is to say, not a part of this creation. He did not enter by means of the blood of goats and calves; but he entered the Most Holy Place once for all by his own blood, having obtained eternal redemption. The blood of goats and bulls and the ashes of a heifer sprinkled on those who are ceremonially unclean sanctify them so that they are outwardly clean. How much more, then, will the blood of Christ, who through the eternal Spirit offered himself unblemished to

God, cleanse our consciences from acts that lead to death, so
that we may serve the living God! (Heb 9:11–14).

Jesus does not merely alleviate the need for the tabernacle, he *is* the
tabernacle. John echoes this idea when he writes in John 1:14, "And the
Word became flesh, and dwelt among us, and we saw his glory, glory as
of the only begotten from the Father, full of grace and truth." This passage
brings the tabernacle into view through the use of the word "dwell," literally
"tabernacle," and the vision of God's glory. The imagery continues in John
when he quotes Jesus saying "Destroy this temple, and I will raise it again in
three days" (John 2:19). Two verses later John clarifies that Jesus equates his
body with tabernacle/temple (John 2:21; Mark 14:58).

According to Paul, after the Pentecost the role of God's presence in
Jerusalem has been replaced by God dwelling within individual followers
of Christ. In several locations Paul explains that the Holy Spirit indwells
the believer, who thus becomes a new temple of God. This is evident when
Paul writes to the church at Corinth "Don't you know that you yourselves
are God's temple and that God's Spirit lives in you? If anyone destroys God's
temple, God will destroy him; for God's temple is sacred, and you are that
temple" (1 Cor 3:16–17; see also 1 Cor 6:19; 2 Cor 6:16; Eph 2:19–22).

Paul also equates the image of the tabernacle/temple with the community of believers. Ephesians utilizes the image of the church as God's
tabernacle to show the unity of both gentiles and Jews in the new body of
believers. Building upon Jesus as the cornerstone of the temple, vv. 21–22
state that "in him (Christ) the whole building is joined together and rises to
become a holy temple in the Lord, in whom you also are being built together
into a dwelling of God in the Spirit." The imagery of a holy building (temple)
being built upon the foundation of Christ is continued in 1 Peter 2:4–8.
In this passage the universal church is built upon a foundation, enacted
through the death of Jesus, which will never fail. Similarly, Paul writes to the
church at Corinth that "we [*referring to all believers*] are the temple of the
living God. As God has said: 'I will live with them and walk among them,
and I will be their God, and they will be my people'" (2 Cor 6:16). Taken
together, these passages demonstrate that the universal body of believers
forms a tabernacle, indwelled by the Holy Spirit, so that God may dwell
within his sacred community.

Finally, the New Testament views the tabernacle in eschatological
terms. After the resurrection, Jesus goes to dwell with God as "a minister
in the sanctuary and in the true tabernacle, which the Lord pitched, not
man" (Heb 8:2; 9:11–12). The earthly counterpart is depicted as a "copy and
shadow" of the heavenly sanctuary (Heb 8:5; 9:24). The return of Jesus will

usher in a new era with a new Jerusalem. In this eschatological age, similar to the garden of Eden, there is no need for a temple as God is, at last, able to be in direct and continuous fellowship with his people. John writes that when the new Jerusalem descends from heaven, "the dwelling of God is with men, and he will live with them. They will be his people, and God himself will be with them and be their God" (Rev 21:3). There was no need for a temple "because the Lord God Almighty and the Lamb are its temple" (Rev 21:22).

We have seen in this section that the tabernacle/temple equates to two key factors. First, the tabernacle demonstrates the presence of God. Second, the tabernacle represents a mechanism by which sinful man can regain holiness and be in fellowship with God. Essentially, the use of the ritual system and sanctuary altar atones for the sins of humans, allowing both God and his creation to occupy the same location. Beginning in the Old Testament and throughout the New Testament, these two factors become increasingly spiritualized. First, during the exile Jews discover that they have not lost God's presence despite being in a strange and foreign land. Second, the Gospel reader discovers that the temple will soon be destroyed. Third, the author of Hebrews clarifies that Jesus made atonement, once and for all, for the sinful behavior of believers. As such, the ritual system is no longer necessary. Fourth, the presence of God is in all believers (regardless of physical location) due to the indwelling of the Holy Spirit. And finally, fifth, in the eschatological future no temple is necessary as God and humans will no longer be separated by sin and both may live together in the new heaven and new earth.

IMPLICATIONS FOR AND IDENTITY WITH THE MODERN CHRISTIAN CHURCH

Neither the tabernacle nor the temple have survived the course of time. However, the truth of the tabernacle is far greater than a mere building or tent. As we have attempted to show above, the meaning of the tabernacle is rooted in the presence of God among his people. This section will explore the ongoing role of sacred presence in a modern Christian context and as it pertains to the individual Christian, the church, and an eschatological hope.

First, the tabernacle symbolically represents God's presence in the life of the individual Christian. We have already noted that Paul' s letters to the Corinthians highlight a personal correlation between the tabernacle and the believer (1 Cor 3:16–17; 6:19; 2 Cor 6:16). A similar message is contained in the letter to the Ephesians, where Paul writes, "Consequently, you are no longer foreigners and aliens, but fellow citizens with God's people and members of God's household, built on the foundation of the apostles and prophets, with Christ Jesus himself as the chief cornerstone. In him the whole building is joined together and rises to become a holy temple in the Lord. And in him you too are being built together to become a dwelling in which God lives by his Spirit" (Eph 2:19–22). Therefore, all Christians exist as a holy temple or tabernacle within which God dwells. In Exodus we learn that, upon the completion of the temple, God's presence descended into the holy of holies like a cloud of smoke. This indwelling of the tabernacle is similar to the indwelling of the Holy Spirit in the believer (Acts 19:5–6; 1 Cor 6:19).

Other often cited symbolic elements in the description of the tabernacle that may apply to the individual include: (1) the entrance gate, which differentiates between the outer unholy world and the inner holy place of God. John 10:9 states that Jesus is the "gate" through which all Christians must pass; (2) the bronze altar symbolizes Jesus's death as a sacrifice making substitutionary atonement for our sins (John 1:29); (3) the bronze basin (called the laver) represents both the cleansing act of water baptism and the cleansing purification of Jesus's blood (Acts 22:16; Heb 19:19; 1 Peter 1:18–23); (4) the table and food in the holy place signify Jesus as the bread of life (John 6:35; Matt 4:4); (5) the lamp, or menorah, represents the Word of God (Ps 119:105; 2 Cor 4:3–4); (6) the acacia incense burner symbolizes our continual prayers (1 Thess 5:17; Rev 5:8); and (7) the ark stands for the throne of God at the center of the Christian's life (Heb 4:16). Each of these elements demonstrates a connection between the presence of God and the life of the individual believer.

Second, the tabernacle provides an example of God's presence in community—bringing God's immanence into view. God choose to locate his tabernacle in the middle of the Israelite camp. God is relational. Three elements are important: (1) God wants to be in fellowship with his creation; (2) the presence of God is wherever his people are located—it is portable like the tent; and (3) God is building a holy temple, the church of believers, upon the death and resurrection of Jesus. Peter highlights this correlation between God's presence, Jesus's death, and the tabernacle when he writes:

> As you come to him, the living Stone—rejected by men but chosen by God and precious to him—you also, like living stones, are being built into a spiritual house to be a holy priesthood, offering spiritual sacrifices acceptable to God through Jesus Christ. For in Scripture it says: "See, I lay a stone in Zion, a chosen and precious cornerstone, and the one who trusts in

him will never be put to shame." Now to you who believe, this stone is precious. But to those who do not believe, "The stone the builders rejected has become the capstone," and, "A stone that causes men to stumble and a rock that makes them fall." They stumble because they disobey the message—which is also what they were destined for. But you are a chosen people, a royal priesthood, a holy nation, a people belonging to God, that you may declare the praises of him who called you out of darkness into his wonderful light. Once you were not a people, but now you are the people of God; once you had not received mercy, but now you have received mercy. (2 Pet 2:4–10)

Third, the image of the tabernacle conveys God's presence for all time in heaven. As we have discussed above, the character of God offers both an immanent (near) and a transcendent (distant) concept of relationship. When exploring the eschatological tabernacle, or heavenly home of God, we visualize the holy, omnipotent, and transcendent God. Christians have the ability to be in fellowship with God now. But we may also look forward to a time that we will share, in heaven, in the holy temple of God. Ultimately, the earth will be transformed and mankind and God will be able to dwell together on the earth without the need for any separation (as viewed in the tabernacle). In that final, eschatological age, mankind will experience the peace, joy, and fellowship with God's presence that was envisioned in the garden of Eden before the fall.

QUESTIONS FOR DISCUSSION

Discussion Questions

1. Read Gen 1–3 and Rev 21. Do you think the garden of Eden represents the perfect view of God's presence? Why or why not?

2. Read Exod 25–40. How does the location of the fiasco with the golden calf impact the account of the design and building of the tabernacle?

3. Read 2 Sam 7. Do you believe that God wanted David to move God's location from the tabernacle to the temple? Why or why not?

Assignments:

1) Prepare a drawing of the tabernacle as described in Exod 25–31 that shows the location of each of the furnishings and sacred objects.

2 Create a continuum of "holiness" showing the areas: (a) outside the Israelite camp; (b) inside the camp; (c) courtyard of the tabernacle; (d) holy place; (e) holy of holies.

3) Create a continuum of "holiness" for different people groups mentioned in Exod 25–40, including non-Israelites, Israelites, priests, and the high priest.

BIBLIOGRAPHY FOR CONTINUED STUDY

Alexander, T. Desmond. *From Paradise to the Promised Land: An Introduction to the Pentateuch.* 3rd ed. Grand Rapids: Baker Academic, 2012.

Babcock, Bryan C. *Sacred Ritual: A Study of the West Semitic Ritual Calendars in Leviticus 23 and the Akkadian Text Emar 446.* BBRSup. Winona Lake, IN: Eisenbrauns, 2014.

———. "Sacred Time in West Semitic Festival Calendars and the Dating of Leviticus 23." *Journal for the Evangelical Study of the Old Testament* 2, no. 1 (2013) 1–23.

Balentine, Samuel E. *The Torah's Vision of Worship.* Overtures to Biblical Theology. Minneapolis: Fortress, 1999.

Bloch-Smith, Elizabeth. "Solomon's Temple: The Politics of Ritual Space." In *Sacred Time, Sacred Place: Archaeology and the Religion of Israel,* edited by Barry M. Gittlen, 83–94. Winona Lake, IN: Eisenbrauns, 2002.

Cross, Frank M. "The Priestly Tabernacle and the Temple of Solomon." In *From Epic to Canon: History and Literature in Ancient Israel,* 84–95. Baltimore: Johns Hopkins University, 1998.

Fleming, Daniel E. "Mari's Large Public Tent and the Priestly Tent Sanctuary." *VT* 50 (2000) 484–98.

George, Mark. *Israel's Tabernacle as Social Space.* Ancient Israel and Its Literature 2. Atlanta: SBL, 2009.

Gorman, Frank H., Jr. *The Ideology of Ritual Space: Space, Time, and Status in the Priestly Theology.* JSOTSup 91. Sheffield: JSOT, 1990.

Haran, Menahem. *Temples and Temple Service in Ancient Israel.* Oxford: Clarendon, 1978.

Hess, Richard S. *Israelite Religions: An Archaeological and Biblical Survey.* Grand Rapids: Baker Academic, 2007.

Hurowitz, Victor A. "The Form and Fate of the Tabernacle: Reflections on a Recent Proposal." *Jewish Quarterly Review* 86 (1995) 127–51.

———. "The Priestly Account of Building the Tabernacle." *Journal of the American Oriental Society* 105 (1985) 21–30.

Jenson, Philip Peter. *Graded Holiness: A Key to the Priestly Conception of the World.* JSOTSup 106. Sheffield: JSOT Press, 1992.

Kaiser, Walter, Jr. *Exodus.* Rev. ed. Expositor's Bible Commentary 1. Grand Rapids: Zondervan, 2008.

Kitchen, Kenneth A. "The Desert Tabernacle." *Biblical Research* 16 (2000) 14–21.

———. "The Tabernacle: A Bronze Age Artifact." *Eretz-Israel* 24 (1993) 119–29.

Klein, Ralph W. "Back to the Future: The Tabernacle in the Book of Exodus." *Int* 50 (1996) 264–76.

Klingbeil, Gerald A. "Ritual Space in the Ordination Ritual of Aaron and His Sons as Found in Leviticus 8." *JNSL* 21 (1995) 59–82.

Knierim Rolf P. "Conceptual Aspects in Exodus 25:1–9." In *Pomegranates and Golden Bells: Studies in Biblical, Jewish, and Near Eastern Ritual, Law, and Literature in Honor of Jacob Milgrom,* edited by David P. Wright et al., 113–23. Winona Lake, IN: Eisenbrauns, 1995.

Knohl, Israel. *The Sanctuary of Silence: The Priestly Torah and the Holiness School.* Minneapolis: Fortress, 1995.

———. "Two Aspects of the 'Tent of Meeting.'" In *Tehillah le-Moshe: Biblical and Judaic Studies in Honor of Moshe Greenberg,* edited by Mordechai Cogan et al., 73–79. Winona Lake, IN: Eisenbrauns, 1997.

Kutsko, John F. *Between Heaven and Earth: Divine Presence in the Book of Ezekiel.* Biblical and Judaic Studies 7. Winona Lake, IN: Eisenbrauns, 2000.

Levenson, Jon D. *Creation and the Persistence of Evil: The Jewish Drama of Divine Omnipotence.* 2nd ed. Princeton: Princeton University, 1994.

Meyers, Carol L. *The Tabernacle Menorah: A Synthetic Study of a Symbol from the Biblical Cult.* Atlanta: Gorgias, 2003.

Van Dam, Cornelis. "Priestly Clothing." In *Dictionary of the Old Testament: Pentateuch,* edited by T. Desmond Alexander and David W. Baker, 643–46. Downers Grove, IL: InterVarsity, 2003.

Wenham, Gordon J. "Sanctuary Symbolism in the Garden of Eden Story." In *Proceedings of the Ninth World Congress of Jewish Studies, 1985: Panel Sessions: Bible Studies and Ancient Near East,* edited by Moshe Goshen-Gottstein, 19–24. Jerusalem: World Union of Jewish Studies, 1986.

Zevit, Ziony. "Preamble to a Temple Tour." In *Sacred Time, Sacred Place: Archaeology and the Religion of Israel,* edited by Barry M. Gittlen, 73–81. Winona Lake, IN: Eisenbrauns, 2002.

9

"GOD WITH US"

RUSSELL L. MEEK

INTRODUCTION

"Therefore Adonai will give you a sign: Behold! The virgin will conceive and bear a son, and she will name him Immanuel" (Isa 7:14).[1] Isaiah delivered this message to Ahaz, king of Judah, while Ahaz was in the midst of an imminent attack because he refused to join the Syro-Ephraimite (Syria and Israel) coalition in their rebellion against the Assyrian Empire.[2] Since Ahaz had refused to ask Yahweh for a sign (Isa 7:12) though Yahweh had commanded that he do so, the Lord gave the sign of Immanuel, "God with us." The sign reassured Ahaz that God would be faithful to his people because, indeed, he would be with them, in their midst. Unfortunately, the king's refusal to obey Yahweh portended another looming crisis—the Assyrian invasion.[3]

---

1. Unless otherwise noted, Scripture quotations in this chapter are the author's translation.

2. For a brief description of the Syro-Ephraimite coalition and its historical context, see Watts, *Isaiah 1–33*, 121. For a fuller discussion, see Na'aman, *Ancient Israel*, 43–47.

3. Stromberg, *Isaiah*, 86.

Isaiah's primary message here is that, despite the king's disobedience, God would continue to be with his people, just as he had been before. God's presence had been with Adam and Eve in the garden; with the people of Israel at Sinai and in the wilderness as he led them by the pillar of fire and the cloud; with his people in the tabernacle and later the temple; and before the temple was destroyed and Judah was exiled, God's presence left the temple, indicating he would also be with them in exile. God's presence was with his people in the incarnation of Christ—the Immanuel who was the ultimate fulfillment of Isaiah's prophecy (Matt 1:22–23)—and is with us now as the Holy Spirit indwells believers as the "temple of the Holy Spirit, whom [we] have from God" (1 Cor 6:16 ESV; see also 1 Cor 3:16). Later there will be no temple, for we will once again dwell in the presence of God as in Eden (Rev 21:3).

For many Christians today, the presence of God is given little thought apart from how one might experience it during a corporate worship service. As a young person growing up in the church, I thought God's presence was that emotion I experienced when the worship band played a particularly moving song while the lights were low and my thoughts were focused on God. And while there is certainly some truth to that—God *does* manifest his presence when believers are gathered together to worship him—this is a partial understanding of the presence of God. Indeed, his presence may be experienced far away from dim lighting and reverberating minor chords. The Old Testament presents a much fuller picture of God's presence, one that induces terror and awe in those who experience it, one that causes people to fall prostrate in worship, to lament their sins, to beg forgiveness. And yet we also see God walking with Adam and Eve in the garden of Eden and meeting with Moses and Joshua in the tent of meeting. We see an imminently good God leading his people in a pillar of cloud by day and a pillar of fire by night, appearing to them in flashes of lightning and rumbling thunder atop Mount Sinai, and finally dwelling among them in the tabernacle and the temple.

God's presence is a powerful thing in the Old Testament, and it continues to be so today. This chapter will investigate the presence of God as it appeared in the Old Testament, how the coming of Christ impacts our understanding of God's presence, and how Christians today should live in light of the reality of God's presence among his people.

THE PRESENCE OF GOD AND THE GOSPEL

In the opening pages of the Bible we read that Yahweh communicated directly with the humans he had created—Adam and Eve—blessing them and commanding them to be fruitful, multiply, and exercise authority over the rest of creation (Gen 1:26–30). God then looked over his creation and noted that it was all "very good" (Gen 1:31). After Adam and Eve disobey God, they hear "Yahweh God walking about in the garden in the cool of the day," and they hide themselves "from the presence of God."[4] This sequence of events indicates that Yahweh's presence dwelled with the humans he had created in his image. Upon confronting Adam and Eve, Yahweh banishes them from the garden of Eden and, consequently, from his presence (Gen 3:22–24). The rest of the Bible is the story of how God would make a way for people to return to that pre-garden existence in which humans dwelled with God. This story culminates in the gospel, wherein the Son of God made it possible for people to live in right relationship with God once again.

The Gospel of Matthew picks up on Isaiah's prophecy regarding the Immanuel.[5] In Isaiah's time this prophecy assured Judah that God would be with them, protecting them from the onslaught of the Syro-Ephraimite coalition. Matthew, however, sees a more complete fulfillment in Jesus Christ, the full embodiment of Immanuel, the God who took on human flesh and dwelled among his people, living a perfect life, dying a sinless death, and making atonement for the sins of the world so that the disobedience of Adam and Eve that fateful day in the garden of Eden might finally be reversed. For Matthew, Jesus Christ was the true Immanuel, the ultimate sign that God would be with his people and finally deliver them from all enemies and all evil. God himself, in human form, walked among his people once again. Jesus Christ was thus the final step in the long journey of God making a way for humans to return once again to the garden of Eden and experience his presence as Adam and Eve had experienced it.

The Gospel of John likewise argues that Jesus Christ is God himself dwelling in human flesh among his people, but instead of citing Matthew's Immanuel passage, John points to the typological pattern[6] of the Old

---

4. The Hebrew reads "from before the face of Yahweh God," a common Hebrew expression that indicates being in a person's presence.

5. On Matthew's use of Isaiah's Immanuel prophecy, see, e.g., Compton, "Immanuel Prophecy," 3–15; Gaffy, "The Coming of the Messiah," 472–75; Wegner, "How Many Virgin Births are in the Bible?," 467–84; Neuner, "Immanuel, God with Us," 562–66.

6. On typology, Duvall and Hays, *Grasping God's Word*, 215–17; Klein, Blomberg, and Hubbard, *Introduction to Biblical Interpretation*, 182–85.

Testament tabernacle.[7] John 1:14 (ESV) states that "the Word became flesh and dwelt among us." The term "dwelt" in the ESV translates the Greek term that means "to dwell in a tent." It's the verbal form of the word for "tabernacle" used in the Old Testament to refer to God's dwelling place among humans—*the* tabernacle. Thus, the phrase could be translated as, "the Word became flesh and *tabernacled* among us."

As we will see below,[8] after leading the people of Israel out of Egypt, God revealed to Moses the plan for building a portable dwelling place for Yahweh. This dwelling place, the tabernacle, is where God's presence would dwell in the midst of his people as they traveled in the wilderness. The ceremonies and rituals surrounding its proper use and the people's cleanness and holiness protected the people from the holiness of God. There were differing levels to the tabernacle (outer courtyard, holy place, most holy place), each of which had stricter requirements for entrance than the previous level. Thus, while God dwelled among his people, his presence was not immediately available to all, and approaching this holy space was exceedingly dangerous.

By using the term "tabernacled" John is indicating to his ancient readers that Jesus is the typological fulfillment of what was only partially possible in the tabernacle. While God's presence was uniquely present in the tabernacle, there were still significant boundaries that prevented all of Israel from experiencing his presence fully. In Christ, God took on bodily form and dwelled among his people in a new, unique way, abolishing the boundaries that once prevented people from fully experiencing God's presence in the tabernacle. Whereas approaching God in the tabernacle with unclean hands or an impure heart would have meant disaster, all could approach Christ and be made clean.

ANALYSIS OF KEY BIBLICAL TEXTS

God's Presence in the Garden of Eden

God's presence dwelled with Adam and Eve in Eden in a way that believers have since longed to experience. Scholars have pointed out that the garden of Eden was essentially a cosmic temple, the first place in which God's

---

7. Of course, John does not recount Jesus's birth narrative, so there was no reason for him to cite the Immanuel passage.

8. For a fuller discussion of the tabernacle in the Old Testament, see the chapter titled "God's Sanctuary" in the current volume.

presence dwelled on earth.[9] There God walked with his creation. There humans were able to commune with God because they had not become entangled in sin. That the garden of Eden was God's first sanctuary—his first dwelling place on earth—is important because the rest of the biblical story chronicles how God would make a way for humans to return to a place where they could once again experience God's presence fully.[10] Further, God's initial presence with Adam and Eve makes the first instance of his absence all the more shocking to our human forebears. They were the first to experience God's presence fully, and with their sin they also became the first to experience his absence as he banished them from the garden. This absence of God's presence will become an important theme later in the biblical witness (e.g., in Psalms and Job) as believers continue to struggle with God's perceived distance from them.

God's Presence at Sinai and in the Tabernacle

We will fast forward through quite a bit of biblical history, skipping the rest of the Primeval History (Gen 1–11) and the narratives of Abraham's family (Gen 12–50), and stop to look at God's presence first at Sinai after he led Abraham's family out of Egypt and then in the tabernacle as he dwelled among Abraham's family in the wilderness. After centuries of slavery in the land of Egypt, "He heard their [the Israelites'] groaning, and God remembered his covenant with Abraham, with Isaac, and with Jacob. God saw the children of Israel, and God knew" (Exod 2:24–25).[11] God heard his people groaning under the weight of pharaoh, he remembered his covenant with their ancestors, and he began the process of leading them out of Israel. That process culminated in Israel's entry into the promised land some forty years later, after the ten plagues, the crossing of the Red Sea, forty years of wandering, and so many more miracles of provision and protection. The most significant miracle of all, however, is that God revealed himself at Mount Sinai and then dwelled among his people in the tabernacle. And while these instances of God's presence were not as intimate as what Adam and Eve experienced before they sinned, they represent important developments in God's plan to live among his people.

---

9. See Beale, "Garden Temple," 3–50; Wenham, "Sanctuary Symbolism," 399–404; Elior, "Garden of Eden," 63–118; Schachter, "Garden of Eden," 73–77.

10. Beginning with the protevangelium in Gen 3:15.

11. For more on the theological significance of the exodus, see the chapter on the exodus in the current volume.

In Exodus 19 we read that Yahweh descended upon Mount Sinai in the midst of thunder and lightning, and the people were terrified. Yahweh called Moses up to the top of the mountain, where he told him for the second time to warn the Israelites not to approach his presence upon pain of death. There was a barrier surrounding the mountain across which the people—even the priests—could not pass (Exod 19:24). God revealed his presence to his people[12]in a way that had not been experienced since Eden, but his presence was limited strictly to Moses first and then to Aaron. Thus, while we see a progression toward the restored relationship between God and humans—God revealed his presence once again—there remained a strict boundary between God and the people (all save Moses and Aaron) that protected the latter from death.[13] God's presence could be felt, but the people could not walk in God's presence as Adam and Eve had; indeed, to do so would result in death for God could not tolerate being in the presence of their sin.

Since people could not survive God's holiness, God gave Moses specific instructions (see Exod 25–40) for constructing a dwelling place, or palace,[14] for God—the tabernacle—so that God could dwell among the people and they could at the same time avoid the death that would result from their entering the presence of a holy God.[15] God states his purpose for building the tabernacle expressly in Exod 25:8: "They shall build me a sanctuary so I can dwell in their midst."[16] Just as God dwelled among his people in the garden of Eden, he wants to dwell among his people after delivering them from Egypt.

This tabernacle, stationed in the middle of the camp, had varying degrees of holiness that required varying degrees of ritual cleanliness and holiness from the people who would enter it. There were three distinct spaces, with each space moving inward toward the presence of God, requiring more ritual purity and holiness, and limiting significantly who could enter that space. The most severe requirements for holiness and purity were reserved

12. Block, "Joy of Worship," 132.

13. For a discussion of the significance of the boundaries that separate the people from God's presence and thus protect them from his holiness and the death that would ensue, see Schnittjer, *Torah Story*, 259–68.

14. See Block, "Joy of Worship," 132.

15. This chapter will not fully explore the theological significance of the tabernacle and temple because God's dwelling place is covered in detail in the chapter, "God's Sanctuary."

16. Yehezkel Kauffman makes the important observation that the purpose of the tabernacle is not so that God can answer the prayers of the people or bless them (though that would happen), but so that he could dwell among them. See Kauffman, *Religion of Israel*, 302.

for those who would enter the inner-most part of the tabernacle—the holy of holies. This is where the manifest presence of God dwelled, and only one person could enter this place—and then only one time each year—on the Day of Atonement. Entering into the most holy place was highly dangerous because God's presence would not tolerate any sin or ritual impurity.[17] Thus, while God's presence was with his people in a way they had not experienced since Eden, there remained strict limitations—for the people's own safety— on the extent to which they could experience his presence. These limitations continued for the duration of the time that God dwelled in the tabernacle and extended into the period during which God dwelled in the temple.[18]

God's Absence from the Temple (Ezekiel 10)

After the people of Israel conquered the land of Canaan, made their home there, and established the monarchy, God's presence transitioned from dwelling in the tabernacle, a movable, temporary dwelling place, to the temple, a permanent structure. King David had requested to build such this house for Yahweh, but instead Yahweh promised David to build his "house," that is, his dynasty (see 2 Sam 7). The task of building the temple would fall to David's son and immediate successor, Solomon (see 1 Chr 22:6–19). Importantly, just as the tabernacle was the place of Yahweh's manifest presence during the wilderness years and conquest, the temple was the "locus" of God's presence after its construction.[19]

The presence of the temple in Jerusalem—and God's presence in it—led to the development of the so-called Temple of the Lord theology.[20] Jeremiah 7 is worth quoting at length to demonstrate this false theology:

> The word that came to Jeremiah from the Lord: "Stand in the gate of the Lord's house, and proclaim there this word, and say, Hear the word of the Lord, all you men of Judah who enter these gates to worship the Lord. Thus says the Lord of hosts, the God of Israel: Amend your ways and your deeds, and I will let you dwell in this place. Do not trust in these deceptive words: 'This

---

17. Pulse, "Ascending to God," 226.

18. As with the tabernacle, the temple will not be discussed in significant detail because it is covered more fully in the chapter, "God's Sancutuary."

19. Greene, "Spirit in the Temple," 720.

20. I am unsure of the origin of this designation, but I first heard it from N. Blake Hearson during a class on the book of Jeremiah at Midwestern Baptist Theological Seminary.

is the temple of the Lord, the temple of the Lord, the temple of the Lord.'

"For if you truly amend your ways and your deeds, if you truly execute justice one with another, if you do not oppress the sojourner, the fatherless, or the widow, or shed innocent blood in this place, and if you do not go after other gods to your own harm, then I will let you dwell in this place, in the land that I gave of old to your fathers forever.

"Behold, you trust in deceptive words to no avail. Will you steal, murder, commit adultery, swear falsely, make offerings to Baal, and go after other gods that you have not known, and then come and stand before me in this house, which is called by my name, and say, 'We are delivered!'—only to go on doing all these abominations?" (Jer 7:1–10 ESV)

Simply put, Yahweh is condemning the idea that Jerusalem and Judah would be safe from harm for no other reason than that the temple of Yahweh was there ("This is the temple of the LORD, the temple of the LORD, the temple of the LORD"). In the people's thought, the temple essentially acted as a lucky charm that would ward off all evil regardless of whether or not the people themselves were genuinely faithful to Yahweh.[21] This theology was founded on heterodoxy that led to heteropraxy and a false security in the *thing* that represented God's presence rather than true faithfulness to Yahweh himself.

The danger of such a theology became terrifyingly clear in the book of Ezekiel. In an otherworldly vision—not uncommon in Ezekiel—the prophet witnesses the glory of the Lord departing from the temple (Ezek 10:18). For Western readers this may not sound like the horrific situation it was—God's "glory" left the temple. However, we must understand that the Old Testament used the Hebrew term for "glory" to refer to "the portion of [God's] essence visible in the terrestrial plane."[22] That is, God's "glory" is God's very presence. And so when his glory departed the temple in Ezekiel, God would no longer dwell in Israel with his people.[23] Whereas God's Spirit had descended to dwell among Israel first in the tabernacle and later in the temple, God's Spirit departs the temple in Ezekiel—just prior to the Babylonian exile—because of the people's idolatry.

---

21. On the danger of using God's presence as a lucky charm, see Anderson, *Christian Doctrine*. I adopt the term "lucky charm" from his essay, "'Apopathic Theology: The Transcendence of God and the Story of Nadab and Abihu."

22. Propp, *Exodus 1–18*, 595.

23. For discussion of Yahweh's glory as Yahweh's presence, see Keck, "Glory of Yahweh," 201–18. See also Greene, "Spirit in the Temple," 723–24.

However, all is not lost. For while the departure of Yahweh's glory from the temple and the exile of God's people from the promised land heralded dark days for God's people, God would not forsake them. And indeed, God's departure from the temple in Ezekiel indicated that he would do the very thing no one expects—he would go with his people into exile. God's presence had been with his people outside of the promised land as they wandered for some forty years, and even outside the tabernacle in the form of the cloud and fire. Although God's people had adopted heterodox belief regarding the inviolability of the temple and God's protection of them and their land, it remained true that God's presence would dwell with them. And that they were wrong about God's relationship to the temple—that no harm could befall it because he was bound to it—is the very thing that sustained them in exile. For although God's presence left the temple, it signaled that his presence would go with his people into exile. Just as Yahweh had been with them before the construction of the temple and tabernacle, so would he be with them after its destruction. As Gordon Fee has noted, "Yahweh's presence, not the law or other identity markers, is what distinguishes Israel as Yahweh's chosen people."[24] Fee's point is crucial: *Yahweh's presence*, not the temple, tabernacle, Torah, or any other thing marks Israel as Yahweh's people. And so while Yahweh's presence left the temple in judgment of the people for their sins, his presence would yet be with them in exile and eventually return with them from exile.

PRESENCE AND ABSENCE IN THE OLD TESTAMENT

We've thus far looked at the concept of God's presence as we've seen it in the garden of Eden, the tabernacle, and the temple. It's clear that since Adam's and Eve's sin in the garden, there has been a consistent tension between God's presence and God's absence among humans. His absence resulted from the first human rebellion against him, and his presence was kept somewhat at bay in the Old Testament because of the same. However, we must not miss the importance of Yahweh's statement in Exod 25:8: "Let them make me a sanctuary that I may dwell in their midst." Yahweh commanded the tabernacle be built *so that* he could dwell among his people.[25] His desire in Eden and afterward has always been to dwell among his people.

Despite God's desire to dwell among his people, sin often prevented such. And even when sin did not prevent God's dwelling among his people

---

24. Fee, *God's Empowering Presence*, 7.

25. See Anderson, *Christian Doctrine*. Specifically, see the chapter, "Mariology: The Mother of God and the Temple."

in the tabernacle or temple, often his people *felt* God's absence. One need only open the books of Job, Psalms, and Ecclesiastes to learn that many of God's faithful experienced (at least some) times of felt distance from him, whether such distance was actual or perceived. God's felt absence is a key theme in these writings, and those of us who have experienced a similar dearth of God's presence are thankful for that. While space does not permit a full examination of the passages that address God's absence in the Old Testament, a representative example will suffice to demonstrate the shared Old Testament experience of God's absence after the fall.

God's absence features prominently in any number of the individual lament psalms we find in the Psalter.[26] However, Ps 88 is an especially startling depiction of the reality that sometimes God seems far too distant and his absence is felt far too keenly. The psalmist despairs. He states repeatedly that he has called out to Yahweh, and yet no answer has come. His "soul is filled with troubles," (v. 4 [Eng. 3]); he is "as a man without strength" (v. 5 [Eng. 4]). Yahweh's "waves have overwhelmed" him (v. 8 [Eng. 7]). Unlike many lament psalms, Ps 88 ends with no resolution, no vow to praise God, no statement of hope that Yahweh will make himself known. There is only rejection, despair, and desolation. From all accounts, Yahweh is no longer present. It seems that in response to the psalmist's unceasing cries, Yahweh has simply multiplied troubles (see esp. Ps 88:13–18).

John Rogerson points out two important considerations for understanding the testimony of psalms such as Ps 88. First, he states that "Psalm 88 is not meant to be a one-off composition, but something representative within the Old Testament experience of God."[27] Thus, while God desired to dwell among his people, his people did not always *experience* that dwelling among them. Second, Rogerson points out that in order to comprehend what is going on in these psalms that lament God's absence, we must realize that they well up from a deep and intimate relationship with God.[28] Even God's absence is predicated on God's presence.

THE NEW TESTAMENT WITNESS TO GOD'S PRESENCE

The Old Testament testifies of a God who wants to dwell among his people and who goes to great lengths to do so. And even when his people do not feel his presence, that very absence is predicated on the reality of his presence.

26. On lament Psalms, including their features and use in Christian worship, see Waltke, Houston, and Moore, *The Psalms as Christian Lament.*

27. Rogerson, *Theology of the Old Testament,* 141.

28. Ibid., 143.

Indeed, while on the one hand the psalmist can lament that Yahweh has hidden his face (that is, removed his presence; Ps 88:14), on the other hand the psalmist must also ask, "Where can I flee from your presence?" (nowhere, of course; Ps 139:7). This Old Testament narrative of a God who created Eden to dwell with his people, made a way to live among them first in the tabernacle and later in the temple, and whose presence went with them into exile and then later returned with them makes it possible for us to understand better the scandalous gospel of Jesus Christ. For the gospel is the ultimate fulfillment of God's desire to dwell among his people. The gospel tells the story of the God who took on human flesh, deigned to dwell among his people, and died so that the dividing walls of the tabernacle could finally be torn down.

As we noted at the outset of this chapter, John's Gospel uses the tabernacle to explain Jesus's dwelling among his people. The Old Testament picture of God's presence dwelling in the tent was fulfilled in the New Testament when God took up another temporary residence—human flesh. This was a remarkable (and shocking!) development in the story of how God would dwell among his people as he had in the garden of Eden for two (and more besides) reasons.

First, God himself took on human flesh(!). The incarnation is a mind-boggling mystery in which the God of the universe is fully God and fully man. And what's more, "being found in human form, he humbled himself by becoming obedient to the point of death, even death on a cross" (Phil 2:8, ESV). The God whose presence had so long dwelled in the tabernacle and temple (though of course the tabernacle never contained him; see 2 Chr 6) now took on an even more intimate residence with humans, dwelling among them in bodily form. This taking on of the new tent—human skin—was God's first step in the final step toward restoring Eden. His disciples would take quite a while to understand, but God's plan in Christ—why he dwelled here on earth with us—was so that the God-man could live a righteous life (as Adam had failed to live), die an atoning death, and offer forgiveness that would finally make it possible for humans to live in God's presence as Adam and Eve had.

Second, whereas in the Old Testament humans had to take great care in approaching the tabernacle (and later the temple) or else risk death, people could approach Christ without fear of sudden death. Of course the Old Testament is clear that people can approach God in prayer, seeking his face from wherever they may be, but the strict guidelines for entering the tabernacle and temple existed to prevent God's holiness from destroying God's people. To approach God unworthily meant certain death, for his holiness could not suffer the presence of impurity or unholiness.[29] Such was not the case with Christ, for he bid both sinners and the impure to come unto him. The woman who had been bleeding for twelve years—and therefore for twelve years had been banished from the temple (see Lev 15:19)—came close enough to touch Christ, and she did not die. What's more, she was healed! In the Old Testament entering into the Holy of Holies—the closest one could get to the presence of God—in an unclean state would have meant certain death. And yet the opposite happens to this woman: she is made whole. The same is true of lepers, gentiles, prostitutes, greedy people, and all other manner of sinners and ritually unclean people. Whereas before they were not allowed to come close to God's presence, they could now *touch God* without hesitation or fear. Let this sink in: approaching Christ (God himself!) made sinners whole; it did not kill them. The magnitude of such a transition in how God interacts with humanity cannot be overstated.

The transition from God's presence dwelling in the tabernacle/temple to becoming flesh and dwelling among us (John 1:14) is not the only significant transition that happens as a result of the gospel story, the culmination of God's grand story of bringing his people back into his presence. If we keep reading the story of Jesus's redemption of humanity, we learn that *humans* become the temple of God. Yes, the Holy Spirit resides in mere human flesh. Those who place their faith in Christ are filled with the Spirit of God in a way that God's people did not experience in the Old Testament. Yes, the Holy Spirit came upon certain people and filled them for certain tasks, but there is no indication that God's Spirit dwelled with humans on a continual basis before Pentecost.[30]

A few important passages help us understand (as much as is possible) this New Testament change in how God dwells among his people. First, Jesus promised to send "another Helper" to be with them and in them. He states, "I will ask the Father, and he will give you another Helper, to be with you forever, even the Spirit of truth, whom the world cannot receive, because it neither sees him nor knows him. You know him, for he dwells with you and will be in you" (John 14:16–17). Note that Jesus says the Spirit was with them already, but in the future he would be *in* them. The disciples—and ultimately all who believe in Christ—would become the residence of the Holy Spirit. Jesus was physically with the disciples—teaching them, walking

29. For example, see the stories of Nadab and Abihu, Uzzah, and the Philistines in 1 Sam 5. See also Anders, *Christian Doctrine*, specifically the chapter, "Apopathic Theology: The Transcendence of God and the Story of Nadab and Abihu."

30. For OT figures being filled with the Holy Spirit, see, e.g., 1 Sam 16:13 and 2 Chr 24:20.

around with them, spending time with them—but after the resurrection the Third Person of the holy Trinity would take up residence in them.

Paul makes Jesus's statements even clearer in his writings.[31] In his rebuke to the Corinthians over divisions in the church, he states, "Do you not know that you are God's temple and that God's Spirit dwells in you? If anyone destroys God's temple, God will destroy him. For God's temple is holy, and you are that temple" (1 Cor 3:16–17 ESV). God once dwelled in the tabernacle and then the temple in Jerusalem, but now he fills the church (that is, the people who are the church), and because the church is the temple of God, there must not be divisions. In a similar vein, Paul in the same letter points to Christians' being God's temple as the reason they should abstain from sexual immorality. He states,

> Do you not know that your bodies are members of Christ? Shall I then take the members of Christ and make them members of a prostitute? Never! Or do you not know that he who is joined to a prostitute becomes one body with her? For, as it is written, "The two will become one flesh." But he who is joined to the Lord becomes one spirit with him. Flee from sexual immorality. Every other sin a person commits is outside the body, but the sexually immoral person sins against his own body. Or do you not know that your body is a temple of the Holy Spirit within you, whom you have from God? You are not your own, for you were bought with a price. So glorify God in your body. (1 Cor 6:15–20 ESV)

Thus, Paul uses the reality that Christians are now the temple of God— the dwelling place of God's presence—to communicate the importance of unity and sexual purity. Just as holiness was required of those who entered into the temple and tabernacle in the Old Testament, so holiness is required of Christians in the new covenant because we are *always* in the presence of God, for we ourselves are the very temple of God.

In sum, the New Testament development of the concept of the presence of God is shocking, but it is not altogether unexpected. In the garden of Eden God dwelled intimately with his people. Again in the temple and tabernacle he lived among his people, although his presence was restricted in order to protect the people from his holiness. In the New Testament Jesus Christ—God himself—dwells bodily among his people, healing the sick, forgiving the sinner, making whole the unclean. After his death and resurrection, which established the new covenant and made a way for God once again to dwell among his people, the Holy Spirit indwells believers as the

---

31. For further discussion on the Holy Spirit in Paul's writings, see Fee, *God's Empowering Presence*; Fee, *Paul, the Spirit, and the People of God*.

temple of the living God. What was foreshadowed in the Old Testament has been completed in the New.

IMPLICATIONS AND APPLICATION
TO THE CHURCH TODAY

The reality of God's presence in the life of believers is a cause for worship of the great God who has made it so. Several implications for believers today arise from our discussion of God's presence in the Old Testament, but we will focus on only a few here.

The biblical story is no longer as well-known as it used to be, so when sharing the story Jesus with others we often have to begin at the very beginning. The presence of God therefore figures prominently in evangelism of the biblically illiterate because the gospel is really the story of how God made it possible to dwell among his people. The gospel is God pursuing *us*, not the other way around. He sought to be near us, we sinned and were thus banished from his presence. And he continued to seek ways to be near us, first in the tabernacle, then in the temple, and finally in the incarnation of Christ and coming of the Holy Spirit. The gospel is the story of God's restored presence among his people.

There are also clear ethical implications for believers today. Paul highlights these in his letter to the Corinthians. If what Jesus said in John 14 about the Holy Spirit dwelling in us is true (and it is), then believers must live holy lives. Peter says the same: "You shall be holy, for I am holy" (1 Pet 1:14 ESV). Interestingly, Peter is quoting from Leviticus, where the phrase appears repeatedly (e.g., Lev 11:44, 45; 19:2; 20:7). And we know what Leviticus is all about: the regulations for God's people so that God may dwell among them without his holiness killing them. The people's holiness in Leviticus is tied directly to their experience of his presence. The people must be holy because God is holy, and their holiness is what will prevent their sudden death should they come near to God. Thus, when we read Peter's command to be holy, we should connect it with the broader context of Leviticus as it relates to living in God's presence. And holiness is even *more* significant in our context, for God's Spirit lives within us, whereas in Leviticus he merely lived among them.

Finally, we must consider how the Old Testament experience of God's absence can be appropriated into the Christian life today. We examined about Ps 88, which does not include the typical conclusion to lament psalms. Most lament psalms end with thanksgiving to God or a statement of confidence in his presence, but Ps 88 concludes without resolving the problem of God's absence. For the majority of the book of Job, Job likewise feels that God is nowhere to be found when Job needs him most. And of course our Lord himself cried out on the cross, "My God, my God, why have you forsaken me?" (Matt 24:46 ESV).

What does this mean for the believer today? How might we understand God's absence when the Holy Spirit indwells us? First, most, if not all, Christians have experience or will experience a time during which it *feels* as if God is no longer present. Some church contexts speak of this as a "dry" time. We can take heart during these times, knowing that saints before us, and even God himself, experienced moments in which God seemed far away. Sometimes all a person needs is simply to know she is not alone. Second, the experiences of Job, the psalmists, and Christ offer examples of how to seek God when he seems absent. Put simply: pray. Even though God *feels* absent, we must continue to pray, pouring out those feelings to God in honest, open communication. If the psalmists centuries before Christ could honestly pray to God about his felt absence, how much more Christians today, who experience an intimacy with God and closeness of his presence that the psalmists could not fathom? Third, though God may seem absent, we must continually remind ourselves that he has come near to us and even lives within us. The truth is that we are the temple of the living God, and of this truth we must remind ourselves when we experience God's absence.

QUESTIONS FOR DISCUSSION

1. How does the Old Testament reveal God's ultimate plan to restore people to Eden and the experience of his presence there?

2. Read Psalm 88 again. Have you experienced the feelings the psalmist is talking about? Are those legitimate feelings for a Christian today? Why/why not? How does the Old Testament theology of God's presence impact your understanding of this psalm?

3. What metaphors and language does the New Testament use to indicate that Jesus is the fulfillment of the Old Testament promise for God's presence to dwell among his people?

4. What does the danger of entering God's presence in the Old Testament indicate about his holiness? Do you think Christians today understand God's holiness in the same way as those in the Old Testament? Why/why not?

BIBLIOGRAPHY AND RECOMMENDED READING

Anderson, Gary A. *Christian Doctrine and the Old Testament*. Grand Rapids: Baker Academic, 2017.

Beale, Gregory K. "Garden Temple." *Kerux* 18 (2003) 3–50.

Block, Daniel I. "The Joy of Worship: The Mosaic Invitation to the Presence of God (Deuteronomy 12:1–14)." *BSac* 162 (2005) 131–49.

Compton, R. Bruce. "The Immanuel Prophecy in Isaiah 7:14–16 and Its Use in Matthew 1:23: Harmonizing Historical Context and Single Meaning." *DBSJ* 12 (2007) 3–15.

Duvall, J. Scott, and J. Daniel Hays. *Grasping God's Word: A Hands-On Approach to Reading, Interpreting, and Applying the Bible*. 3rd ed. Grand Rapids: Zondervan, 2012.

Elior, Rachel. "The Garden of Eden is the Holy of Holies and the Dwelling of the Lord." *SS* 24 (2014) 63–118.

Fee, Gordon. *God's Empowering Presence: The Holy Spirit in the Letters of Paul*. 1994. Repr., Grand Rapids: Baker Academic, 2009.

———. *Paul, the Spirit, and the People of God*. Grand Rapids: Baker Academic, 1996.

Gaffy, A. "The Coming of the Messiah." *PrPe* 8 (1994) 472–75.

Greene, Joseph R. "The Spirit in the Temple: Bridging the Gap between Old Testament Absence and New Testament Assumption." *JETS* 5 (2012) 717–42.

Kauffman, Yehezkel. *The Religion of Israel: From Its Beginnings to the Babylonian Exile*. Translated and abridged by Moshe Greenberg. New York: Schocken, 1972.

Keck, Elizabeth. "The Glory of Yahweh in Ezekiel and the Pre-Tabernacle Wilderness." *JSOT* 37 (2012) 201–18.

Klein, William W., Craig L. Blomberg, and Robert L. Hubbard Jr. *Introduction to Biblical Interpretation*. Rev. ed. Nashville: Nelson, 2004.

Na'aman, Nadav. *Ancient Israel and Its Neighbors: Interaction and Counteraction*. Collected Essays 1. Winona Lake, IN: Eisenbrauns, 2005.

Neuner, J. "Immanuel, God with Us (Is 7:14; Mt 1:23)." *Vid* 62 (1998) 562–66.

Propp, William H. C. *Exodus 1–18*. AB 2. New York: Doubleday, 1999.

Pulse, Jeffrey H. "Ascending to God: The Cosmology of Worship in the Old Testament." *CTQ* 79 (2015) 221–32.

Rogerson, John W. *A Theology of the Old Testament: Cultural Memory, Communication, and Being Human*. Minneapolis: Fortress, 2010.

Schachter, Lifsa Block. "The Garden of Eden as God's First Sanctuary." *JBQ* 41 (2013) 73–77.

Schnittjer, Gary E. *The Torah Story: An Apprenticeship on the Pentateuch*. Grand Rapids: Zondervan, 2006.

Stromberg, Jake. *An Introduction to the Study of Isaiah*. T. & T. Clark Approaches to Biblical Studies. London: T. & T. Clark, 2011.

Waltke, Bruce K., James M. Houston, and Erika Moore. *The Psalms as Christian Lament: A Historical Commentary*. Grand Rapids: Eerdmans, 2014.

Watts, John D. W. *Isaiah 1–33*. WBC 24. Nashville: Nelson, 2005.

Wegner, P. D. "How Many Virgin Birth are in the Bible? (Isaiah 7:14): A Prophetic Pattern Approach." *JETS* 54 (2011) 467–84.

Wenham, Gordon W. "Sanctuary Symbolism in the Garden of Eden Story." In *I Studied Inscriptions from Before the Flood: Ancient Near Eastern, Literary, and Linguistic Approaches to Genesis 1–11*, edited by Richard S. Hess and David Toshio Tsumura,

399–404. Sources for Biblical and Theological Study 4. Winona Lake, IN: Eisenbrauns, 1994.

10

LOYALTY AND OBEDIENCE

Russell L. Meek

INTRODUCTION

Obedience is easy to understand because we all either have children or have been children—parents teach their children to obey, and as children we learned to obey. As Christians we also know that we should what God requires—be obedient. The concept of loyalty is perhaps more foreign. It may conjure visions of a dog—earth's most loyal animal—or maybe the sacred bond between husband and wife. The biblical concept of loyalty contains these ideas—devotion to a master and commitment to a spouse—but they are subsumed under the much larger idea of covenant, a particular type of relationship that Yahweh established with his people.[1]

The concepts of loyalty and obedience—along with their opposites, disloyalty and disobedience—are ubiquitous in the Old Testament. Yet Christians often misunderstand how these concepts communicate the way God acts toward his people and how his people should respond to him. This chapter will unpack these ideas and their importance for a Christian

---

1. For a discussion of the importance of covenant in the Old Testament, see Eichrodt, *Theology*.

theology of the Old Testament by examining the ancient Near Eastern context of covenant making. Because of this historical-cultural context, loyalty and obedience dictated how Israel understood its relationship with Yahweh.

We will first address the intersection of loyalty and obedience with the gospel. We will then examine the historical-cultural context for Yahweh's covenant at Mt. Sinai. This discussion sets the stage for understanding how loyalty and obedience undergird Yahweh's covenant with his people. We will then show how loyalty and obedience are interwoven throughout the Old Testament, forming the foundation for how God's people were to interact with him throughout history. Finally, we will discuss loyalty and obedience in the New Testament and what these concepts mean for the modern Christian church.

LOYALTY, OBEDIENCE, AND THE GOSPEL

The gospel is God's gift of grace to all those who call on the name of Jesus Christ. It is given freely, not on account of any good works. Since it cannot be earned, why should Christians be concerned about things such as loyalty and obedience? Are these not works that are added to the gospel? Not at all, for loyalty and obedience are the appropriate responses to Yahweh's *hesed*, or covenant faithfulness, to us. Indeed, the gospel is the culmination of Yahweh's covenant faithfulness, and as such requires loyalty and obedience from those who embrace it.

The term *hesed* is used 246 times in the Old Testament. This term—translated variously as "steadfast love" (ESV), "goodness" (KJV), "lovingkindness" (NASB), "faithful love" (HCSB), and "unfailing love" (NLT)—implies that Yahweh acts in a particular way toward his people. However, there is no single word in English that communicates exactly what the word means, and thus how Yahweh acts toward his people. *Hesed* can refer to Yahweh's relationship to his people or to people's relationships with each other; therefore, investigating its use in horizontal relationships (relationships between humans) may illuminate what it communicates about the vertical relationship (Yahweh's relationship with his people). This, in turn, will help us to understand how loyalty and obedience intersect with the gospel.[2]

Will Kynes states that *hesed* "always involves an interpersonal relationship between either individuals or groups, whether that is between family members (Gen. 20:13), a host and guest (Gen. 19:19), friends (1 Sam. 20:8,

---

2. The labels "horizontal" to describe the human-human relationship and "vertical" to describe the Yahweh-human relationship are borrowed from Kynes, "God's Grace," 6–7, 20.

14), or a sovereign and his subjects (2 Sam. 2:5). A degree of mutuality can be assumed since a response in kind is often expected (e.g., Gen. 21:23; Josh. 2:12, 14)."[3] Additionally, the term describes a relationship between people in which they are required to act for the other person's benefit. For example, in Gen 19:19 Lot uses *hesed* to describe the angels who saved him from Sodom and Gomorrah; in Gen 21:23 Abimelech uses it to describe how he has treated Abraham;[4] and in Gen 40:14 Joseph uses the word in requesting the cupbearer to remember him. In each of these instances *hesed* communicates that a person has, or should, promote another person's overall wellbeing. Authors throughout the Old Testament use the term to describe how Yahweh treats his people, and how they are therefore to treat him.

The importance of *hesed*—which includes loyalty and obedience—for the gospel is this: it describes God's goodwill toward his people. God made a covenant that he would deal with his people in *hesed*. That covenant promise culminates in God's most incredible act of love and loyalty: the death and resurrection of Jesus Christ.[5] God's people, in response to Jesus's death and resurrection, act with loyalty and obedience. This brief overview of *hesed* will be filled out below as we examine the ancient Near Eastern context of covenant making and Yahweh's covenant with Israel at Mt. Sinai.

ANALYSIS OF KEY BIBLICAL TEXT:
THE SINAITIC COVENANT

Exodus chronicles the story of Yahweh's bringing Abraham's descendants out of Egypt to make them a nation unto himself. It is much more than a simple story of deliverance, though, for it shows the type of relationship—a covenant relationship—that Israel and Yahweh were to have. He was to be their sovereign and they were to be his vassal. As such, Yahweh would have certain obligations toward his people and they would in turn owe him loyalty and obedience. Reading the book of Exodus (and also Deuteronomy) alongside roughly contemporary examples of treaties between suzerains and vassals shows that Yahweh established a covenant relationship with his people that included elements common to their broader culture.

The Hebrew term *berit*, or covenant, is "an agreement enacted between two parties in which one or both make promises under oath to perform or refrain from certain actions stipulated in advance."[6] Sandra Richter points

---

3. Ibid., 7.
4. Note Weinfeld's discussion ("Berit," 124).
5. See Kynes, "God's Grace," 20.
6. Mendenhall and Herion, "Covenant," 1:1178.

out that the concept of covenant is important in Israelite society and the ancient Near East because the level of responsibility between people is determined by their blood relationship, with ultimate responsibility falling on the family's patriarch.[7] To establish a relationship between two unrelated parties, one must *create* a familial relationship.[8] Thus, "on the individual, tribal and, eventually, national level, if you needed someone to *act* like a family member, and you were willing to give that person the privileges of family in return, you would invite that individual (tribe or nation) into a covenant agreement which created *fictional* kinship."[9]

In order to bind two parties together, such as Yahweh and the people of Israel, a covenant would be made whereby a kinship was created that was as strong as the bonds of a family. In modern society this idea is communicated most clearly in adoption and marriage. When two people become married, they create a family relationship—with all the attendant responsibilities—that previously did not exist. Likewise, when a family adopts a child, that child becomes as if she were physically born to the parents. Marriage and adoption join people as family members who were once not family members. Similarly, covenants in the ancient Near East made families out of those who were not family.

Two basic types of covenants existed in the ancient Near East: the parity treaty (between equal parties) and the suzerain/vassal treaty (between a greater and a lesser party).[10] In suzerain/vassal treaties, the greater party (i.e., the suzerain) provided benefits such as military protection and land grants to the lesser party (i.e., the vassal).[11] In response, the vassal owed the suzerain financial tribute and "consummate loyalty."[12] Consequently, vassals could have only one suzerain, for to take another "lord" or "father" would be tantamount to treason.[13]

The covenant Yahweh established with Israel at Mount Sinai exhibits striking parallels with Hittite suzerain/vassal treaties,[14] which had six basic features: 1) a preamble that identifies the suzerain; 2) a historical prologue that recounts the previous relationship between the parties; 3) covenant

7. Richter, *The Epic of Eden*, 70–71.

8. Ibid., 71.

9. Ibid., 72.

10. Ibid., 73.

11. Ibid., 73–74.

12. Ibid., 74.

13. Ibid., 74–75.

14. Hittites were an ancient Near Eastern people group. For discussion see Hoffner, "Hittites," 127–55; Hoffner, "Hittites and Hurrians," 197–228.

stipulations to which the vassal must agree; 4) provisions for periodic reading and safekeeping of the covenant; 5) witnesses to the covenant; and 6)
blessings and curses should the vassal either keep or fail to keep the covenant.[15] The Sinaitic covenant contains all six of these characteristics.[16]

First, Exod 20:2a and Deut 5:6a record the preamble that identifies
Yahweh as the suzerain: "I am Yahweh your God." Second, in Exod 20:2b and
Deut 5:6b Yahweh reminds the people that he rescued them from slavery in
Egypt. Third, the covenant stipulations, or the requirements for relationship with Yahweh, are recorded in Exod 20:3–17 and Deut 5:7–21, among
other places. Fourth, provisions for storing the covenant in the tabernacle
and periodically reading it are recorded in several places (Exod 24:7; 25:21;
Deut 10:5; 31:10–12). Fifth, Yahweh called heaven and earth as witnesses to
the covenant (Deut 4:26; 30:19–20; 31:28). Sixth, Deuteronomy records an
extensive list of blessings that accompany covenant faithfulness and curses
that result from unfaithfulness to the covenant (Deut 27:11–28:68).[17] In
sum, the Sinaitic covenant was a suzerain/vassal treaty between Yahweh and
Israel.

The ancient Near Eastern context of covenant making and its relationship to the Sinaitic covenant helps us understand Yahweh's relationship with
Israel. In rescuing Israel from Egypt and entering into a covenant with them,
he proclaimed that he was their suzerain, their Lord and Father, and as such
he required their loyalty. He would protect them and give them land, and in
response they were to be loyal and obedient to him. First and foremost, this
loyal obedience meant that Israel would worship Yahweh alone. To worship
anyone else would be treason. Moreover, Yahweh outlined how Israel was
to act toward others in order to demonstrate their loyalty and obedience to
him.

It is crucial to note that the covenant Yahweh made with Israel was of
his own initiative. Their loyal obedience—the proper response to the covenant relationship—was required, but it was not the basis of the covenant.
The basis of the covenant was Yahweh's gracious acts toward Israel, not their
obedience to him. As we move through the Old Testament, we will see the

15. Hahn, *Kinship by Covenant*, 49. Hahn also notes that these features and language used to describe them are consistent across ancient Near Eastern cultures.

16. Not all scholars agree on this point. For discussion, see Nicholson, *God and His
People*, 56–82; Kraus, *Worship in Israel*, 136–40; Whitely, "Covenant and Commandment in Israel," 37–43.

17. See the helpful chart in Richter, *Epic of Eden*, 84. For further discussion and explanation of these aspects of the Sinaitic covenant and their relationship to ancient Near
Eastern treaties, see Kitchen, *Ancient Orient*, 90–102; Levenson, *Sinai and Zion*, 23–36.

importance the biblical authors placed on Israel's obedience and loyalty to Yahweh in response to his establishing himself as their suzerain.

UNITY WITHIN THE OLD TESTAMENT

The Sinaitic covenant required the vassal (Israel) to exhibit covenant faithfulness to its suzerain (Yahweh) by keeping the covenant stipulations. This understanding of the historical-cultural context of Yahweh's relationship with Israel forms the foundation for how we understand the rest of the Old Testament, which recounts the history of that relationship between Israel and Yahweh.[18] This history focuses largely on whether and to what extent Israel exhibited loyalty and obedience to Yahweh. Though Israel's loyalty and obedience were often in question, Yahweh's *hesed*, or covenant faithfulness, never was. Despite the covenant curses that would later come upon Israel, Yahweh remained faithful, which ultimately culminated in the death and resurrection of his son, Jesus Christ.

The Historical Books (Joshua–Esther) chronicle Israel's failure (and sometimes success) at maintaining covenant loyalty. To take one example, Joshua records Israel's entrance into and conquest of the promised land,[19] which is entirely contingent upon their loyalty and obedience to Yahweh.[20] The Jericho narrative (Josh 2–8) provides a stunning illustration of this truth.[21]

In Josh 2 we meet Rahab, the Canaanite prostitute whose faith saves her.[22] The next several chapters recount the conquest of Jericho, in which the people of Israel are successful despite a dubious battle plan. The celebration is cut short with Josh 7:1: "But the sons of Israel acted faithlessly in regard to the ban."[23] The rest of the chapter details how Achan—an Israelite—disobeyed Yahweh, caused the nation's defeat in battle against an inferior foe, and, along with his family, was stoned to death by the people of Israel.

18. See the discussion in Schnittjer, *The Torah Story*, 495–517.

19. For discussion of the conquest and various issues surrounding it, see Hess, "Early Israel in Canaan," 125–42.

20. See House, *Old Testament Theology*, 200–206.

21. On *herem*, or "ban," see Thomas, Evans, and Copan, eds., *Holy War in the Bible*; Cowles, ed., *Show them No Mercy*; Copan and Flannagan, *Did God Really Command Genocide?*

22. Hubbard (*Joshua*, 111) notes that "the mercy accorded Rahab in chapter 2 clearly contradicts the expectation that all Canaanites are to be killed."

23. Unless otherwise noted, Scripture quotations in this chapter are the author's translation.

By bookending the battle of Jericho with these two narratives of covenant loyalty and covenant disloyalty, the author of Joshua demonstrates the gravity of obedience to the Lord. Rahab, who should have been excluded from Yahweh's favor because of her national heritage and profession, instead received Yahweh's favor through faithful obedience to him. Achan, who should have received Yahweh's favor as a member of the covenant community, instead incited God's wrath through disloyalty and disobedience. The magnitude of these two narratives should not be lost on us, for they demonstrate that God both welcomes the non-Israelite into the covenant *and* holds the Israelite accountable to the covenant. Just as loyalty and obedience can overcome ethnic barriers to a relationship with Yahweh (Rahab), disloyalty and disobedience can bring about God's wrath and punishment despite one's ethnic heritage (Achan).

Israel is established in Canaan by the end of Joshua, though the question remains whether they will follow the examples of Joshua, Caleb, and Rahab—covenant loyalty and obedience—or whether they will follow the example of Achan—covenant disloyalty and disobedience. Unfortunately, Judges shows that the people are primarily disloyal and disobedient, with the result that Yahweh "emerges as the 'hero' of the book" for his continual faithfulness to Israel in spite of her unfaithfulness.[24]

In the book of Judges, Israel turns away from Yahweh to worship other gods, is oppressed by enemies, and cries out to God, who raises up a deliverer, or judge, to save Israel.[25] This cycle of apostasy → negative consequence → cry for deliverance → deliverance is repeated throughout the book. In order to properly understand loyalty and obedience, we must realize that Judges demonstrates clearly the interrelationship between the two concepts: "Israel's sense of obedience is always *more than* commandments, but it is never *less than* fulfillment of commands."[26] In order for obedience to be genuine, it must be rooted in loyalty, which becomes even more apparent in the prophetic books.

The implications of Israel's cycle of sin are significant for understanding the theology of loyalty and obedience. First, Israel suffers the consequences of sin. The nation's disloyalty does not go unpunished; rather, when the people break faith, Yahweh punishes them by delivering them unto other nations. Thus, Israel's security and peace in the land is tied directly to

24. Howard Jr., *Historical Books*, 119.

25. On the judges in the book of Judges, see Hamilton, *Historical Books*, 98–99; House, *Old Testament Theology*, 221–22.

26. Birch, Brueggemann, Fretheim, and Petersen, *Theological Introduction*, 187; emphasis original.

its loyalty and obedience to Yahweh, its suzerain.[27] Second, once the people repent of their sin and call out for deliverance, Yahweh responds favorably. Rather than lord his righteousness over them, as humans are apt to do (see Matt 18:21–35), Yahweh forgives and rescues Israel. Despite their disobedience, Yahweh is faithful and continues to honor the stipulations of their covenant.[28]

In sum, Judges teaches two important truths about the concepts of loyalty and obedience in the Old Testament that carry through to the New Testament and remain essential for believers today: 1) sin—that is, disloyalty and disobedience—has consequences, and 2) "If we confess our sins, he is faithful and just to forgive us our sins and to cleanse us from all unrighteousness" (1 John 1:9).

During the period of the Judges, the people were faithful to Yahweh while a strong, faithful judge led them, but the cycle of sin continued when the faithful judge died (Judg 2:19). This pattern holds true for the period of the united and divided monarchies, as Israel continues to vacillate between loyalty and disloyalty to Yahweh.[29] David and Solomon, though not without their faults, led the united kingdom in covenant loyalty and obedience to Yahweh, but during the divided kingdom only a few of the kings of Judah and none of the kings of Israel followed suit.[30] The divided monarchy is therefore marked primarily by disloyalty and disobedience, which the prophetic books highlight in their repeated calls for repentance and a return to Yahweh.

The ministries of the writing prophets spanned the period of the monarchy in Israel and Judah, with some prophets ministering in the exilic and

27. This statement is not meant to indicate that a one-to-one correspondence between actions and rewards is a strict theological construct. Indeed, the book of Job shows that apparent punishment from the Lord does not always result from sin. We must therefore examine the concept of loyalty and obedience carefully, holding in tension the reality that God is mysterious and we cannot understand all his ways this side of eternity. For further discussion along these lines, see Bartholomew and O'Dowd, *Old Testament Wisdom Literature*, 127–66.

28. Concerning Yahweh's loyalty in despite the disloyalty of the bulk of the nation of Israel, House (*Old Testament Theology*, 226) states that "faith and obedience, the twin pillars of the theology revealed to this point in the canon, are evident in only a few Israelites. The existence of a minority of believers means the promises to Abraham are not defunct even on the human side."

29. On the united and divided monarchies, see Hill, "History of Israel 3," 442–52; and McKenzie, "History of Israel 4," 452–58.

30. The kings of Judah who displayed covenant loyalty were Asa (1 Kgs 15:11–14), Jehoshaphat (1 Kgs 22:42–43), Uzziah (2 Chr 26:3–4), Jotham (2 Kgs 15:32–34), Hezekiah (2 Kgs 18:1–6), and Josiah (2 Kgs 22:1–2).

postexilic periods, after the fall of both Israel and Judah.[31] Despite the wide range of time in which the prophets ministered, the basic consistency of their overall message highlights the importance of loyalty and obedience. J. Scott Duvall and J. Daniel Hays have summarized the prophetic message in three points: "1. You have broken the covenant; you had better repent! 2. No repentance? Then judgment! 3. Yet, there is hope beyond the judgment for a glorious, future restoration."[32] The collective prophetic voice calls God's people back to covenant faithfulness, or in other words, loyalty and obedience.

To take one example, Jeremiah devotes his ministry to prophesying against the people of Israel because they "went after worthlessness, and became worthless" (Jer 2:5 ESV). Rather than walking with Yahweh in loyalty and obedience—as the covenant demanded—Israel forsakes the Lord in favor of other gods. J. A. Thompson points out that Israel's apostasy was neither new nor novel; rather, it "had begun as long ago as the days of the Conquest (v. 7) and had continued ever since."[33] Jeremiah, like the other prophets, calls Israel to repent or to face the consequences of covenant disloyalty and disobedience.[34] However, Jeremiah's repeated cries of judgment and destruction are interspersed with statements of hope and restoration (e.g., Jer 4:1–2; 30–33). Ultimately the people refuse to repent and are exiled to Babylon, from which they would return some seventy years later. Despite God's judgment on his people, he remembers his covenant and restores them, thus demonstrating the covenant loyalty that the people failed to show.

Covenant loyalty and obedience to Yahweh are fundamental concepts in the Old Testament. The Pentateuch lays out the requirements for living in relationship with Yahweh (loyalty and obedience); the Historical Books chronicle Israel's cycle of disloyalty and disobedience; and the prophetic books indict God's people for their faithlessness, call them to repentance, and foretell a time during which right relationship with the Lord would be restored.

---

31. On the chronology of these periods, see Kitchen, "Chronology," 181–88.

32. Duvall and Hays, *Grasping God's Word*, 403.

33. Thompson, *Jeremiah*, 167.

34. Chapters 1–25 record multiple prophecies against Judah and Jerusalem in which the Lord calls the people to repentance and threatens judgment if repentance is not forthcoming.

LOYALTY AND OBEDIENCE IN THE NEW TESTAMENT

> "Behold! The days are coming," declares Yahweh, "when I will
> cut a new covenant with the house of Israel and the house of
> Judah. It will not be like the covenant that I cut with their fathers
> when I seized them by the hand to lead them out of the land
> of Egypt—my covenant that they broke though I had married
> them," declares Yahweh. "Instead this is the covenant that I will
> cut with the house of Israel after those days," declares Yahweh.
> "I will put my Torah in their inner part, and upon their heart
> I will write it. And I will be their God and they will be my
> people. And a man will no longer teach his neighbor—or a man
> his brother—saying, 'Know Yahweh.' For all of them will know
> me, from the least of them until the greatest of them," declares
> Yahweh, "for I will forgive their iniquity and their sin I will no
> longer remember." (Jer 31:31–34)

Yahweh declared that he would one day establish a new covenant with
his people.[35] This covenant would not be like the Sinai Covenant, which we
have been examining thus far. As we saw above, Israel's history is a continual
pattern of disloyalty and disobedience interspersed with brief periods of
loyalty and obedience. In order to remedy this issue, the Lord states that he
will cut a new covenant with his people, one that he himself would put on
their hearts and in their inner parts. In so doing, the people will know the
Lord and he will forgive them.[36]

The Sinaitic Covenant was the previous covenant that established the
relationship between Yahweh and his people. This relationship was to be
marked by loyalty and obedience, but was instead characterized by disloyalty and disobedience. This covenant was meant to be written on the heart
(Deut 6:6); the people were supposed to teach their children the Torah (Deut
6:7) and think of the Torah constantly (Deut 6:6–9).[37] Similarly, loyalty and
obedience typify the new covenant—followers of Christ should indeed do
what Christ says. The new covenant is also going to be written on the heart;

---

35. For further discussion on the new covenant in Jeremiah, see, among many
resources, Pettegrew, "New Covenant," 251–70; Mulzac, "Remnant and the New Covenant," 239–48; Lee, "New Covenant," 24–29; Robinson, "Jeremiah's New Covenant,"
181–204.

36. For discussion of forgiveness of sins in the new covenant, see Willis, "'I Will
Remember Their Sins No More,'" 1–15.

37. For discussion of the concept of loving God with one's heart/mind, soul, and
might, see Bruckner, "Human Wholeness," 1–19.

however, in the new covenant the agent of internalization is different—the Lord himself writes his Torah on the hearts of those who know him.

In looking at the gospel implications of loyalty and obedience, we must first of all recognize that the Father inaugurated the new covenant through the death and resurrection of his Son, Jesus. The new covenant *is* the gospel. It is the ultimate expression of Yahweh's covenant loyalty, or *hesed*. He has been faithful to his covenant to the greatest degree possible, even sending his Son to die on a cross in place of us, who are continually and repeatedly disobedient and disloyal to the covenant.

The gospel, or the new covenant, drastically changes our understanding of loyalty and obedience. What mere humans could not do, Jesus Christ—fully God and fully human—did. Whereas we were unable to be loyal to the covenant, he was loyal. Whereas we could not be obedient, he was. Jesus descended to earth, lived a sinless life that fulfilled all the demands of the Torah—that is, he was loyal and obedient in all things—and died as propitiation for sin so that the wrath of God would be turned away from believers.[38]

The magnitude of atonement should not be lost on us, especially as we reflect on loyalty and obedience in the Old Testament. Because of the gospel, it is as if those who follow Christ have perfectly kept the Torah. When we place our faith in Christ, the wrath of God—that wrath we deserve because of disloyalty and disobedience—is turned away from us. Christ takes what we deserved—judgment—and gives us what we would never deserve—grace and mercy (see Rom 4:23–25).[39] Because of the gospel, loyalty and obedience to the covenant are not something we must strive for. Rather, they are something that we already have. When the Father looks upon Christians, he does not see the pattern of sin—disloyalty and disobedience—instead, he sees the perfect obedience and righteousness of his Son, Jesus Christ. The gospel therefore frees Christians from the inability to please God. It bathes us in the righteousness of Christ and allows us access to the Father that we previously did not have.

The gospel also reinforces the Old Testament's teaching on loyalty and obedience. In fact, the gospel's demands are even more strenuous than those of Torah.[40] Think of the Sermon on the Mount (Matt 5:1–7:29), in which Christ interpreted the true meaning of Torah. Being loyal to Torah does

38. On the concept of propitiation, and general discussion of Christ's work of atonement, see Boice, "Propitiation," 31–47; Patterson, "Work of Christ," 545–602; McDonald, *Atonement*; Morris, *Atonement*; Letham, *Work of Christ*.

39. This is called "double imputation." For discussion of this doctrine, see references cited above.

40. See the chapter on Torah in this volume.

not mean that we simply won't murder someone. Christ showed that to be obedient to the command not to murder, we must also not be angry with our brother (Matt 5:21–26). Loyalty to the covenant means not committing adultery, but it also means not committing lust (Matt 5:27–30). Learning the true intent of Torah, and what it actually means to be loyal and obedient to the Lord, makes Christ's statement about our ability to enter heaven even more daunting: "unless your righteousness exceeds that of the scribes and Pharisees, you will never enter the kingdom of heaven" (Matt 5:20 ESV). However, the good news of the gospel is that we do not have to fulfill the demands of the Torah because Christ fulfilled them perfectly. Our righteousness does exceed that of the scribes and Pharisees, for we have the righteousness of Christ (see Rom 8:1–11; 2 Cor 5:21; Gal 3:10–13; Phil 3:9).

In sum, the gospel implications for the Old Testament theme of loyalty and obedience could not be more significant. Christ was perfectly obedient and perfectly loyal. His death on the cross made propitiation for our disloyalty and disobedience, and through faith he imputed his righteousness to us and turned away the wrath of God by taking our sin. Thus, we now have the righteousness of Christ through faith, and it is therefore as if we were perfectly loyal and obedient to the Father.

LOYALTY, OBEDIENCE, AND
THE CHRISTIAN LIFE TODAY

Since the Old Testament has continuing relevance for Christians today (2 Tim 3:16), and since Jesus changes everything, we must determine how we are to appropriate the Old Testament concepts of loyalty and obedience. As discussed above, the significance of loyalty and obedience are essentially the same, and yet drastically different, for the modern Christian church.

Continued Relevance

The continuing relevance of loyalty and obedience lies primarily in that the New Testament's demands the same from Christians. We saw above that when Jesus interpreted the Torah, he showed that the standard for loyalty and obedience is much greater than we once thought. Outward obedience is certainly necessary ("do not commit adultery"), but is insufficient until coupled with inward obedience ("do not lust"). The implication of Jesus's interpretation of Torah—that it is primarily a heart issue—is that we must have a new heart in order to be loyal and obedient to the covenant. Our outward obedience must stem from a changed heart, which only the Father accomplishes through the new covenant.

Given the church's correct emphasis on God's grace and the changed heart that accompanies it, the Christian may be tempted to think that outward obedience is inconsequential, that all that matters is whether his "heart is in the right place." Both James and Paul confronted this issue head-on. Paul argued that continuing to sin in light of God's grace was absurd (Rom 6:1–14). James stated that "faith by itself, if it does not have works, is dead" (Jas 2:17 ESV). Thus, the basic idea that we must be loyal and obedient to the Lord and the covenant he has made with us remains consistent in the New Testament.

Significant Difference

While we must not overlook the continued relevance of loyalty and obedience, we must also recognize that the gospel has brought with it a significant change in how we apply this concept. Righteousness has always been by faith, even in the Old Testament (see Gen 15:6; Rom 4:3; Gal 3:5–9; Heb 11). Obedience and loyalty did not earn righteousness, yet they were still required by members of the covenant community. The people were essentially unable to keep these requirements, so the Lord promised a new covenant in which he would write his Torah on the heart. Jesus inaugurated this new covenant with his death and resurrection, and now those who place their faith in Christ are clothed in his righteousness.

The significant difference, therefore, is that Christians today live in right relationship with God because of the sacrifice of Christ. While we must maintain covenant loyalty, our ability to do so comes from God having written his Torah on our heart. Furthermore, regardless of the Christian's ability or inability to be loyal and obedient, the Father will always see them covered in the blood of his Son, Jesus Christ. There is great liberty for the Christian because of the love poured out on the cross. As Paul stated, "For I am sure that neither death nor life, nor angels nor rulers, nor things present nor things to come, nor powers, nor height nor depth, nor anything else in all creation, will be able to separate us from the love of God in Christ Jesus our Lord" (Rom 8:38–39).

QUESTIONS FOR DISCUSSION

1. What is God's *hesed*, or loyal love? How was it displayed in the Old Testament, and how is it displayed today?

2. In what ways does Christ's perfect loyalty and perfect obedience impact the role of loyalty and obedience in the Christian life?

3. What is the theological significance of the Sinaitic Covenant?

4. Read the Sermon on the Mount. In what ways does it require greater loyalty and obedience from followers of Christ? How does the Christian's righteousness surpass that of the Pharisees?

BIBLIOGRAPHY AND RECOMMENDED READING

Bartholomew, Craig G., and Ryan P. O'Dowd. *Old Testament Wisdom Literature: A Theological Introduction*. Downers Grove, IL: IVP Academic, 2011.

Birch, Bruce C., Walter Brueggemann, Terrence E. Fretheim, and David L. Petersen. *A Theological Introduction to the Old Testament*. Nashville: Abingdon, 1999.

Boice, James Montgomery. "The Nature of the Atonement: Propitiation." In *Atonement*, edited by Gabriel N. E. Fluhrer, 31–47. Phillipsburg, NJ: P & R, 2010.

Bruckner, James K. "A Theological Description of Human Wholeness in Deuteronomy 6." *ExAud* 21 (2005) 1–19.

Copan, Paul, and Matt Flannagan. *Did God Really Command Genocide: Coming to Terms with the Justice of God*. Grand Rapids: Baker, 2014.

Cowles, C. S., ed. *Show Them No Mercy: Four Views on God and Canaanite Genocide*. Counterpoints: Bible and Theology. Grand Rapids: Zondervan, 2010.

Duvall, J. Scott, and J. Daniel Hays. *Grasping God's Word: A Hands-On Approach to Reading, Interpreting, and Applying the Bible*. 3rd ed. Grand Rapids: Zondervan, 2012.

Eichrodt, Walter. *Theology of the Old Testament*. 2 vols. Translated by J. A. Baker. OTL. Philadelphia: Westminster John Knox, 1967.

Hahn, Scott W. *Kinship by Covenant: A Canonical Approach to the Fulfillment of God's Saving Promises*. New Haven: Yale University Press, 2009.

Hamilton, Victor P. *Handbook on the Historical Books*. Grand Rapids: Baker Academic, 2001.

Hess, Richard. "Early Israel in Canaan: A Survey of Recent Evidence and Interpretation." *PEQ* 125 (1993) 125–42.

Hill, Andrew E. "History of Israel 3: United Monarchy." In *Dictionary of the Old Testament: Historical Books*, edited by Bill T. Arnold and H. G. M. Williamson, 442–52. Downers Grove, IL: InterVarsity, 2005.

Hoffner, Harry A. "Hittites." In *Peoples of the Old Testament World*, edited by A. J. Hoerth, G. L. Mattingly, and E. M. Yamauchi, 127–55. Grand Rapids,: Baker, 1994.

———. "The Hittites and Hurrians." In *Peoples of Old Testament Times*, edited by D. J. Wiseman, 197–228. Oxford: Clarendon, 1973.

House, Paul R. *Old Testament Theology*. Downers Grove, IL: IVP Academic, 1998.

Howard, David M., Jr. *An Introduction to the Old Testament Historical Books.* Chicago: Moody, 1993.

Hubbard, Robert L. *Joshua.* NIVAC. Grand Rapids: Zondervan, 2009.

Kitchen, Kenneth A. *Ancient Orient and Old Testament.* Chicago: InterVarsity, 1966.

———. "Chronology." In *Dictionary of the Old Testament: Historical Books,* edited by Bill T. Arnold and H. G. M. Williamson, 181–88. Downers Grove, IL: InterVarsity, 2005.

Kraus, Hans-Joachim. *Worship in Israel: A Cultic History of the Old Testament.* Translated by Geoffrey Buswell. Richmond, VA: Knox, 1996.

Kynes, Will. "God's Grace in the Old Testament: Considering the *Hesed* of the Lord." *Knowing and Doing* (2010) 6–7, 20.

Lee, J. W. "The New Covenant in Jeremiah." *BI* 12 (1986) 24–29.

Letham, Robert. *The Work of Christ.* Contours of Christian Theology. Downers Grove, IL: IVP Academic, 1997.

Levenson, Jon D. *Sinai and Zion: An Entry into the Jewish Bible.* Minneapolis: Winston, 1985.

McDonald, H. D. *The New Testament Concept of Atonement: The Gospel of the Calvary Event.* Grand Rapids: Baker, 1994.

McKenzie, Steven L. "History of Israel 4: Division of the Monarchy." In *Dictionary of the Old Testament: Historical Books,* edited by Bill T. Arnold and H. G. M. Williamson, 452–58. Downers Grove, IL: InterVarsity, 2005.

Mendenhall, George E., and Gary A. Herion. "Covenant." *ABD* 1:1178–202.

Morris, Leon. *The Atonement: Its Meaning and Significance.* Downers Grove, IL: InterVarsity, 1983.

Mulzac, Kenneth. "The Remnant and the New Covenant in the Book of Jeremiah." *AUSS* 34 (1996) 239–48.

Nicholson, E. W. *God and His People: Covenant and Theology in the Old Testament.* Oxford: Clarendon, 1986.

Patterson, Paige. "The Work of Christ." In *A Theology for the Church,* edited by Daniel L. Akin, 545–602. Nashville: B & H Academic, 2007.

Pettegrew, Larry D. "The New Covenant." *MSJ* 10 (1995) 251–70.

Richter, Sandra. *The Epic of Eden: A Christian Entry into the Old Testament.* Downers Grove, IL: IVP Academic, 2008.

Robinson, Bernard P. "Jeremiah's New Covenant: Jer 31,31–34." *SJOT* 15 (2001) 181–204.

Schnittjer, Gary. *The Torah Story: An Apprenticeship on the Pentateuch.* Grand Rapids: Zondervan, 2006.

Thomas, Heath, Jeremy Evans, and Paul Copan, eds. *Holy War in the Bible: Christian Morality and an Old Testament Problem.* Downers Grove, IL: InterVarsity, 2014.

Thompson, J. A. *The Book of Jeremiah.* NICOT. Grand Rapids: Eerdmans, 1980.

Weinfeld, Moshe. "Berit—Covenant vs. Obligation." *Bib* 56 (1975) 120–28.

Whitely, C. F. "Covenant and Commandment in Israel." *JNES* 22 (1963) 37–43.

Willis, Timothy M. "'I Will Remember Their Sins No More': Jeremiah 31, the New Covenant, and the Forgiveness of Sins." *ResQ* 53 (2011) 1–15.

11

SUFFERING[1]

RUSSELL L. MEEK

INTRODUCTION

Why does God allow—or as some might say, cause—suffering in the world? This question is as relevant today as it was millennia ago when the biblical authors struggled with it. The Old Testament offers no pat answers to the problem, opting instead to place human suffering and God's blessing right next to each other, with often little effort to resolve the ensuing tension. We find in the Pentateuch, Proverbs, and portions of the Prophets that God blesses obedience and that those who follow him may expect to live a long, full life with plenty of resources and children with whom to share their abundance. Yet, we also encounter people such as Joseph and Job, who suffered greatly despite their faithfulness to Yahweh.

This tension caused by unjust suffering and explored in Ecclesiastes and Job is finally resolved when in the New Testament we meet a Savior who suffers to redeem humanity. And yet, the New Testament modifies the idea

1. A slightly different version of this chapter was originally published as "Truly God Is Good: Suffering in Old Testament Perspective," *Journal of Spiritual Formation and Soul Care* 9.2 (2016) 151–63. I thank the journal and its editors for permission to include the article here.

that obedience leads to earthly rewards by stating clearly that the righteous will suffer greatly in this life. It is no longer a singular Joseph or Job who suffers—an anomaly in the biblical narrative—or even a nebulous group of "the oppressed" (Eccl 4:1).[2] Now *all* followers of God can expect suffering (Matt 10:16–25).

There are several possible reasons for human suffering: direct sin (God's discipline or punishment), indirect sin (the result of living in a fallen world), and righteousness. Job's friends were most familiar with suffering that resulted from direct sin, holding to the bitter end that Job's sin *must* have resulted from his own sinfulness. They had good reason to believe this because the theology with which they—and we—were familiar teaches that the wicked will receive their just deserts.[3] For example, Bildad states in Job 8:20 that "Behold, God will not reject a guiltless person." As we will see, such sentiment is common throughout the Bible, and indeed the human experience bears this out. We know intuitively that poor choices usually result in undesirable consequences. Yet, we also know that sometimes "bad things happen to good people," a theme that features prominently in the Bible.[4]

Second, sometimes people suffer as a result of the human condition: we live in a fallen world that "has been groaning together in the pains of childbirth" (Rom 8:22 ESV), surrounded by fallen people. While there was certainly a larger plan at work with Job's suffering, we may point to the fact that his very existence in a world riddled with sin enabled his suffering to occur.

Finally, people may experience suffering because of their faith in Jesus Christ and proclamation of the gospel. The New Testament promises us repeatedly that such will be the fate of Jesus' followers. Christians living in the United States live a peculiar sort of existence because we experience religious freedom that is unparalleled throughout the rest of the world, and indeed throughout history. For our brothers and sisters living in the majority world, however, suffering through persecution is often a very real possibility.

In the following pages we will discuss suffering in the Old Testament. First, we will look at passages in the Pentateuch that describe life before the Fall, which paints a picture of human existence before suffering. We will then look at what the Pentateuch and Proverbs teach about avoiding suffering through living a life of faithful obedience. Next, we examine suffering

2. Unless otherwise noted, Scripture quotations in this chapter are the author's translation.

3. Dhorme, *Job*, cxxxv.

4. Kushner, *Job: When Bad Things Happen to Good People.*

in the books of Job and Ecclesiastes, which tackle head-on the issue of the suffering of the righteous. We will then move to the New Testament to examine how suffering differs on this side of the cross and how modern day Christians must live in light of the reality of suffering. We will conclude the chapter with a few proposals for how to apply the biblical theology of suffering. First, though, we turn to the relationship between suffering and the gospel.

SUFFERING AND THE GOSPEL

Jesus promises those who follow him will experience suffering, but that is not all. The gospel brings resolution to the dilemma of human suffering in that God took on flesh and suffered mightily so that his followers might experience salvation in him. Thus, Jesus' suffering is significant for Old Testament theology because Jesus represents the greatest extreme of the unjust sufferer—the one with no sin became sin, so that we might be counted righteous in him (2 Cor 5:21). If we are to make sense of righteous suffering, then we must take into account the ultimate Sufferer. Not only that, but Jesus's suffering demonstrates that something is to be learned through suffering, as Heb 5:8–9 makes clear. The Bible is clear that suffering will happen, and that it will happen to Jesus's followers as a result of their faith in him and sometimes for no apparent reason. As Bartholomew and O'Dowd point out, Jesus helps to resolve this tension because

> Central to the biblical narrative is the slain lamb upon the throne; his death will ultimately remove all suffering, but in the time between his inauguration of the kingdom and its consummation, believers will continue to suffer and continue to read a book like Job. In a far fuller way we know that our Redeemer lives and that we shall yet live to see him.[5]

Our treatment here of the relationship between suffering and the gospel is brief because these issues will be developed fully when we engage the New Testament texts that relate to suffering in the believer's life today. These initial paragraphs about suffering and the gospel serve to orient us to the cross as we move through the Old Testament texts that deal with suffering.

---

5. Bartholomew and O'Dowd, *Old Testament Wisdom Literature*, 158.

ANALYSIS OF KEY BIBLICAL TEXTS

Sin Enters the World: Genesis 3

The first passages of the Pentateuch present readers with a good world. In this good creation there is no sin, no suffering, and no death. God walks with Adam and Eve in the cool of the day, indicating the perfect relationship they enjoy together. God gives Adam and Eve the simple command not to eat from the tree of the knowledge of good and evil, about which Robin Routledge states, "This command gave human beings an opportunity to play an active part in their relationship with God. It gave a choice: obey God's word and maintain the relationship, or disobey and reject the relationship. This shows that God wants a relationship with human beings that is entered into freely. It also emphasizes that a key element within that relationship is obedience."[6] It takes a mere three chapters for humanity's perfect relationship with God to change, as Adam and Eve choose to rebel against God by disobeying his command not to eat of the fruit from the tree of the knowledge of good and evil. Suddenly sin enters the world, and with it suffering.

Blessing and Curses: Deuteronomy

The book of Deuteronomy confirms what we see in Gen 3: suffering results from sin. Deuteronomy 30:16–17, for example, clarifies the relationship between actions and consequences: "I command you today to love Yahweh your God, to walk in his ways, and to keep his commandments, statues, and judgments. Then you shall live and multiply and Yahweh your God will bless you in the land that you are entering to possess. But if your heart turns away and you do not obey, but you allow yourself to be led astray and if you worship other gods and serve them, I declare to you today that you will utterly perish." Throughout Deuteronomy the people of Israel are reminded that they are heirs to a special relationship with Yahweh that is based in his gracious choice of Abraham, Isaac, and Jacob (see Deut 1:8). Israel cannot choose to be *un*chosen by Yahweh, yet their choice either to obey or disobey God plays a significant role in the quality of life they will experience in the land. Deuteronomy 7:11–15 delineates the type of blessing Israel may expect for their faithfulness to the covenant: Yahweh's love, large families, abundant harvests, increased livestock, and no sickness.[7] Conse-

---

6. Routledge, *Old Testament Theology*, 147.

7. See also Deut 30:11–20, where Moses assures the Israelites that the commandments

quently, Deut 28:15–68 promises that they may expect the opposite if they disobey: sickness, disease, death, defeat in war, famine, barrenness, and lack of provision (unfruitful crops and the inability to eat from one's livestock). As with blessing, the curses are conditional upon the people's behavior and come from the hand of Yahweh.

Unjust Suffering: Job

In the very first verse of Job, we learn that Job is a righteous man who feared God and shunned evil (Job 1:1), going so far as to offer sacrifices for his children in case they sinned against God (Job 1:4–5). Incidentally, Job was also fantastically wealthy (Job 1:2–3). The text does not say explicitly that Job's wealth resulted directly from his obedience to Yahweh, but Job's friends thought as much. Satan's view was a bit more nuanced; he argued that Job worshiped Yahweh because of Yahweh's blessing rather than Job's blessing being a result of his faithfulness. Both Job's friends and Satan incorrectly judged the situation.

Deuteronomy presents the worldview that things will generally go well for those who fear and obey Yahweh and that the righteous may rightfully expect to receive blessings for their faithful lives. The book of Job, however, seeks to rectify the common misunderstanding and misappropriation of this theology, as Robin Routledge states, "what [Job's friends] are saying is not wrong, and similar principles are stated in other parts of Scripture. The error is in their rigid *application* of it."[8]

Job's friends present two basic reasons for Job's suffering: either he has sinned and God is rightly punishing him (Job 4:8). Or, he has sinned and God is using his suffering to discipline him.[9] Eliphaz sums up the first explanation for Job's suffering: "plowers of iniquity and sowers of trouble will reap it" (Job 4:8). Certainly Eliphaz is correct, and the New Testament confirms that the wicked can expect God's punishment, as was the case with Ananias and Sapphira in Acts 5. However, Job has committed no sin. Thus, while the principle of suffering as a result of sin holds true in general, Job demonstrates that it does not hold true in each particular instance of suffering.

---

are doable—the commandments are near to them, in their hearts (11–14). The people, therefore, cannot charge Yahweh with making the conditions of blessing too difficult. The passage goes on to explain what blessing consists of: descendants, reputation, physical provision (both sustenance and victory over enemies), land, and long life.

8. Routledge, *Old Testament Theology*, 257.

9. Ibid., 256–57.

Elihu sums up the friends' second explanation to Job's problem: "And he opens their ears to discipline and commands that they return from wickedness. If they obey and serve him, they will finish their days in goodness, and their years in singing. But if they do not obey, they will perish by the sword and die without knowledge" (Job 36:10–12). Again, Job's friend is expounding biblical truth. God disciplines in order to teach his children obedience, which the Old Testament demonstrates and the book of Hebrews reiterates (Heb 12:5–11). Elihu and Eliphaz are both correct: God does sometimes, perhaps even often, use suffering as a method of both discipline and punishment. However, they fail to recognize that God is not limited to a strict set of principles that we humans use to understand his dealings in the world. Jesus brings this out when he states that his Father "makes his sun rise on the evil and on the good, and sends rain on the just and the unjust" (Matt 5:45 ESV). Deuteronomy gives believers a general set of principles by which to live, but we must understand that God's ways are mysterious, as Job learns when he encounters the Almighty.

Despite the best efforts of his friends to convince Job of his guilt, Job holds steadfastly to his conviction that he has committed no sin deserving of such treatment from God. Rather, he argues that if he has indeed sinned then he will gladly accept the recompense due him (Job 31). God finally reveals himself to Job in the mighty whirlwind, but God's presence brings resolution to Job's misery in a surprising way. We expect God to reveal his conversation with Satan perhaps give him a nice commendation. Instead, God inundates Job with questions he cannot answer until finally Job repents. While Job's repentance seems strange, Norman Habel points out that "Job had sought to arraign God so as to bring the matter of his human integrity before the highest possible court of appeal. Yahweh's speech from the whirlwind, however, did not focus on the question of Job's innocence, but on the subject of Yahweh's cosmic design and governance which Job had belittled as chaotic and cruel."[10] Thus, it becomes clear to Job that he has misjudged Yahweh's right to rule the world as he sees fit, which explains the barrage of questions Yahweh hurled at Job and to which Job had no response. In the final summation, Job repents because he has not understood God's ways nor admitted that God is free to do as he sees fit. God's will is often mysterious. Therefore, we must avoid the mistake of Job's friends in rigidly applying the retribution principle to all instances of suffering as well as Job's mistake in thinking that we might be better suited to rule the world in God's place. As humans, we must seek to live by the general principles that God has

10. Habel, *Job*, 581.

outlined in his word, yet we must also remain faithfully obedient to him and trust in his goodness even when life events seem to point to the contrary.

Unity within Diversity:
The Two Sides of Righteous Living in the Old Testament

Deuteronomy presents one side of the issue of suffering in the Old Testament: suffering results from disobedience. Job presents the other side: sometimes the righteous suffer. These two aspects of suffering come together in a unique way in the book of Ecclesiastes, which aptly demonstrates the unity of the Old Testament's treatment of suffering within its great diversity.

Ecclesiastes addresses the issue of unjust suffering and ultimately comes to the same conclusion as Job: God is sovereign; humans must trust and obey him. However, Ecclesiastes blends the Deuteronomic understanding of suffering with the problem of righteous suffering in a way that gets to the heart of the Old Testament's view of how one should relate to God in the face of life's mysteries. One of the primary themes of Ecclesiastes is death.[11] For Ecclesiastes, the concept of death is closely related to the concept of injustice, which for Ecclesiastes means the breakdown between one's actions and the expected consequences of such actions.[12] These two issues—death and injustice—speak to the issue of unjust suffering in a meaningful way because of Ecclesiastes's response: fear God, obey his commands, and enjoy the gifts God has given you to enjoy.

Ecclesiastes recognizes that in the fallen world life does not always turn at we think it should: "I turned and I saw under the sun that the race is not to the swift and the battle is not to the strong, and also food is not to the wise, and also wealth is not to the discerning, and also favor is not the knowledgeable, for time and chance happen to all of them" (Eccl 9:11). The book's author furthers this idea when he laments that the wise and foolish both die (Eccl 2:16) and that humans and animals meet the same end (Eccl 3:19). These sentiments are why some scholars view the book as the musing of an unorthodox sage who is raging against the theological traditions handed down to him.[13] However, once we read these statements in the context of the book's overall theological message, we find that the author is in fact an orthodox sage who is simply grappling with the realities of life in a world turned upside-down by sin. In essence, Ecclesiastes paints a refresh-

---

11. See, e.g., Dor-Shav, "Ecclesiastes, Fleeting and Timeless. Part 1," 215.

12. Meek, "Meaning of הבל in Qohelet," 253–55.

13. See, e.g., Gese, "Crisis of Wisdom in Koheleth," 141–53; Fox, "The Meaning of *Hebel*," 409–27.

ingly honest portrait of "real life" then offers two suggestions for how to deal with the suffering that humans face.

First, we find in Ecclesiastes six passages in which the author commends joy as a response to various types of injustice (Eccl 2:24–26; 3:10–15, 16–22; 5:18–20[ET 17–19]; 8:10–15; 9:7–10; 11:7–10). Craig Bartholomew describes these passages as "the vision evoked with Eden in Gen. 2 and in the promises to the Israelites about the good land of Israel," stating that they present "an alternative vision set in contradictory juxtaposition to the conclusion of *hebel* that Qohelet's epistemology leads him to."[14] The *carpe diem* passages therefore represent an essential component to Qohelet's vision for how life should be lived in light of the suffering and injustice that confronts believers.[15] In six key places in Ecclesiastes Qohelet states that humans should take enjoyment in the temporal gifts of God—if God so allows it. Each of these "enjoy" statements comes after Qohelet has reflected on some aspect of the reversal of retribution theology. His answer to the fact that life does not always work out as it should is therefore that humans should take pleasure in the things in which God allows them to take pleasure, such as eating, drinking, working, and one's spouse. Essentially, Qohelet encourages his readers—and us today—to acknowledge that suffering can and will occur even to the most righteous of individuals, and then to do all that is within our power to enjoy life. Rather than worrying over things outside of human control—such as Job's intense suffering—we should take hold of the good things in life as they come.

Second, Qohelet urges his readers to be steadfastly obedient to God and to trust fully in God and his sovereignty. These two aspects of Qohelet's message are most clear in Eccl 12:13–14, the book's hermeneutical lens: "The end of the matter; everything has been heard. Fear God and keep his commands, for this is the whole of humanity. For all deeds God will bring into judgment, every secret thing whether good or evil." Though this statement is almost universally taken to be the words of an author other than Qohelet, we find that the importance of fearful obedience to God manifests itself throughout the rest of the narrative. Thus, we read in Eccl 3:14 that God has acted so that people would fear him;[16] in 5:1–7 Qohelet outlines

14. Bartholomew, *Ecclesiastes*, 152.

15. Following scholarly convention, I am using "Qohelet" to refer to the main speak in the book of Ecclesiastes.

16. Note that in Crenshaw's (*Ecclesiastes*, 100) estimation, fear in Ecclesiastes is terror induced by "an unpredictable despot . . . jealously guarding divine prerogatives." Longman (*Ecclesiastes*, 124–25) concurs, stating that "Qohelet believes that God acts the way that he does to frighten people into submission, not to arouse a sense of respectful awe of his power and might." However, neither the immediate nor larger

the importance of approaching God's house circumspectly; and in 8:10–13 he reiterates his confidence that ultimately the righteous will fare better than the wicked. These passages, taken with 12:13–14 highlight the importance of both God's sovereignty and the appropriate human response: fearful obedience. Therefore, while Qohelet commends that humanity take joy in God's gifts, he is careful to warn people that their enjoyment must not exceed the bounds established by God. Ultimately, then, the human response to suffering is simply to walk in faithful obedience to God and trust him, the very same lesson that Job learned when God revealed himself from the whirlwind.

Taken together, Job and Ecclesiastes present a stunning picture of the appropriate human response to suffering. Humans are free to acknowledge openly that individual circumstances do not always turn out the way that Deuteronomy teaches that they should. Deuteronomy, along with Proverbs, supplies *general* principles that should be followed, but they are not iron-clad promises of long life and material blessing. In response to suffering, Job and Ecclesiastes teach that we are to fear God, obey God, trust God, and if possible, enjoy God's gifts. Indeed, this is the whole of humanity.

In sum, the Old Testament presents two primary voices in regard to suffering. Deuteronomy outlines what is commonly called retribution theology. That is, a person's experience of either blessing or reward in this life is directly related to that person's obedience to God. The wicked person should expect to suffer for his wickedness and the righteous person should expect blessing because of his righteousness. However, we also learned that it is vital to understand that this theological framework represents the way that life generally happens. That is, on the grand scale, retribution theology rings true. Nevertheless, individual circumstances vary from person to person. It is certainly true that suffering may result from a person's direct sin, as Job's friends held, and represent either the discipline or punishment of the holy God.

However, when we examined the books of Job and Ecclesiastes we learned that suffering is not always the result of direct sin. Suffering could simply be the result of living in a world that operates under the curse that resulted from Adam's and Eve's sin in the Garden of Eden. Ecclesiastes addresses this issue directly by acknowledging the presence of injustice and suffering—even for the righteous—and then outlining the proper response to unjust suffering: trust in and obedience to God and enjoyment of his gifts. Similarly, Job explores the problem of righteous suffering, though it leaves readers with a less obvious program for coping with suffering. Rather

---

context demands such a reading.

than answer Job's accusations, the Lord reveals himself to Job in a way that highlights his divine sovereignty and demonstrates Job's lack of faithful trust in him. Ultimately, Job's answer to suffering is the same as Ecclesiastes's answer: trust the sovereign God.

There is great unity in the diversity of these four Old Testament voices. Instead of a canonical cacophony, they complement each other in a way that equips believers both ancient and modern to deal with life's vagaries. Proverbs and Deuteronomy urge faithful obedience to the covenant God Yahweh, complete with stern warnings for those who would choose to disobey. Underlying faithful obedience to the Lord is the concept that God is sovereign, which was clearly demonstrated to the Israelites as he led them out of Egypt and provided for them throughout the wilderness experience and would continue to do as they conquered the promised land. God's sovereignty over all things demands that we humans trust in him, which is the basic response to suffering of both Job and Ecclesiastes. Essentially, the Old Testament teaching about suffering and its relationship to righteous living is therefore that it is best, and most appropriate, to walk in faithful obedience to the Lord, which in the most normal circumstances will result in a life of blessing. However, when such blessing does not occur, the best and most appropriate response remains to walk in faithful obedience to God. The underlying premise of the Old Testament response is therefore that God is sovereign, humans are not, and that we must put our faith fully in him, which works itself out in living a life characterized by obedience to him.

Suffering in Light of the Gospel Message

Moving forward into the New Testament we find a great deal of continuity in the teaching on suffering, but with one significant difference. Rather than the obedient life being characterized by material blessing, as Deuteronomy and Proverbs teach, the New Testament teaches that suffering characterizes the obedient life. In Matthew's Gospel Jesus speaks to the Christian's new reality regarding suffering:

> Behold, I am sending you out as sheep in the midst of wolves, so be wise as serpents and innocent as doves. Beware of men, for they will deliver you over to courts and flog you in their synagogues, and you will be dragged before governors and kings for my sake, to bear witness before them and the Gentiles. When they deliver you over, do not be anxious how you are to speak or what you are to say, for what you are to say will be given to you in that hour. For it is not you who speak, but the Spirit of your

Father speaking through you. Brother will deliver brother over to death, and the father his child, and children will rise against parents and have them put to death, and you will be hated by all for my name's sake. But the one who endures to the end will be saved. When they persecute you in one town, flee to the next, for truly, I say to you, you will not have gone through all the towns of Israel before the Son of Man comes. A disciple is not above his teacher, nor a servant above his master. It is enough for the disciple to be like his teacher, and the servant like his master. If they have called the master of the house Beelzebul, how much more will they malign those of his household. (Matt 10:16–25 ESV)

Here Jesus indicates that his followers should expect suffering as normal. Christians in the Western world for the most part do not suffer on account of their faith in Christ, but this is not the case for much of the rest of the world. Thus, though Western Christians are accustomed to a life of creaturely comforts, such as excesses of food and clothing, we should not forget that our situation is unique both in the current world situation and in the history of Christianity. Therefore, we turn now to the New Testament to examine its view of suffering in the Christian life.

Christ as Our Example

First, we may look to Christ as the ultimate example of suffering. Bartholomew and O'Dowd point out that, like Job, Christ protested—albeit briefly—the suffering he was to endure on the cross.[17] In Gethsemane, knowing that he would soon face the humiliation and cruelty of the cross, he asked God if he would take from him the cup of suffering: "Father, if you are willing, remove this cup from me. Nevertheless, not my will, but yours be done" (Luke 22:42 ESV). It was indeed the Father's will that Christ would take on the sins of the world and the suffering included therein, culminating in Christ's stunning statement on the cross: "My God, my God, why have you forsaken me?" (Matt 27:46 ESV; Mark 15:34). Jesus's death was the height of all suffering, as he experienced in the most real way the separation from his Father for the sake of those who would be called children of God (1 John 3:1).

The author of Hebrews reflects on Christ's immense suffering and teaches that his willingness to suffer offers an example to his followers today (Heb 5:8). Rather than question the sovereignty of God, as Job did, Christ understood that the Father was in control of his life and destiny throughout

17. Bartholomew and O'Dowd, *Wisdom Literature*, 158.

all of his suffering. Therefore, as Christians today work through the unjust suffering we face, we should look to Christ as our example. Christ did not cry out against the Father, nor did he resist the Father's will. Instead, he submitted his life to God, knowing that his Father was—and still is—trustworthy. Such trust and faithful obedience serves as the ultimate example for how to cope with suffering, and coheres with the teaching of the Old Testament: trust and obey, no matter what.

Christ as Our Liberator

A second key aspect of the New Testament view of suffering is that Christ suffered so that he might once and for all remove suffering. Bartholomew and O'Dowd are again helpful here, for they point out that Jesus's burden contrasts significantly with that of Job, another righteous sufferer:

> Unlike Job, Jesus, in his suffering, takes on himself the burden of the world's guilt and sin. Unlike Job, Jesus dies, crushed by that burden, but rises triumphantly to open the gates of the kingdom to all. Central to the biblical narrative is the slain lamb upon the throne; his death will ultimately remove all suffering, but in the time between his inauguration of the kingdom and its consummation, believers will continue to suffer and continue to need a book like Job. In a far fuller way we know that our Redeemer lives and that we shall yet to see him.[18]

Christ, as the conqueror of sin and death, will one day wipe away every tear and remove all suffering (Rev 21:4). However, such will occur only at the consummation of his kingdom. Until then, believers must live their lives in trust and obedience, taking the long view of retribution. The promises of Proverbs and Deuteronomy—that a life lived in obedience to God will result in blessing—still represent the norm; however, we must realize that now even more so these promises are related to the next life.

Application to the Modern Church

The Old and New Testaments clearly teach that bad things happen to good people, that God's mysterious plans often remains mysterious, and that suffering will be the norm for followers of Christ in the New Testament age. What, then, should believers today do? How are we to reconcile our belief in a good God with our belief in an omnipotent God? What are the

18. Ibid.

options for dealing with the issue of theodicy in ministry both to believers and unbelievers?

First, we see clearly that retribution theology, as outlined above and seen throughout the Bible, teaches Christians today that we must remain steadfastly obedient to the Lord in all circumstances. Sinful choices will certainly result in negative consequences, whether in this life or the next. If we are experiencing suffering, we must search our hearts to see if there is any sin for which God is either punishing or disciplining us. Suffering may be used of God to lovingly bring us back into right relationship with him. However, we must be careful not to misinterpret this theology as a guarantee that righteous people will face no suffering, as Jesus himself so wonderfully demonstrates.

Second, from the book of Job and Christ's work on the cross we learn that our suffering may not be the result of sin. However, even if our particular circumstances do not work out *in this life* according to the broad principles of retribution theology, we must remain faithfully obedient to Christ. The New Testament adjusts the retribution principle so that Christians are now *expected* to experience suffering for their righteousness. Our reward for obedience to Christ and faithful proclamation of the gospel will come in the next life, not necessarily this one. Persecution is promised, so we should not balk when faced with it.

Third, the book of Ecclesiastes teaches that we are to rejoice in all the gifts that God has given us. These gifts include the simple things of life, such as food, work, and a spouse. If God so allows it, then we must take great pleasure in these things because we know very well that suffering may lie ahead. Rather than fret about those things over which we have no control, we should seize every opportunity for joy that God has given.

Fourth, Ecclesiastes and Job teach us that God is both sovereign and mysterious. Our present suffering—if not the result of direct sin—serves a larger purpose in God's plan. We should certainly be honest with God about how we feel, but we must not wring our hands at him and question his goodness or sovereignty. Instead, we must humbly submit to him and trust that he rules over us with grace and mercy. Such a posture is difficult to maintain in the face of suffering, but we must nevertheless trust in God's sovereignty. A robust theology of suffering must take into account the various causes of suffering but ultimately must submit to God's sovereignty and mystery and trust that in his great goodness he has allowed us to suffer for purposes greater than we can understand. Furthermore, a theology of suffering must embrace the good things when God allows it, and above all must live a blameless life no matter the consequences.

Fifth, and finally, those Christians living without persecution, such as those in the North American context, must pray for and identify with our brothers and sisters across the world who are suffering for the cause of Christ. The body of Christ knows no national boundaries, so we must not turn a blind eye to the suffering of believers in faraway places that we may never visit. Beyond simply praying for the persecuted, may we also support them in whatever way possible, which can include financial support, the sending of missionaries, or even leaving our own comfortable context to go serve in a place where persecution is a genuine threat. Maranatha.

QUESTIONS FOR DISCUSSION

1. What is retribution theology? Demonstrate your answer with biblical texts from both the Old and New Testaments. How, in your experience, has retribution theology been used contrary to its intended meaning?

2. Read the book of Job. How do the friends' responses demonstrate a flawed understanding of retribution theology? Using texts from the Old and New Testament, correct their misguided theology.

3. Read each of the Passion Narratives. In what way do they demonstrate God's goodness and personal involvement with the suffering of humans? How does Christ's sacrificial death enable him to sympathize with us? How does it change your view of your own suffering?

BIBLIOGRAPHY AND RECOMMENDED READING

Bartholomew, Craig. *Ecclesiastes*. Baker Commentary on the Old Testament Wisdom and Psalms. Grand Rapids: Baker Academic, 2009.

Bartholomew, Craig, and Ryan O'Dowd. *Old Testament Wisdom Literature: A Theological Introduction*. Downers Grove, IL: IVP Academic, 2011.

Dhorme, Édouard. *A Commentary on the Book of Job*. 1926. Reprint, Nashville: Nelson, 1984.

Habel, Norman C. *The Book of Job: A Commentary*. OTL. Philadelphia, Westminster, 1985.

Kushner, Harold. *The Book of Job: When Bad Things Happened to a Good Person*. Jewish Encounters. New York: Schocken, 2012.

Plantinga, Alvin. "The Free Will Defense." In *The Analytic Theist: An Alvin Plantinga Reader*, edited by J. F. Sennett, 22–49. Grand Rapids: Eerdmans, 1998.

Routledge, Robin. *Old Testament Theology: A Thematic Approach*. Downers Grove, IL: InterVarsity, 2008.

Stump, Elenore. "Faith and the Problem of Evil." In *Seeking Understanding: The Stob Lectures 1986–1988*, 491–550. Grand Rapids: Eerdmans, 2001.

Van Leeuwen, Raymond C. "Wealth and Poverty: System and Contradiction in Proverbs." *HS* 33 (1992) 25–36.

Walton, John. "Theodicy." In *Dictionary of the Old Testament: Wisdom, Poetry and Writings*, edited by Tremper Longman III and Peter Enns, 808–17. Downers Grove, IL: InterVarsity, 2008.

Wilson, Gerald. *Job*. NIBC. Peabody, MA: Hendrickson, 2007.

Wright, Christopher J. H. *The God I Don't Understand: Reflections on Tough Questions of Faith*. Grand Rapids: Zondervan, 2009.

Wright, N. T. *Evil and the Justice of God*. Downers Grove, IL: InterVarsity, 2006.

12

EXILE AND HOPE

Bryan C. Babcock

INTRODUCTION

The exile was a prominent event in the history of Israel and, more generally, in the formation of Old Testament theology. Several of the prophets like Jeremiah and Ezekiel spread God's warnings that Israel and Judah would be punished if the nation and its people did not turn away from sin and turn back to God. The people ignored God's message and were exiled to Assyria and Babylon. Once in exile, the prophets began to preach a message of hope that the people might be reconciled to God and returned to the promised land.

In this chapter we will explore the prophet Jeremiah's message of hope to Israel in Jer 31:31–34, where he proclaims: "'The days are coming,' declares the LORD, 'when I will make a new covenant with the people of Israel and with the people of Judah . . . I will put my law in their minds and write it on their hearts. I will be their God, and they will be my people . . . For I will forgive their wickedness and will remember their sins no more.'"

Ezekiel 36:16–38 echoes this message of hope for a renewed relationship with God. The prophet summarizes the justification for the exile and the hope of return:

> Son of man, when the people of Israel were living in their own land, they defiled it by their conduct and their actions. Their conduct was like a woman's monthly uncleanness in my sight. So I poured out my wrath on them because they had shed blood in the land and because they had defiled it with their idols. I dispersed them among the nations, and they were scattered through the countries; I judged them according to their conduct and their actions . . . For I will take you out of the nations; I will gather you from all the countries and bring you back into your own land . . . I will give you a new heart and put a new spirit in you; I will remove from you your heart of stone and give you a heart of flesh. And I will put my Spirit in you and move you to follow my decrees and be careful to keep my laws. Then you will live in the land I gave your ancestors; you will be my people, and I will be your God. (Ezek 36:17–28)[1]

After a hermeneutical exploration of Jeremiah and Ezekiel, we will examine the relationship between exile and hope in the balance of the Old Testament and its connection to the New Testament. We will demonstrate that there is a great theme at work—one revolving around mankind's relationship with God. We will find that sin undermines mankind's relationship with God, resulting in 'exile from God. The Lord then provides hope for renewal of the estranged relationship through a free gift of sovereign grace.

We will conclude our study by exploring the impact of an Old Testament theology of exile and hope for the contemporary church.

EXILE AND THE GOSPEL

Both the Bible and archaeological record demonstrate that the Israelites were exiled from the land that God gave them. During the exile, the prophets spoke with hope of a time when the people would return to the land. After several decades in Assyria and Babylon, this message was fulfilled when the Persians allowed the people of God to return to their land with a renewed sense of faith. Cyrus the Great not only allowed the Israelites to return the land, but he provided funding to rebuild Jerusalem's walls and

---

1. Unless otherwise noted, Scripture quotations in this chapter are the author's translation.

the temple, ushering in a time of peace and prosperity known as the Second Temple period.

However, we must ask whether this return under Cyrus fulfilled the prophetic message or whether God was foreshadowing another, greater fulfilment. The apostle Paul reads these passages about the new covenant in Ezekiel and Jeremiah and finds that they are ultimately fulfilled with the covenant that is founded upon Jesus the Messiah. Echoing Ezekiel and Jeremiah, Paul writes to the church at Corinth "It is clear that you are a letter from Christ, the result of our ministry, written not with ink but with the Spirit of the living God, not on tablets of stone but on tablets of human hearts" (2 Cor 3:3). Here Paul evokes the power of both passages to teach that God's new covenant would be written upon the hearts of believers.

Luke records the comments of Jesus to the disciple at the Last Supper: "In the same way, after the supper he took the cup, saying, 'This cup is the new covenant in my blood, which is poured out for you'" (Luke 22:20). Jesus is confirming that he is the fulfillment of Jeremiah's prophecy and that through his blood future generations will be justified before God.

The author of Hebrews restates the entire passage of Jer 31:31–34. In Heb 8:13 the author argues that Jesus "in speaking of 'a new covenant,' he has made the first obsolete." He goes on to argue that "if that first covenant had been faultless, there would have been no need to look for a second one" (Heb 8:7).

Therefore, an initial review of the New Testament reveals that the prophetic hope given by Jeremiah and Ezekiel to the Israelites must have a deeper meaning than merely a return to the promised land after the exile. To uncover the intent of God's new covenant with his people and the reception of God's message upon our hearts we must more closely examine where and how their prophetic words are used.

ANALYSIS OF KEY PASSAGES

After decades of warnings from God that the Israelites needed to repent and turn away from their sin, God acts in the early eighth century BC to separate the people from the land promised to Abraham.

Despite God's warnings, the Israelites refuse to repent, so God uses the surrounding nations to accomplish his retribution upon the nation. The Assyrians waged war with, defeating the nation in 722 BC. God warned of the impending raid by the Assyrians through the prophets Isaiah, Amos, Joel, and Hosea. The foreign nation took significant numbers of the Israelite population from their land and transplanted them back to Assyria. They then relocated many Assyrians into the newly captured Israelite lands, resulting in a blended population. The result was a mixed-culture population later known as the Samaritans in the New Testament.[2]

A century and a half later, the Babylonian empire under Nebuchadnezzar invaded Judah. God warns the nation a last time through Jeremiah; however, the people refuse to change their ways. Jeremiah 1:14–16 reads:

> The LORD said to me, "From the north disaster will be poured out on all who live in the land. I am about to summon all the peoples of the northern kingdoms," declares the Lord. "Their kings will come and set up their thrones in the entrance of the gates of Jerusalem; they will come against all her surrounding walls and against all the towns of Judah. I will pronounce my judgments on my people because of their wickedness in forsaking me, in burning incense to other gods and in worshiping what their hands have made."

Using Babylon as God's hand of judgment, the foreign army put Jerusalem under siege in 597 BC and again in 586 BC. The walls of the city finally failed and most of the educated and skilled members of the community were taken into exile. The prophet Ezekiel was among them, while Jeremiah likely remained in Judah until he was forcibly taken to Egypt.

It is during the time of exile in Babylon that God speaks through Ezekiel and Jeremiah. While earlier prophets shared a message of impending judgment, Ezekiel and Jeremiah shift to a message of hope for a return home and renewed relationship with God. God uses the sack of Jerusalem and resulting exile to demonstrate his judgment. However, God's judgment is always tempered with mercy. As such, Ezekiel shares that despite the current hard times, there will be a new shepherd who will usher in a time of restored relationship with God and renewal of time in the land. Likewise, Jeremiah speaks of a new covenant and a time when God's message will be written on the hearts of mankind. While the initial fulfilment for these prophecies is in the time of the return from exile and resulting Second Temple period, there is more going on. Let's turn to explore two key passages and unpack the hermeneutical understanding.

---

2. In the first century AD the Samaritans were considered "half-breeds": not quite Assyrian and not quite Israelite. While they worshiped Yahweh, the Israelites treated them as second-class citizens. This understanding helps to better inform the parable of the Good Samaritan in Luke.

Jeremiah 31:31–34

The prophet Jeremiah first receives the word of the Lord in the thirteenth year of the reign of the Josiah, about 627 BC, and continues to prophesy until the destruction of Jerusalem and its temple (586 BC) and into the following months of the Babylonian exile. To understand Jeremiah, it is important to understand the political context of the era.

The book reflects the historical crisis of the last days of Judah, culminating in the destruction of Jerusalem and the temple in 587 BC. A century earlier the Assyrians had raided and displaced Israel. However, by the last days of the seventh century BC, the Assyrian Empire collapsed and was promptly displaced by the Babylonians under Nebuchadnezzar.

The Judean crisis needs to be understood in the context of multiple political pressures. First, Nebuchadnezzar sought to expand Babylonian territory, creating an empire throughout the region. This created continual tension to the north of Judah. Second, Judah was a vassal of the Egyptian empire, whose desire was to maintain Judah as a buffer against Babylonian pressure.

Therefore, Judah was in the unenviable position of being placed between two major powers—Babylon and Egypt. King Josiah rules wisely, maintaining a strong relationship with Egypt. However; the Judahite kings after Josiah (639–609 BC) vacillated between alliances with Babylon and with Egypt. Finally, Babylon tired of Judah's ambivalence and forced a political decision. Josiah's son, Jehoiakim (609–598), was unable to maintain the political standoff (especially in light of Egypt's declining power), and Babylon invaded Judah, reaching Jerusalem in 598 BC. In addition to the destruction of Judah's major defenses, Jehoiachin (Jehoiakim's son) was relocated to Babylon as a king in exile. In addition, many prominent citizens of Judah were deported with him. For the period of 598–587, yet another son of Josiah, Zedekiah, presided over the affairs of Jerusalem but in the end had no chance for independent action in the face of Babylonian power. During these years there was an intense rivalry between the community in Jerusalem (over which Zedekiah presided) and the exilic community in Babylon (where Jehoiachin was understood as the legitimate leader).[3]

Judah was again overrun by Babylon in 587 BC, ending Judah's existence as an independent nation. Jerusalem and the surrounding territory was merged within the Babylonian empire as a wholly controlled state. During this time Babylon enacted another wide-spread deportation of Jerusalem's influential citizens. The goal was to divide the strongholds of

---

3. Brueggemann, *A Commentary on Jeremiah*, 80.

Judah's power and create an ethnic melting pot—one where Babylonian political and religious culture might maintain control. According to Walter Brueggemann,

> this radical displacement raised in Judah and Jerusalem a range of critical questions, moral and religious as well as political. It is therefore possible to understand and explain the events around 587 BC in terms of Realpolitik, that is, in terms of political tensions between states and the overriding military and imperial power of Babylon. The realities of the political, military, and historical process provide convincing proof of Judah's helplessness in the face of Babylonian power, a helplessness exacerbated by the unwise and weak leadership it received from its monarchy.[4]

Jeremiah wrote with an awareness of these political realities. However, the prophet sees beyond the political maneuvering to two great empires (Egypt and Babylon). Replacing an historical-political viewpoint, Jeremiah interprets the era through a theological lens. As such, the prophets Isaiah, Amos, and others made clear that the earlier fall and exile of Israel was a divine punishment for their unrepentant sins. During that time Josiah led Judah into repentance and revival and the nation was spared judgment.

However, in the years that followed Judah shared the religious apostasy of Israel and God called Jeremiah to speak. Early in the prophet's visions he sees both a boiling pot from the north and an almond tree (1:4–19). These place the visions in the context of the impending invasion of Babylon.

The next several chapters relate God's warning to Judah. The proclamations are rooted in the salvation of Israel after leaving Egypt and wandering in the desert. During this period the Israelites followed God (2:1–3). However, the people all too quickly turned back to idolatry (2:4–3:5). This resulted in their deportation and exile from the land (3:6–6:30).

After providing a theological framework for the historical events, Jeremiah turns to the nation of Judah. The people have wrongly believed that they would always be protected due to their special relationship with God and the sacred site of the temple of David. However, God proclaims in Jer 7:4–8: "Do not trust in deceptive words and say, 'This is the temple of the LORD, the temple of the LORD, the temple of the LORD!' If you really change your ways and your actions and deal with each other justly, if you do not oppress the foreigner, the fatherless or the widow and do not shed innocent blood in this place, and if you do not follow other gods to your own harm, then I will let you live in this place, in the land I gave your ancestors for ever and ever. But look, you are trusting in deceptive words that are worthless."

4. Ibid.

Jeremiah goes on to outline Judah's sins. In addition to worshiping false idols, the people are stubborn, prideful, and immoral. God will therefore bring upon Judah and Jerusalem judgement that will destroy the land and deport the people (ch. 12). However, there is redemption for those who would repent (chs. 13–15).

Leading into our passage we find the response of the nation to Jeremiah's call for repentance. The words of the prophet are largely ignored and God continues to predict the coming judgment. Finally, in 27:1–8 God declares his decision that judgment is at hand. Jeremiah relays God's word to Judah and the surrounding nations—

> This is what the Lord said to me: "Make a yoke out of straps and crossbars and put it on your neck. Then send word to the kings of Edom, Moab, Ammon, Tyre and Sidon through the envoys who have come to Jerusalem to Zedekiah king of Judah. Give them a message for their masters and say, this is what the Lord Almighty, the God of Israel, says: Tell this to your masters: With my great power and outstretched arm I made the earth and its people and the animals that are on it, and I give it to anyone I please. Now I will give all your countries into the hands of my servant Nebuchadnezzar king of Babylon; I will make even the wild animals subject to him. All nations will serve him and his son and his grandson until the time for his land comes; then many nations and great kings will subjugate him. If, however, any nation or kingdom will not serve Nebuchadnezzar king of Babylon or bow its neck under his yoke, I will punish that nation with the sword, famine and plague, declares the Lord, until I destroy it by his hand."

It is in this context that Jeremiah turns to a message of hope. The people will be deported and exiled to Babylon for several decades; however, their sins will be forgiven and they will be returned to the promised land. Jeremiah records in 31:31–40:

> "The days are coming," declares the LORD, "when I will make a new covenant with the people of Israel and with the people of Judah. It will not be like the covenant I made with their ancestors when I took them by the hand to lead them out of Egypt, because they broke my covenant, though I was a husband to them," declares the LORD. "This is the covenant I will make with the people of Israel after that time," declares the Lord. "I will put my law in their minds and write it on their hearts. I will be their God, and they will be my people. No longer will they teach their neighbor, or say to one another, 'Know the LORD,' because

they will all know me, from the least of them to the greatest," declares the LORD. "For I will forgive their wickedness and will remember their sins no more." This is what the LORD says, he who appoints the sun to shine by day, who decrees the moon and stars to shine by night, who stirs up the sea so that its waves roar—the LORD Almighty is his name: "Only if these decrees vanish from my sight," declares the Lord, "will Israel ever cease being a nation before me." This is what the Lord says: "Only if the heavens above can be measured and the foundations of the earth below be searched out will I reject all the descendants of Israel because of all they have done," declares the LORD.

"The days are coming," declares the LORD, "when this city will be rebuilt for me from the Tower of Hananel to the Corner Gate. The measuring line will stretch from there straight to the hill of Gareb and then turn to Goah. The whole valley where dead bodies and ashes are thrown, and all the terraces out to the Kidron Valley on the east as far as the corner of the Horse Gate, will be holy to the LORD. The city will never again be uprooted or demolished."

When seeking the essence for the theme of the exile and hope in Jeremiah, we discover the following cycle:

1) God's people in fellowship with God

2) Humanity acts (or has the potential to act) against God (sin), marring God's name and relationship

3) God provides a warning to repent and return to God

4) God acts in judgment, separating himself from mankind

5) God provides hope of a time when the relationship will be restored.

Except for humanity's sin, these steps are uniquely accomplished by God. Further, when God restores the relationship, it is through divine unmerited grace with no work required by God's people.

J. Andrew Dearman argues that the "collection of prophecies in chapters 30–31 is actually the prediction of a new world, that is, a new age and a new time unlike that known to the hearers. It includes restoration of exiles from Assyrian and Babylonian territories, surely a hopeful and gracious word to Jeremiah's contemporaries. But there is more to the prophetic depictions of a new world than that, for nothing less than an ideal community (a new Jerusalem and new David) and a fully realized covenant relationship with God are announced."[5]

5. Dearman, *Jeremiah and Lamentations*, 269.

These predictions gave rise to the hope for national healing in the postexilic period and served as the beginnings of a new community in a restored Jerusalem. In addition, these prophecies point beyond the initial restoration to a time beyond the postexilic period.

Ezekiel 36:16–28:

Similar to Jeremiah, Ezekiel speaks to those exiled in Babylon and Assyria during the sixth century BC. The prophet begins with the justification for judgment: "Son of man, when the people of Israel were living in their own land, they defiled it by their conduct and their actions. Their conduct was like a woman's monthly uncleanness in my sight. So I poured out my wrath on them because they had shed blood in the land and because they had defiled it with their idols. . . And wherever they went among the nations they profaned my holy name, for it was said of them, 'These are the Lord's people, and yet they had to leave his land.' I had concern for my holy name, which the people of Israel profaned among the nations where they had gone" (Ezek 36:17–21).

The Lord then turns to offer a message of hope: "therefore say to the Israelites, 'This is what the Sovereign Lord says: It is not for your sake, people of Israel, that I am going to do these things, but for the sake of my holy name, which you have profaned among the nations where you have gone . . . For I will take you out of the nations; I will gather you from all the countries and bring you back into your own land. I will sprinkle clean water on you, and you will be clean; I will cleanse you from all your impurities and from all your idols. I will give you a new heart and put a new spirit in you; I will remove from you your heart of stone and give you a heart of flesh. And I will put my Spirit in you and move you to follow my decrees and be careful to keep my laws" (Ezek 26:22–27).

This part of the prophecy is packed with theological implications. First, we find that the basis for reconciliation is not found in any action by the Israelites. Instead, the foundation is solely grounded in the actions of God—and for God to clear his own holy name. It is purely through God's unmerited grace that the land and relationship will be restored. Ian Duguid finds that, "as long as Israel was scattered among the nations, they continually profaned the divine name (Ezek 36:20). This was now not because of anything particular they were doing, although there is no suggestion that the shock of exile in and of itself brought about a radical change in their behavior. Rather, they profaned God's name simply by being in exile instead of in the land of promise!"[6]

Second, while the nation will be gathered as a whole, the action focuses on the individual. Sprinkling with clean water (v. 25) means more than just forgiveness of sins. John Tylor argues that "its symbolism is derived from ritual washings with water which were intended to remove ceremonial defilement (cf. Exod 30:17–21; Lev 14:52; Num 19:17–19), and this is applied to the people's cleansing from the defilement of idolatry (from all your idols I will cleanse you, v. 25)."[7]

Third, these now justified individuals are given a new heart and filled with God's Spirit. God's people must be redeemed not merely outwardly but inwardly.[8] They are not so much parts of humanity's make-up as aspects of his total personality. The ancient Near Eastern understanding of the heart includes what we would understand as the mind and the will as well as the emotions. These facets of the body are the essence of the personality and the nature of humanity. The spirit is the focus that urges action and then regulates our desires. Both heart and spirit will be replaced and renewed so that a heart that is stubborn, rebellious, and insensitive (a heart of stone) will be replaced by one that is soft, impressionable, and responsive (a heart of flesh), and the spirit of disobedience will be replaced by the Spirit of God.

According to Taylor, "the result of this psychological transplant will be that Israel will experience a real 'change of heart' and will become, by God's gracious initiative, the kind of people that they have in the past so signally failed to be. The implanting of God's Spirit within them will transform their motives and empower them to live according to God's statutes and judgments (v. 27)."[9] Daniel Block expands on this change in behavior when he writes that "God will no longer gamble with Israel as he did in old times, and Israel rebelled against him; in the future—no more experiments! God will put his spirit into them, he will alter their hearts (their minds) and make it impossible for them to be anything but obedient to his rules and his commandments."[10]

While the Jeremiah passage makes no reference to the gift of the Spirit, it does contain the idea of putting "my law within them" and writing it "upon their hearts." "The enduement with the Spirit was a sign of the Messianic age (cf. Isa 42:1; 44:3; 59:21; Joel 2:28f.), and Ezekiel was aware of this and

6. Duguid, *Ezekiel*, 370.
7. Taylor, *Ezekiel*, 126.
8. Duguid, *Ezekiel*, 371.
9. Taylor, *Ezekiel*, 152.
10. Block, *Book of Ezekiel*, 264.

mentioned it on later occasions (Ezek 37:14; 39:29). For him therefore the restoration of Israel was the beginning of the last days, the age of the Messiah. In keeping with that idea, therefore, the covenant relationship between God and Israel."[11]

The passage in Ezekiel continues with God acting to provide and care for his people. The land and towns will be restored. All of these things will be accomplished by God so that the Israelites and those nations surrounding Israel will know the power of God.

So, what can we take away from Ezekiel's prophecy of hope? There are four truths to keep in mind as we complete our study of hope:[12]

1) Although the Lord's ways may be mysterious, they are not hidden. His activity is played out in the public arena for the world to observe and to draw their conclusions.

2) God's actions in human history are driven by revelatory aims: that his people and the world may know that he is Yahweh.

3) The only solution for the fallen human race is a fundamental cleansing, a heart transplant, an infusion of the divine Spirit.

4) The future of Israel rests in the eternal, immutable promises of God.

The restored Israel and Jerusalem depicted in both Ezekiel's and Jeremiah's messages of hope is far greater than the communities built after the exile. Stated somewhat differently, the Jews of the exilic and postexilic periods would not see the significance of these prophecies fully realized in the return to Judah from Babylon. "God has yet more to accomplish with and through his people. The future depicted in these chapters still has hopes as yet unrealized. At a fundamental level this puts modern readers in a similar context to that of the first hearers/readers: All alike wait in anticipation of the fuller realization of God's grand design."[13]

We find that Jer 31 and Ezek 36 are ultimately eschatological in nature, depicting in the language and thought-forms of the day a prophecy that God will gain ultimate victory over alienation and sin.

> The postexilic restoration was the firstfruits of the promises, the prelude to and a type of the greater restoration to come. In light of Christ's first advent, the New Testament provides further guidance on the significance of these prophecies; nevertheless, modern Christians still await (in hope, just like their spiritual

---

11. Ibid.

12. Ibid., 266.

13. Dearman, *Jeremiah and Lamentations*, 269.

ancestors of Jeremiah's day) the final consummation of the new world glimpsed by Jeremiah. Here is a perspective that places the current generation of God's people in a mode of expectation similar to that of Jeremiah's own day.[14]

UNITY OF EXILE AND HOPE
AS A THEME WITHIN THE OLD TESTAMENT

While the theme of exile and hope is prominent in the prophetic books, it is present from the very beginning of Genesis. The first instance of this theme is found in Gen 1–4 and the narrative of creation. God creates mankind and places them in fellowship with him. Then, "the LORD God took the man and put him in the garden of Eden to till it and keep it" (Gen 2:15). While man (and woman) are created and in fellowship with God, they have the potential for sin and God warns that the pair can eat from anywhere in the garden, but they cannot eat from the tree of knowledge of good and evil (v. 17).

In Gen 3 we learn that through the encouragement of the snake Eve and then Adam rebel against God and eat from the tree of knowledge. They gain knowledge of their nakedness and become self-conscious—sewing fig leaves together to cover their nakedness (Gen 3:7). The first sign that a separation from God is taking place comes from the human pair as they hide from God as the Lord seeks them in the garden. Over the next several verses, God confronts the sin, sending judgment in the form of a transformed relationship to creation. The animals will no longer be in relationship with humans, and some will change form (vv. 14–15). God's people will be exiled from what was once a peaceful existence and will now be placed in an environment of pain and stressful toil (vv. 17–19). Finally, even the relationship between man and woman will be separated, such that man and woman will contend with each other (v. 16).

In addition to each of these transformed relationships, God physically exiles the man and woman from their home in Eden: "So the LORD God banished him from the Garden of Eden to work the ground from which he had been taken. After he drove the man out, he placed on the east side of the Garden of Eden cherubim and a flaming sword flashing back and forth to guard the way to the tree of life" (Gen 3:23–24). The exile from the garden is clearly physical; however, the deeper loss is a loss of fellowship with God.

14. Ibid.

The hope appears in two forms. First, despite God's judgment and during the height of God's anger we find that God's mercy overrules his judgment. As we mentioned, the key point of knowledge identified as a result of eating the fruit is the shame of being naked. The couple sew vegetation leaves together as an inadequate, makeshift cover. At the height of God's anger, v. 21 relates that God recognizes the couple's self-consciousness and replaces their makeshift coverings with clothing made from more lasting animal skins. In this way God provides hope for the couple despite the tarnished relationship. The hope for the restoration of land is found when God promises Abraham the land of Canaan and a restored relationship with the Lord.

Another example of exile and hope appears in the Moses narrative. The second half of the book of Genesis relates God's relationship to Abraham and the hope for the possession of the promised land of Canaan and blessing of future generational growth. Over the next two generations, we learn of the growth of the family through the patriarchs Isaac and Jacob. However, the promises and hope are never completely fulfilled. As the book of Genesis ends, Joseph invites his brothers and the Israelites to Egypt where they settle and become numerous, but the people find themselves separated from the land promised to them by God.

In Exod 2:23 the Israelites cry out to God about their position in Egypt and God provides a leader in Moses. Moses is called to deliver a message of hope that the Israelites are still God's chosen people and heirs to the hope and blessings given to Abraham. Moses is sent to free the Israelites from their exile in Egypt and return them to the promised land. Throughout the time of wandering in the desert, God is faithful. When they need protection, God provides a passage through the Sea of Reeds (Red Sea) (Exod 14). When they are starving, God provides manna (Exod 16:1–35). When they need meat, God provides quail (Exod 16:13; Num 11:4–32).

Ultimately, at the end of the generation God leads the people to the boarder of Canaan where Moses is able to look upon the final destination before he dies. Joshua then leads the people into the promised land, thus fulfilling God's promise.

A final example is found in 2 Chronicles regarding the exile and hope for return to the promised land. In 2 Chr 36:11–14 we learn that Zedekiah leads Judah into sin against God and rebellion against the Babylonian Nebuchadnezzer. The king and the people hardened their heart against God and even the priests were "unfaithful, following all the abominations of the nations; and they polluted the house of the Lord that he had consecrated in Jerusalem" (2 Chr 36:14).

God sends multiple prophets to warn of impending judgment, and we are told that God was slow to act because of his enduring compassion. Nevertheless, the people merely mocked the messengers until God's anger caused him to act by sending the Babylonian army to conquer Judah's defenses, destroy the temple of David, and exile the population.

After several years in exile, the Lord raises a "messiah" to fulfill the word of hope proclaimed by Jeremiah. The book of Chronicles ends with this passage (2 Chr 36:20–23):

> He carried into exile to Babylon the remnant, who escaped from the sword, and they became servants to him and his successors until the kingdom of Persia came to power. The land enjoyed its sabbath rests; all the time of its desolation it rested, until the seventy years were completed in fulfillment of the word of the Lord spoken by Jeremiah.
>
> In the first year of Cyrus king of Persia, in order to fulfill the word of the LORD spoken by Jeremiah, the Lord moved the heart of Cyrus king of Persia to make a proclamation throughout his realm and also to put it in writing:
>
> This is what Cyrus king of Persia says:
>
> "The LORD, the God of heaven, has given me all the kingdoms of the earth and he has appointed me to build a temple for him at Jerusalem in Judah. Any of his people among you may go up, and may the LORD their God be with them."

This passage comprises the last verses of the Hebrew Bible as it brings the people of God through the exile and highlights the message of hope that the people will soon return to the promised land. While this is clearly a partial fulfillment of the hope discussed in Jeremiah, more remains unfulfilled. Let's now turn to a review of the New Testament to see if we can gain more information on the theme of exile and hope.

IMPLICATIONS FOR READING THE NEW TESTAMENT

The exile of God's chosen people was a dramatic low point for the nations of Israel and Judah. In the middle of the sixth century BC, King Cyrus of the Persians seized control of Babylon, and in 538 BC he puts forth a decree ending the exile. The essence of the decree is recorded at the end of 2 Chronicles, and the actual decree (not mentioning Israel or Judah) was discovered in AD 1879 and is known as the Cyrus Cylinder.

The books of Ezra and Nehemiah recount the period of the returning exiles and the renewed religious zeal. While the return to the promised land, rebuilding of the temple, and improved economic condition is clearly a partial fulfillment of Jeremiah's prophecy of hope, at no time during the Second Temple period do the people experience the level of renewal and relationship with God foreshadowed by Jeremiah and Ezekiel.

Therefore, we now turn to explore passages in the New Testament that point to the texts of Jeremiah and Ezekiel and demonstrate how the texts are fulfilled through Christ.

First, in the late first century, around AD 85, Luke pens a Gospel of Jesus and an historical account of the early spread of the gospel (Acts). Luke records Jesus's words at the Passover meal of the Last Supper after sharing bread with the disciples. Luke 22:20 reads: "In the same way, after the supper he took the cup, saying, 'This cup is the new covenant in my blood, which is poured out for you.'" Jesus is relating the sacrifice of his blood to the hope of a restored relationship through a new covenant in Jeremiah. The parallel accounts in Mark 14:24 and Matt 26:28 record the same message.

Writing in the mid-50s AD, Paul also quotes Jeremiah as part of the tradition he received and handed on to the Corinthians surrounding the remembrance of Christ's sacrifice. Paul writes that "in the same way, after supper he [Jesus] took the cup, saying, 'This cup is the new covenant in my blood; do this, whenever you drink it, in remembrance of me'" (1 Cor 11:25).

While these passages quote Jeremiah, Jesus says that his blood is the blood of the new covenant. However, the passages do not clarify *how* Jesus's blood represents the new covenant. In 2 Cor 3:4–18 Paul provides the church at Corinth with more information. Paul begins by providing the basis for the power of the new covenant in vv. 4–6. The passage reads: "Such confidence we have through Christ before God. Not that we are competent in ourselves to claim anything for ourselves, but our competence comes from God. He has made us competent as ministers of a new covenant—not of the letter but of the Spirit; for the letter kills, but the Spirit gives life." Similar to Jer 31:31–33, the passage equates hope to both the arrival of the new covenant and the presence of the Holy Spirit.

Paul continues in vv. 7–18:

> Now if the ministry that brought death, which was engraved in letters on stone, came with glory, so that the Israelites could not look steadily at the face of Moses because of its glory, transitory though it was, will not the ministry of the Spirit be even more glorious? If the ministry that brought condemnation was glorious, how much more glorious is the ministry that brings righteousness! For what was glorious has no glory now in comparison with the surpassing glory. And if what was transitory

came with glory, how much greater is the glory of that which lasts! Therefore, since we have such a hope, we are very bold. We are not like Moses, who would put a veil over his face to prevent the Israelites from seeing the end of what was passing away . . . Now the Lord is the Spirit, and where the Spirit of the Lord is, there is freedom. And we all, who with unveiled faces contemplate the Lord's glory, are being transformed into his image with ever-increasing glory, which comes from the Lord, who is the Spirit. (NRSV)

This passage picks up several key points. First, the old covenant is determined to be the Sinai covenant with Moses; while the new covenant is connected to Jesus. Second, the old covenant consisted of letters written on stone tablets. It brought death and condemnation. This is consistent with Jeremiah's prophecy that the old covenant was written on stone while the new would be a lasting covenant written on the heart. Third, the glory of the old covenant was fading and had the effect of putting a veil over the Scriptures. By contrast, the new covenant was guided by the Holy Spirit. Paul's view was that it brought life, righteousness, and freedom. And it offered a permanent kind of splendor, removed the veil, and allowed the God's word to be properly interpreted as referring to what God had done in Christ.

A final example comes from the book of Hebrews, where the author quotes the entire passage of Jer 31:31–34. As we mentioned earlier, the quotation is the longest quotation of any Old Testament passage found in the New Testament. Hebrews 8:1–7 highlights that Jesus is the ultimate High Priest standing as intercessor between us and God. As the ultimate intercessor, he does not need to have an offering like was called for in the old covenant. The final two verses bring this section to a close stating that "the ministry Jesus has received is as superior to theirs [Moses's] as the covenant of which he is mediator is superior to the old one, since the new covenant is established on better promises. For if there had been nothing wrong with that first covenant, no place would have been sought for another" (vv. 6–7).

In Heb 8:13 the author argues that Jesus "in speaking of 'a new covenant,' he has made the first obsolete." The author of Hebrews also argues that God will remember their sins no longer and that in speaking of new covenant God has made the old covenant obsolete.

In Hebrews 9 the author contends that the sacrifices and the priesthood of the old covenant were powerless to bring about the forgiveness of sins. A new sacrifice and a new priesthood were needed and the author finds them in Christ's atoning death on the cross. Viewing Christ as the ultimate High Priest, the author of Hebrews continues:

> But when Christ came as high priest of the good things that are
> now already here, he went through the greater and more per-
> fect tabernacle that is not made with human hands, that is to
> say, is not a part of this creation. He did not enter by means
> of the blood of goats and calves; but he entered the Most Holy
> Place once for all by his own blood, thus obtaining eternal re-
> demption. The blood of goats and bulls and the ashes of a heifer
> sprinkled on those who are ceremonially unclean sanctify them
> so that they are outwardly clean. How much more, then, will the
> blood of Christ, who through the eternal Spirit offered himself
> unblemished to God, cleanse our consciences from acts that
> lead to death, so that we may serve the living God!
>
> For this reason, Christ is the mediator of a new covenant,
> that those who are called may receive the promised eternal in-
> heritance—now that he has died as a ransom to set them free
> from the sins committed under the first covenant. (Heb 9:11–15)

We can now put each of these New Testament passages together. Jesus, acting as the ultimate High Priest has shed his blood as the atoning media-tor for our sins and in fulfilment of the old covenant. Paul and the gospel writers record that Jesus commands all believers to remember this atoning sacrifice of his blood at the time of fellowship among the Christian com-munity. Through a person's acceptance of the sacrifice of Jesus their heart is transformed and they receive the Holy Spirt—all in fulfillment of the prophecies of Jer 31:31–34.

IMPLICATIONS FOR AND IDENTITY WITH
THE MODERN CHRISTIAN CHURCH

After our analysis, we find that the theme of exile and hope is centered in the exile of mankind's relationship to God on account of sin and the hope of salvation through Jesus's atonement. With this theme in mind we might explore three possible applications for the modern church.

First, God makes clear throughout Scripture that he desires a relation-ship with mankind. In Genesis 1–2 God creates mankind to be the steward of the pinnacle of creation. As chief steward God desired that mankind be in continual fellowship. Mankind rebelled and was separated from both the garden of Eden and God. However, God reached out to Abraham and cre-ated a covenant and giving of both blessings and land. This relationship too was unsustainable and the people left the land for Egypt.

God again reached out to his people and developed the old covenant with Moses to renew the closeness of relationship and ability to live together in the land. Despite these attempts, mankind continued to choose sin and idolatry in place of obedience and relationship. Finally, God acted by exiling the sinful nations of Israel and Judah—and again God acts unilaterally through Jeremiah to provide a message of hope that the special relationship between humans and God would ultimately be restored through a new covenant.

In each of these cases, God is the actor seeking relationship. Therefore, we can say to the modern church that we know that if there is a separation between us and God, then it is not because God desires the separation. Indeed, God stands ready and desires that we accept the sacrifice of Jesus and enter into a new and close relationship with the Lord.

Second, our ongoing relationship with God is all about grace. Adding to the thought of the prior paragraph, God is the actor and God is the one providing grace. Ezekiel 36:22–30 clarifies that God is not saving the nations because they have acted. Instead, God is acting solely out of his mercy and grace to provide hope.

And third, being a Christian means that each of us is literally transformed. The prophets proclaimed that God is changing the bodies of those who follow him. Jeremiah 31:33 says that God is placing his law "inside" the believer. In Ezek 36:26 God gives his followers a new heart and his Holy Spirit. God will then remove from their body the heart of stone and provide a heart of flesh (vv. 26–27). In these ways, God is forever changing the body of the believer.

QUESTIONS FOR FURTHER STUDY

1) Why is it good and right that God acts most for his name and not ours? If we considered your actions, then whose name would we think you lived for most?

2) Have you ever struggled with the truth that God is free to extend or withhold his mercy? How did the Lord bring you to peace on the issue?

3) If the point of reconciliation is relationship, then how's that going between you and God? Are you more excited about secondary blessings or the fact that God gives himself to you?

4) Jeremiah 31:34 states that "No longer will they teach their neighbor, or say to one another, 'Know the LORD,' because they will all know me, from the least of them to the greatest." What do you think this means?

BIBLIOGRAPHY AND RECOMMENDED READING

Block, Daniel I. *The Book of Ezekiel Chapters 25–48*. NICOT. Grand Rapids: Eerdmans, 1998.

Brueggemann, Walter. *A Commentary on Jeremiah: Exile and Homecoming*. Grand Rapids: Eerdmans, 1998.

Dearman, J. Andrew. *Jeremiah and Lamentations*. NIVAC. Grand Rapids: Zondervan, 2002.

Duguid, Iain M. *Ezekiel*. NIVAC. Grand Rapids: Zondervan, 1999.

Hess, Richard S. *The Old Testament: A Historical, Theological, and Critical Introduction*. Grand Rapids: Baker Academic, 2016.

Taylor, John B. *Ezekiel: An Introduction and Commentary*. TOTC 22. Downers Grove, IL: InterVarsity, 2009.

13

RESTORED COMMUNITY

Bryan C. Babcock

INTRODUCTION

How does it all end? As Christians, that is a question we often ask. Most of us would respond by exploring the book of Revelation and explaining something about Armageddon and Jesus's return. We might add that we personally have little interest in the confusing language of Revelation and we trust that everything will turn out—as Jesus returns and "wins."

But is Armageddon the real end? This chapter explores the concept of eschatology in the Old Testament. While the term eschatology means "doctrine of the end," the Old Testament does not envision the end of the world, of time, or of history. Donald Gowan notes that the Old Testament instead "promises the end of sin (Jer 33:8), of war (Mic 4:3), of human infirmity (Isa 35:5–6), of hunger (Ezek 36:30), of killing or harming of any living thing (Isa 11:9)."[1] In this future there will be a new heaven and a new earth (Isa 65:17; 66:22) where humans and animals will again live in peace and prosperity together. Each of these passages shares a common understanding

---

1. Gowan, *Eschatology in the Old Testament*, 2.

that the present world is radically wrong. Therefore, radical changes are necessary to make things right.

Every part of creation was made by God, and when God says "it was good" (Gen 1:4, 10, 12, 18),[2] that means it was perfect. Therefore, creation is not bad in itself. However, the fall of mankind allowed sin to invade every aspect of creation leaving it hopelessly corrupted. These Old Testament eschatological texts promise transformation as the radical victory over evil and restoration of God's perfect plan.

So, how does it all end? According to the Old Testament the answer is essentially the end of evil and the ushering in of a renewed community. Isaiah 65:17–18 typifies this understanding: "See, I will create new heavens and a new earth. The former things will not be remembered, nor will they come to mind. But be glad and rejoice forever in what I will create, for I will create Jerusalem to be a delight and its people a joy" (NRSV).

RENEWED COMMUNITY AND THE GOSPEL

Jesus's ministry began at a time of heightened eschatological hope and expectation. The writers of the New Testament identified that Christ was the beginning and the end of eschatological theology because all of God's plan was focused in Jesus. The writer of Hebrews confirms that God's work from the beginning of creation was completed with the coming of Jesus (Heb 4:1–4).

> Therefore, since the promise of entering his rest still stands, let us be careful that none of you be found to have fallen short of it. For we also have had the good news proclaimed to us, just as they did; but the message they heard was of no value to them, because they did not share the faith of those who obeyed. Now we who have believed enter that rest, just as God has said,
>
> "So I declared on oath in my anger, 'They shall never enter my rest.'"
>
> And yet his works have been finished since the creation of the world. For somewhere he has spoken about the seventh day in these words: "On the seventh day God rested from all his works." (Heb 4:1–4; NRSV)

Jesus proclaims this same message when he says that "the time has come . . . The kingdom of God has come near. Repent and believe the good news!" (Mark 1:14–15). In this passage Jesus is inviting all Israel to

2. Unless otherwise noted, Scripture quotations in this chapter are the author's translation.

participate in the restoration of God's relationship with humans; however, few actually answer the call at that time. Luke goes on to connect Jesus with the Suffering Servant of Isaiah.

> The Spirit of the Lord is on me,
>> because he has anointed me
>> to proclaim good news to the poor.
> He has sent me to proclaim freedom for the prisoners
>> and recovery of sight for the blind,
>> to set the oppressed free, to proclaim the year of the Lord's favor.
> (Luke 4:18–19, NRSV; cf. Isa 61:1–2)

At one level, judgment and an eschatological end is determined at the cross. Darkness at noon symbolized the darkness of the "day of the Lord" over the entire world. The cry of declaration demonstrated Jesus's full identification with human estrangement from God (Mark 15:33–34). The conflict with Jerusalem's temple leadership "brought God's judgment on the very heart of the temple system through the death of the messiah. This judgment also carried with it the conviction that God's purposes for the temple would be realized through Jesus and his new covenant community."[3] In addition, the temple veil was rent; from that moment on the dwelling place of God among his people was Jesus and the new community.

On another level, a future resurrection is the key to God's plan. In Second Temple Judaism, belief in resurrection was linked not merely to personal survival beyond death but to God's perfect plan for restoring his creatures to their proper destiny. In the resurrection, the whole story from creation onward has reached its climax. Jesus came to announce and usher in the kingdom of God. The last days are here and the day of deliverance is at hand. Jesus is "God with us" in his saving power. "He is the embodiment of God's eschatological purposes, promised by the prophets and realized in the new covenant community with the promised in-the-heart Torah."[4]

Paul provides a clear message about the significance and centrality of Christ's resurrection (1 Cor 15). He goes so far as to say that "if Christ has not been raised, our preaching is useless and so is your faith" (1 Cor 15:15). On the one hand, the resurrection confirms that Jesus is God's final solution to the plight of humanity. In Jesus's resurrection, the eschatological future of humanity has already been realized. Christ is the paradigmatic new creation and those who are in Christ are also new creatures (2 Cor 5:17). The coming of Jesus marked the decisive turn of the ages; the age to come has already

---

3. Brower, *Reader Must Understand*, 143.
4. Ibid.

dawned and is being experienced during this present age. In Christ, all of God's promises find their fulfillment.

On the other hand, Paul is also clear that the resurrection of Christ is but the firstfruits and there is more to come (1 Cor 15:20). Humanity awaits the resurrection and redemption of our bodies (Rom 8:23). Likewise, creation itself awaits the final re-creation, which will be the culmination of God's purposes (Rom 8:19–21).

> For the creation waits in eager expectation for the children of God to be revealed. For the creation was subjected to frustration, not by its own choice, but by the will of the one who subjected it, in hope that the creation itself will be liberated from its bondage to decay and brought into the freedom and glory of the children of God. (Rom 8:19–21; NIV)

The New Testament writers believe that the kingdom is a present reality. Before Jesus ascended to his father, he promised to send the Spirit. The same Spirit who had been with Jesus would now be poured out on all flesh, again in fulfillment of Old Testament prophecy and as a public confirmation that the last days had arrived (Acts 2:16–17). However, there is a dynamic tension between the "already" and the "not yet." This concept is integral to biblical eschatology as the kingdom is both present and coming. The resurrection of the body, the defeat of death, the end of all opposition to God's reign, and the redemption of the whole created order in a new heaven and a new earth all await fulfillment in God's timing.

ANALYSIS OF KEY PASSAGES

Understanding that Jesus ushered in some aspects of the promised kingdom and yet some aspects of the promise remains, we now turn back to explore the Old Testament promises for a renewed community in more detail.

Isaiah 65:17–25 A New Heaven and New Earth

This section of Isaiah is one of the final passages of hope, and it stands in opposition to the book's earlier sections of judgment. The passage begins, "See, I will create new heavens and a new earth. The former things will not be remembered, nor will they come to mind" (Isa 65:17). Reminiscent of Genesis 1–2, God will create a new reality for humanity. The existing fallen world will not be cleansed, but replaced. Like Isa 43:14–21, God demonstrates his lordship over both human nations and nature. In addition, God shows that he has both the desire and the ability to intervene for his purposes. And we are reminded that God is not predictable, as he works in new ways and the old will not be remembered.

In this way the passage announces a radically new vision of the future: "new heavens and a new earth." The vocabulary of the passage extends the theme of the suffering servant who will provide salvation and usher in a new divine order. As found earlier in Isaiah, the reference to God as creator (*bôrē*) of the heavens and earth is carried forward here as a dominant theme (cf. 42:5; 45:7, 12, 18). The use of this verb is important as it is not only used to designate God's initial creation of the heavens and earth but also the continuous maintenance and preservation of the earth (42:5–6). Earlier in Isaiah the verb is associated with the promise of the new things (48:6), which will replace the former things. Therefore, v. 17 intentionally joins with the theme of the former things (48:18). This passage in Isaiah elevates the theme of God as creator in speaking of a new world order different in kind from the past. The break here is so strong that the new vision may be designated as apocalyptic.

Brevard Childs explains that "the present social order as an unmitigated evil had to be completely expunged to purge the human sphere and to usher in a new apocalyptic vision of a supernatural divine order (cf. Rev. 21:1ff.). As part of this pattern the imagery of chapter 65 is understood as an eschatological return to the primordial age. Accordingly, the verses that follow develop the mythical themes of a return to paradise, which later abound in the apocryphal and pseudepigraphical books."[5]

The passage continues in vv. 18–20: "but be glad and rejoice forever in what I will create, for I will create Jerusalem to be a delight and its people a joy. I will rejoice over Jerusalem and take delight in my people; the sound of weeping and of crying will be heard in it no more. Never again will there be in it an infant who lives but a few days, or an old man who does not live out his years; the one who dies at a hundred will be thought a mere child; the one who fails to reach a hundred will be considered accursed."

In these verses the reality of the present concedes its position to a new reality. The new earthly expression is not merely a duplication of what already exists in heaven. Isaiah envisions something entirely new, and because it is new, the tragic realities of this world need not be repeated there. Humanity can experience the true reality of joy and delight without the old reality of weeping and crying (65:18–19). Equally, we may experience a full life without the despair of an early death (65:20). Isaiah alludes to the

5. Childs, *Isaiah*, Loc 13953.

early chapters of Genesis where humans lived for hundreds of years (cf. Gen 5:1–32).

The passage continues in Isa 65:21–23: "They will build houses and dwell in them; they will plant vineyards and eat their fruit. No longer will they build houses and others live in them, or plant and others eat. For as the days of a tree, so will be the days of my people; my chosen ones will long enjoy the work of their hands. They will not labor in vain, nor will they bear children doomed to misfortune; for they will be a people blessed by the LORD, they and their descendants with them."

Isaiah reveals that the satisfaction of building will not be accompanied by the fear of destruction and conquest. All too often in Israel's past the Israelites had struggled to build cities and plant crops only to be invaded by its neighbors (cf. Judg 6:1–6). This ever-present fear will be replaced with peace and the assurance of safety. In contrast to Gen 3:17–19, where the ground was cursed and the sewing crops was a constant struggle, now humans will enjoy the work of their hands. This new reality will last from one renewed generation to the next. Those who believe God's word, obey him, and live his life will be "blessed" (Isa 65:23).

The passage concludes in vv. 24–25: "'Before they call I will answer; while they are still speaking, I will hear. The wolf and the lamb will feed together, and the lion will eat straw like the ox, and dust will be the serpent's food. They will neither harm nor destroy on all my holy mountain,' says the LORD."

This passage reverses the fear placed upon animals after the fall and further recounted in Gen 9:2. Now natural predators will live in harmony. The passage depicts a full reversal of the curses of Gen 3:14–19 with one exception. While the descendants of Adam and Eve are restored, the serpent remains under the curse of having to eat "dust" (Gen 3:14). This continuation of a curse on the serpent is understandable, as Jesus is the fulfillment and restoration through the crushing the serpent in Rom 16:20: "The God of peace will soon crush Satan under your feet."

The language of Rev 65:24–25 is closely related to the vision of the messianic kingdom in Isaiah 11, with the final line of the verse being an exact duplicate of the first colon of 11:9. This makes it plain that what we have here is not merely a poetic expression of the certainty of justice in some general sense but a prediction of real events in the age to come.

UNITY OF RENEWED COMMUNITY AS
A THEME WITHIN THE OLD TESTAMENT

We identified above that the eschatological core of the Old Testament is the renewal of God's perfect creation and a renewed relationship of God with humanity. This eschatological hope is strongly present throughout the Old Testament and includes four distinct segments: a renewed city of the future (Zion), restoration of peace, new humanity, and a renewed ecology.[6]

Zechariah speaks in the postexilic era about the restoration promised by earlier prophets. At the time of Zechariah's prophecy, many of the exiles had returned to Jerusalem and construction had already begun on the new temple. Over the previous century many prophets had spoken of a glorious time when the people would return from exile to a new and prosperous city of Jerusalem (known as Zion). As the people now lived in the period after the exile, they looked around and could see that the reality of the return from exile did not usher in all the glorious things promised for Zion by these earlier prophets and they wanted to know if they should continue the practice of mourning, essentially asking if this current time fulfilled the earlier prophecies.

Zechariah responds with a combination of both "realized" and "future" eschatology when he says "This is what the Lord Almighty says: 'I am very jealous for Zion; I am burning with jealousy for her.' This is what the Lord says: 'I will return to Zion and dwell in Jerusalem. Then Jerusalem will be called the Faithful City, and the mountain of the Lord Almighty will be called the Holy Mountain . . . Once again men and women of ripe old age will sit in the streets of Jerusalem, each of them with cane in hand because of their age. The city streets will be filled with boys and girls playing there'" (Zech 8:2–5). In this passage the prophet repeats Zion (twice) and Jerusalem (three times), demonstrating the importance of the city as the focal point of the message.

The passage reveals how a postexilic prophet saw the relationship between past, present, and the ideal future with Zion as the eschatological symbol. The good life that Zechariah projects for the inhabitants of Jerusalem is a mixture of the material and the spiritual. Peace, prosperity, and security are dominant themes, but this is no secular city. What makes it all possible is God, who carries out his plan (8:2), and the source of the good life in Zion is the presence of the Lord in its midst.

A similar message is demonstrated in Micah where Zion is exalted and restored as God's throne. Micah 4:1–4 reads:

6. These four themes and the following discussion are adopted from the work of Gowan, *Eschatology in the Old Testament*.

In the last days the mountain of the LORD's temple will be established as the highest of the mountains; it will be exalted above the hills, and peoples will stream to it. Many nations will come and say, "Come, let us go up to the mountain of the LORD, to the temple of the God of Jacob. He will teach us his ways, so that we may walk in his paths." The law will go out from Zion, the word of the LORD from Jerusalem. He will judge between many peoples and will settle disputes for strong nations far and wide. They will beat their swords into plowshares and their spears into pruning hooks. Nation will not take up sword against nation, nor will they train for war anymore. Everyone will sit under their own vine and under their own fig tree, and no one will make them afraid, for the LORD Almighty has spoken.

These verses provide a vivid depiction of the coming age; however, the passage omits many of the anticipated features of eschatology. There is no mention of a dramatic transformation or a messianic king. In addition, the prophecy is realistic in that it envisions that people and nations will have disputes. However, in the new age the disputes will be settled by God without the need for war. As with Zechariah 8, the key to the passage lies in the renewed city of Jerusalem (Zion). However, Mt. Zion is a small hill not even as high as the Mount of Olives next to it. The passage uses this literal distinction to a theological advantage as this modest hill will become the highest mountain on earth! Theologically, the language symbolizes that God's resting place is the most important place on earth. In this eschatological view, God will be in complete control of the renewed community and Zion/Jerusalem will be the location.

The restoration of peace and the transformation of human society is a second eschatological theme associated with God's renewed community in the Old Testament. The new city that Israel hoped God would establish on earth "in that day" was described in such a way as to include radical changes in human nature as well as renewal of social institutions and the natural world. This change was fundamental to a change in the nature of society and a coming peace.

Isaiah incorporates this theme by building upon God's salvific act in a new exodus. God's marvelous care for his people in the wilderness is the part of the tradition Isaiah wished to emphasize, and for him the new exodus will be a triumphal procession across a transformed land. Isaiah writes "They will neither hunger nor thirst, nor will the desert heat or the sun beat down on them. He who has compassion on them will guide them and lead them beside springs of water. I will turn all my mountains into roads, and my highways will be raised up" (Isa 49:10–11).

Throughout the central chapters of Isaiah there is rejoicing because God has already forgiven (40:2; 43:1) and because all obstacles, spiritual and material, are in the process of being overcome. The prophet highlights this idea when he writes "Those the LORD has rescued will return. They will enter Zion with singing; everlasting joy will crown their heads. Gladness and joy will overtake them, and sorrow and sighing will flee away" (Isa 51:11).

The third theme depicts a renewed humanity. This theme begins with the fall of mankind in Gen 3 and God's just response, tempered with mercy, revealing God's character. The character of God is further revealed in Exod 34 when God passes before Moses on the mountain saying "The LORD, the LORD, the compassionate and gracious God, slow to anger, abounding in love and faithfulness, maintaining love to thousands, and forgiving wickedness, rebellion and sin. Yet he does not leave the guilty unpunished; he punishes the children and their children for the sin of the parents to the third and fourth generation" (Exod 34:6–7). In this passage we find that God is both just and merciful towards his fallen creation.

The transformation of mankind involves the re-creation of our presently distorted position, requiring a new heart. This requires a gift from God and is more than simply a restoration to an uncorrupt state. It requires a new spirit and calls for the establishment of a relationship between God and humanity on different grounds from those at present (necessitating a new covenant).

The Old Testament does not suggest that these changes should eliminate human freedom of choice. Instead, the prophets found that the problem of sin is the root and that humanity can never attain the ideal society planned by God unless the Lord intervenes to make a change in human nature itself. Deuteronomy foreshadows this type of change when Moses writes "The LORD your God will circumcise your hearts and the hearts of your descendants, so that you may love him with all your heart and with all your soul, and live" (Deut 30:6). The term "circumcision of the heart" was a common expression in Hebrew and indicated that what was "blocked-up" is now free to operate as it was designed. This idea is also found in Jer 4, where the prophet tells the people "Circumcise yourselves to the LORD, circumcise your hearts, you people of Judah and inhabitants of Jerusalem, or my wrath will flare up and burn like fire because of the evil you have done—burn with no one to quench it." (Jer 4:4). Unlike in Jeremiah, the circumcising is now being done by God, resulting in Israel's ability to love God without qualifications or restraints. Love for God means far more than to have warm feelings about hm. Loving God is intimately connected with obedience. Conversely, to hate or despise God means to disobey him.

God relates this eschatological and fundamental change of human condition in Jer 31. The Lord states through the prophet:

> "The days are coming," declares the LORD, "when I will make a new covenant with the people of Israel and with the people of Judah. It will not be like the covenant I made with their ancestors when I took them by the hand to lead them out of Egypt, because they broke my covenant, though I was a husband to them," declares the LORD. "This is the covenant I will make with the people of Israel after that time," declares the LORD. "I will put my law in their minds and write it on their hearts. I will be their God, and they will be my people. No longer will they teach their neighbor, or say to one another, 'Know the LORD,' because they will all know me, from the least of them to the greatest," declares the LORD. "For I will forgive their wickedness and will remember their sins no more." (Jer 31:31–34)

The mechanism for the new relationship with humans begins with a new covenant. This new covenant will be written on the heart with an inscribed law that humanity is now able to follow. The beginning of the passage explains that obedience is the concern of the prophet, and it concludes with a surprising promise about the extent of the knowledge of God which writing the covenant on the heart will provide. The advent of this new covenant is the beginning of the eschatological hope for a renewed community.

Our final theme for the transformation of creation is a renewed ecology. While the Old Testament does not ascribe sin to any of creation except humans, it does acknowledge the presence of two kinds of evil in the non-human world. First, there is an element of threat to all that is stabled and ordered. This chaotic element is felt lurking just beyond the edges of the normally dependable world that God created.[7] Second, the naturally ordered world has challenges including crops that fail, hunger, floods, and earthquakes each that destroys life and property. In the same way, wild animals endanger life and health. The Old Testament takes the theological position that human sin is the culprit as sin has inflicted a curse on the natural world so that it suffers because of mankind's misdeeds. Because humanity is dependent upon nature, the curse rebounds from nature back upon mankind. Making the divinely intended fullness of life impossible until the curse is removed. The eschatology of the Old Testament conveys that it is God's intention to renew nature as part of a renewed community.

Two examples convey this idea. First, Hos 2 relates that the relationship between humans and animals will be restored. The prophecy reads:

7. Ibid., 97.

"In that day I will make a covenant for them with the beasts of the field, the birds in the sky and the creatures that move along the ground. Bow and sword and battle I will abolish from the land, so that all may lie down in safety" (Hos 2:18). The passage relays the eschatological hope that mankind and animals will each live in harmony and safety.

A second passage in Isaiah further expounds on this message:

> The wolf will live with the lamb,
>> the leopard will lie down with the goat,
> the calf and the lion and the yearling together;
>> and a little child will lead them.
> The cow will feed with the bear,
>> their young will lie down together,
>> and the lion will eat straw like the ox.
> The infant will play near the cobra's den,
>> and the young child will put its hand into the viper's nest.
> They will neither harm nor destroy
>> on all my holy mountain,
> for the earth will be filled with the knowledge of the Lord
>> as the waters cover the sea. (Isa 11:6–9)

This passage describes total peace in nature. Earlier in Isaiah the prophet connects this renewed ecology with the coming messianic king (11:1–5). These passages form a fitting conclusion to our earlier study of Isa 65, where a more comprehensive picture of the "new" world is represented. It begins with the creation of new heavens and a new earth then moves to the new Jerusalem, in which everyone enjoys a long-life span, in which houses, vineyards, fruitful work, and children are the key blessings.

IMPLICATIONS FOR READING THE NEW TESTAMENT

When writing to the Galatians, Paul explains, "neither circumcision nor uncircumcision means anything; what counts is the new creation" (Gal 6:15). This new creation was established in Jesus's incarnation, human life, death, resurrection, and ascension. By it, Christians are presently given new eyes through which to interpret the world. Paul teaches that "if anyone is in Christ, the new creation has come: The old has gone, the new is here!" (2 Cor 5:17). It is the hope to which we are called, it is a new heaven and a new earth.

Paul speaks about the new creation as both a reality made possible because of Jesus's resurrection, and as a future hope; however, Paul tends to highlight the latter (Rom 8). For Paul, the Holy Spirit has ushered in some aspects of the new creation, and yet this new creation is not fully present and will not be fully present until the time of Jesus's triumphant return. Paul writes, "We know that the whole creation has been groaning as in the pains of childbirth right up to the present time. Not only so, but we ourselves, who have the firstfruits of the Spirit, groan inwardly as we wait eagerly for our adoption to sonship, the redemption of our bodies. For in this hope we were saved. But hope that is seen is no hope at all. Who hopes for what they already have? But if we hope for what we do not yet have, we wait for it patiently" (Rom 8:22–25) In this way the Spirit resides in each of us, transforming us, as in Gal 6:5. However, we hope for another transformation in fulfillment of God's prophecy.

Isaiah and other Old Testament prophets seem to convey that more is to come. They point to a return to something like Eden. The New Testament encompasses this view and expands the image to a fruitful city inhabited by a multitude. John records this scene in the book of Revelation:

> Then I saw a new heaven and a new earth, for the first heaven and the first earth had passed away, and there was no longer any sea. I saw the Holy City, the new Jerusalem, coming down out of heaven from God, prepared as a bride beautifully dressed for her husband. And I heard a loud voice from the throne saying, "Look! God's dwelling place is now among the people, and he will dwell with them. They will be his people, and God himself will be with them and be their God. He will wipe every tear from their eyes. There will be no more death' or mourning or crying or pain, for the old order of things has passed away." He who was seated on the throne said, "I am making everything new!" Then he said, "Write this down, for these words are trustworthy and true." (Rev 21:1–4; NRSV)

In this passage we learn of the final fulfillment of Old Testament prophecy. Jesus's return will usher in a renewed community. Not one where the old is "washed" and "cleansed," but one where God creates a new heaven and earth. The creation is returned to being "good" and the sinful nature of mankind is restored to its desired state. Most importantly, humanity is again able to be in full fellowship with God in a renewed community.

We find that biblical eschatology ends in the victory of God in Christ (1 Cor 15:28). The new heaven and new earth in which the holy God dwells in the midst of a holy people (Rev 21–22) is the glorious hope of those who are in Christ. With this hope in view, the people of God face the present with confidence in God. They can "perceive God's purpose in the present situation and the role that Christians are called to play in that purpose with a view to the coming of the kingdom."[8] Those who suffer now hope for the future described in Rev 20:1–6 and often called the millennium. John expects the martyrs to be vindicated, but the millennium depicts the meaning rather than the manner of their vindication.[9]

Even if countless details of biblical eschatology are open to different interpretations, its central theme is clear enough: God's perfect goal for his created order is fulfilled in Christ, the perfect representative of redeemed humanity. We do not yet see everything in subjection to him, but we do see Jesus (Heb 2:8–9). This is the nucleus of our Christian hope.

IMPLICATIONS FOR AND IDENTITY WITH THE MODERN CHRISTIAN CHURCH

So, what applications can we take away from this study for the modern church as these eschatological passages that await fulfillment? The best place to start is to place our study in context. This study explored the final expression of God's relationship with humanity. However, there are other periods and different ways that God has related to his creation. The first was with Adam and Eve in the garden of Eden. In this first period of innocence, humanity and God experienced a direct and personal relationship surrounded by God's perfect creation. Mankind rebelled, leading to the fall and the advent of sin. This action resulted in a progression of different periods of relationship. In each period God connected with his creation in a different way.

After the fall, God allowed humans to act upon their own conscience (Gen 3:8–8:22). Communication was still direct (Gen 4:6; 5:13), but the frequency of the communication decreased as sin permeated every action. In this time the human conscience of mankind was to keep them from evil, but it became corrupt (evil became good and good was condemned). This period ended with the flood and the promises to Noah for a new period of government. The Bible relates little about the communication between humanity and God during this period except to show that humanity further desires to be like God. Ultimately the people come together to build a great tower and reach the heavens. God thwarts the effort, scattering people and confusing language.

8. Bauckham, *Theology of the Book of Revelation*, 158.
9. Ibid., 108.

Abraham ushers in a period of promise in Gen 11 during which God acted through the lives of the patriarchs. This period ended with the exodus of God's chosen people from Egypt. During this section of history God developed a great nation that he had chosen as his people. God is associated with a chosen people and relates to the growing nation through dreams, visions, and leaders/prophets.

Moses initiated a period of law encompassing the bulk of the Israelite history from the exodus to the ministry of Jesus. God's relationship with his people was governed by the Mosaic Covenant, or the Law, found in Exod 19–23. The community and relationship to God involved temple worship directed by priests, with further direction spoken through God's mouthpieces, the prophets. Eventually, due to the people's continued disobedience to the covenant, the nations of Israel and Judah lost their land and were subjected to exile in Assyria and Babylon.

The sixth period, the one in which we now live, is a time of grace. It began with the new covenant in Christ's blood (Luke 22:20). This "Age of Grace" or "Church Age" starts with the coming of the Spirit on the Day of Pentecost and ends with the rapture of the church (1 Thess 4). The scope of the relationship is worldwide and includes both Jews and the Gentiles. Mankind's responsibility during this period is to believe in Jesus, the Son of God (John 3:18). In addition, the Holy Spirit indwells believers as the Comforter (John 14:16–26). This period describes our current relationship to God and will be explored more below.

The final period is the eschatological future period of relationship explored in this paper. We will experience a new creation and a return to a full and intimate relationship with God. This period will include a time known as the millennium and the ultimate judgment by God concluding with return of Jesus.

Now that we understand the eschatological future for a renewed community within the context of our current relationship, we can unpack two implications for the modern church. First, we will explore the current call for community, and then, second, we will explore the hope for the future.

As mentioned above, the current relationship between God and his community is defined by grace and structed through the new covenant of Jesus. This community is centered in the church. Derek J. Tidball writes that "although the church is often thought to be a human institution, a social arrangement to facilitate the interests and mission of likeminded people, as indeed it is, the Bible presents it as primarily a consequence of the character and purposes of the Trinitarian God."[10] Its origins lie in God's desire to have

---

10. Tidball, "Church," 407.

a people of his own (Deut 7:6). It is a community of those who acknowledge Jesus Christ as Lord (1 Cor 12:3). It is a fellowship where the Holy Spirit lives (1 Cor 3:16), directing and energizing its community life.

The plan of God was not completely fulfilled under the old covenant but came to full realization in Jesus (Eph 1:3–10; 2:11–22). He brought the church into being and it is his church (Matt 16:18). The church of the new covenant is entered by faith in him (Gal 3:1–14; Eph 2:1–10) and, consequently, is international in membership and allows no ethnic, gender, or social divisions (Gal 3:28; Eph 2:11–22; Col 3:11). The church is his body on earth, and he is the head (Rom 12:5; 1 Cor 12:12–31; Col 1:18). The church takes its alignment from him as a building takes its alignment from the cornerstone (Ehp 2:20–21). It derives unity and growth from Jesus (Eph 2:19–22; 4:15–16). The life of the church is maintained by its vital union with Christ and exists only insofar as it is "in him" (Rom 6:1–4; Eph 2:21–22; 4:15–16). The person and work of Christ are therefore at the heart of the New Testament view of the *ekklēsia* (church). They enable us to understand both the continuities and the discontinuities between the old and new covenant people of God.[11]

Therefore, we are right to understand that the church is at the heart of God's relationship with his community. As Paul writes: ". . . Christ loved the church and gave himself up for her to make her holy, cleansing her by the washing with water through the word, and to present her to himself as a radiant church, without stain or wrinkle or any other blemish, but holy and blameless" (Eph 5:25–27). It is through the church, of which Christ is the head, that God's wisdom is made known to his community (Eph 1:22; 3:10; 5:23; Col 1:18).

Our second application for the modern church is hope. If the story ended with the resurrection of Christ, that would be enough because we know that our relationship with God is restored through Jesus's atoning sacrifice. However, there is more! As Paul talks of a new kingdom in terms of "already and not yet," we also are satisfied with the current relationship and yet know that a time is coming when God will restore his perfect relationship to his community, a time when there will be a new heaven and a new earth, where humans will discover a renewed community and people will live together in peace and security. The relationship between humanity and the animal kingdom will no longer be one of fear but now one of fellowship. Both predator and prey will exist in peaceful fellowship, and the environment will be restored. Most importantly, humanity will rejoice in the direct and constant relationship with God.

11. Ibid., 408.

Therefore, we live knowing that the future will bring a renewed community in God's perfect creation.

QUESTIONS FOR FURTHER STUDY

1) Read Rev 21–22. What do you think the "new heaven and new earth" will be like?

2) What is the purpose of community in the context of being a Christian?

3) What is your personal responsibility for engagement in community as a Christian? Reflect on whether you are fulfilling these responsibilities.

4) How do you believe the church fulfills the biblical understanding of community? How can that be improved?

5) Can there be a virtual church? Does social media and remote preaching impact the biblical understanding of community?

6) What is the difference between the coming new creation and our current situation?

BIBLIOGRAPHY AND RECOMMENDED READING

Bauckham, Richard. *The Theology of the Book of Revelation.* New Testament Theology. Cambridge: Cambridge University Press, 1993.

Brower, Kent E. "Eschatology." In *New Dictionary of Biblical Theology: Exploring the Unity and Diversity of Scripture,* edited by T. Desmond Alexander, 459–64. Downers Grove, IL: InterVarsity, 2000.

Brower, Kent E., and Mark W. Elliott. *The Reader Must Understand: Eschatology in Bible and Theology.* Eugene, OR: Wipf & Stock. 2013.

Childs, Brevard S. *Isaiah.* OTL. Louisville: Westminster John Knox, 2001.

Enns, Paul. *The Moody Handbook of Theology.* Rev. and exp. ed. Chicago: Moody, 2008.

Godwan, Donald E. *Eschatology in the Old Testament.* Philadelphia: Fortress, 1986.

Hess, Richard S. *The Old Testament: A Historical, Theological, and Critical Introduction.* Grand Rapids: Baker Academic, 2016.

Humphrey, Edith M. "New Creation." In *Dictionary for Theological Interpretation of the Bible,* edited by Kevin J. Vanhoozer, 536–37. Grand Rapids: Baker Academic, 2005.

Oswalt, John N. *Isaiah: From Biblical Text to Contemporary Life.* NIVAC. Grand Rapids: Zondervan, 2003.

———. *The Book of Isaiah: 40–66.* NICOT. Grand Rapids: Eerdmans, 1998.

14

OLD TESTAMENT THEOLOGY FOR A MULTI-ETHNIC CHURCH

JAMES SPENCER

INTRODUCTION

Often when the topic of multi-ethnicity is discussed in relation to biblical and theological disciplines, there is a strong emphasis on social justice, on the benefits of diverse perspectives to the theological enterprise, or on the development of a more localized body that looks like the worldwide church of Christ. Though such emphases are appropriate and important, diversity of all sorts derives its rationale from a more central point of doctrine which is, at times, assumed rather than made explicit. That doctrine is the catholic nature of the body of Christ as God's vehicle for proclaiming the gospel of Christ and glorifying his name. This body is diverse in gifts, experience, and ethnicities with each member contributing to the body and to the accomplishment of God's purposes. The diversity of the body of Christ provides the context for mutual edification, instruction, correction, and the pursuit of holiness. It is within this body that Old Testament theology is practiced. Understanding the relationship between the church and the academic practice of Old Testament theology is crucial to recognizing the impact the church, local or worldwide, which is already a multi-ethnic body, may have on Old Testament theology.[1]

The presence of difference within the church is not new. The church has historically been comprised of a diverse group of individuals seeking to glorify God in various cultural contexts around the world. The current capacity to connect these previously separated individuals and local congregations through advances in technology offers avenues of influence to believers who have not previously had ready access to participate in academic discourse dominated largely by European and North American male authors. Whether that influence comes by participating in the academic guild, writing and publishing theological research, sharing stories of challenge and victory in Christ from a particular geographic locale, prompting the investigation of new theological themes, or offering commentary through various forms of social media, God's people are now more available to speak into Old Testament theology than ever before. The field of Old Testament theology may now more easily connect with global voices and allow the influence of such voices to impact the questions that Old Testament theology seeks to answer.

Finding ways to integrate the experiences and concerns of the global church into the field of Old Testament theology is one of the greatest challenges facing a predominantly Western academy. In order to effectively engage cultural difference within the church, there needs to be a clear understanding of the manner in which Old Testament theology engages the church more generally. What role does Old Testament theology play in the life of a given congregation or in the life of God's people as a whole? As an academic discipline, how might Old Testament theology understand itself as a discipline within the broader academe, as well as recognizing and exercising its crucial role in relation to the body of Christ? How can Old Testament theologians cultivate a disposition within Old Testament theology to shape and reshape Old Testament theology from within and for the church?

THE FIELD OF OLD TESTAMENT THEOLOGY

As an academic discipline, Old Testament theology functions as a field, or network within which individuals, groups, and institutions relate according to practices structured by the field itself. In other words, a field is a bounded

---

1. Though Old Testament theology does not derive solely from the academy, it would be naïve to ignore the heavy influence the academy exerts on the practice of Old Testament theology more generally. The emphasis placed on the academy in this work is a matter of scope and focus and is not intended to diminish Old Testament theology that takes place in other settings and fields.

space that conditions the behaviors of those seeking to act within it in a way similar to the field of play in sports. Soccer players do not use their hands unless they are in the goal because it is illegal to do so within the field of play. To become an excellent soccer player one must condition one's actions within the field of play so that they conform to those allowed by and advantageous within that field.

As a field, Old Testament theology exerts some level of influence over those who seek to practice Old Testament theology by defining boundaries, rewarding certain scholarly activities, and reinforcing patterns of thought through formalized education systems. Like other fields, the field of Old Testament theology constitutes the space within which agents (individuals, groups, or institutions) receive (and compete for) field-based power and capital. Based on the accumulation of that power and capital, agents gain access to "specific profits that are at stake in the field, as well as by their objective relation to other positions (domination, subordination, homology, etc)."[2] If fields define, as Pierre Bourdieu and others would suggest, the space in which field-based power and capital are distributed, it makes sense that agents within the field would orient their energies toward behaviors that would allow for the accumulation of that field-based power and capital.[3] Such an understanding of fields in general and of Old Testament theology in particular suggests that the field of Old Testament theology structures the sorts of interactions that take place within its boundaries and rewards certain behaviors, works, and patterns of thought more than others.

While there is not sufficient space to discuss the historical development of academic disciplines within the context of the academy, it is important to understand certain dynamics of the field of Old Testament theology and the potential impact those dynamics have on Old Testament theology's capacity to incorporate and speak to multiethnic voices within the church. For instance, frequent, substantive, academic publication is valued within the field of Old Testament theology, which may make it more difficult for authors from the global south to find recognition within the field of Old Testament theology. Similarly, the willingness to interact with the accepted

---

2. Bourdieu and Wacquant, *An Invitation to Reflexive Sociology*, 97.

3. Much of Bourdieu's work is influenced by Marx and focused on relationships, particularly relations of power. Bourdieu's use of language such as "power" and "competition," while featuring heavily in his work, are not essential to the notion of field in the same way as relationality. While power relations may well exist within fields, it should not be assumed that individual actors will simply seek to overturn power relations or to occupy positions of power within a given field. At the same time, it should not be assumed that the current structure of power relations or the use of power within the field is appropriate. Challenging the status quo, however, entails more than a reordering of power relations.

tomes of Western scholarship has become something of a rite of passage for Old Testament scholars. There has been comparatively less emphasis, however, placed on the willingness to situate one's reading of the Old Testament within one's own personal history or within the history of one's particular ethnic group. In some sense, this latter dynamic does not account for the manner in which ethnic difference may well inspire approaches or emphases complementary to those more prevalent within Old Testament theology.

The field of Old Testament theology, then, is not neutral. Rather, it is a structured and structuring space with boundaries and rules that favor those with certain dispositions and skillsets. The rules and boundaries are also often defined and reinforced by those in whom the "certain dispositions and skillsets" have been cultivated. At the same time, the field of Old Testament theology is only relatively autonomous and can be influenced and changed. As Karl Moton notes, "A field's *autonomy* is illustrated by the way it generates its own values and markers of achievement, but the *relative* nature of this autonomy means these values are not alone in shaping the field."[4] This relative autonomy suggests that the body of Christ has the capacity, if not the obligation, to shape the field of Old Testament theology. Old Testament theology cannot exist apart from the church. The question, to paraphrase Stanley Hauerwas, is "whether the church exists that can provide the material conditions that can make such an alternative . . ." discipline "possible."[5]

The structure of Old Testament theology as a discipline, as well as the common language and ongoing dialogues of intelligent men and women, are surely beneficial. That same structure, however, has the potential of excluding individuals or groups that do not speak the languages of the academic guild. If, however, Old Testament theology is to serve a multiethnic church, those participating in Old Testament theology must develop the capacity to bridge across "structural holes" because, as Burt hypothesizes "people who live in the intersection of social worlds are at higher risk of having good ideas."[6] The discipline of Old Testament theology must also fight to remain pliable and responsive to the body of Christ.

---

4. Maton, "A Question of Autonomy," 689.

5. Hauerwas, *State of the University*, 105. The original quote question whether a church was available to allow such an "alternative university" to be possible.

6. Burt, *Brokerage and Closure*, 16–18.

THE CHURCH'S ROLE IN SHAPING
OLD TESTAMENT THEOLOGY

What Church?

If it is the case that (1) the church is capable of influencing the field of Old Testament theology and (2) the capacity for Old Testament theology to thrive within a multiethnic community depends, in part, on the discipline's relationship with the church, the question of what is meant by "the church" must be addressed. While it is tempting to think of the church as an institution, the church is not, first and foremost, an institution. Instead, the church is the body called and redeemed to follow Christ together so as to glorify God through the empowering of the Holy Spirit. In this more universal sense of "church," the body called consists of disciples past and present both around the world and in local congregations. The catholic nature of the body reflects both the significance of individuality within the church, as well as the connected, interdependent nature of the body called. In other words, catholicity does not create a generic singularity, but an eclectic community of uniquely essential members coordinating to offer testimony of the God it serves within a fallen world.

This body has a vital relationship to the Scriptures. As Karl Barth suggests, ". . .the constitution and preservation of the Church rests in this, that man hears God. . .In the Church man hears God because He has spoken and he gives ear to what God has spoken. The Church exists wherever this is done. . ."[7] This relationship develops through time being informed by the conversations of previous generations, shaped by past and present social and political contexts, influenced by local and global concerns, and conditioned by the knowledge and hope that God will act on behalf of his people in the future. The church's concerns, then, transcend the boundaries of any given time or geographic locale even as the particular articulations of the Christian faith are lived out by bodies of believers in diverse and distinct environments worldwide.

It is important to understand and to think about the church as an historical congregation that engages in an ongoing conversation through time and across a variety of cultures and contexts. Equally important is to recognize that the Scriptures serve as the final authority, or "norming norm," governing the church's dialog.[8] This dialog is expressed in a variety

---

7. Barth, *God in Action*, 21–22.

8. Vanhoozer speaks to the role of both the church and the Scriptures noting, "While Scripture alone is the norming norm, catholicity—the scope of agreement about what Scripture teaches—is a helpful secondary normed norm insofar as it draws

of ways each of which is linked in some way to the Scriptures and none of which is comprehensive enough to express the full counsel of God.[9] Sermons, creeds, works of (Old Testament) theology, rituals, and even faithful Christian action are utterances of the church that become part of an imperfect, intergenerational, multiethnic dialog constituting the testimony of the church through the ages and around the globe.

The Church, the Academe, and Old Testament Theology

While it would be unfair to suggest that Old Testament theologians have done nothing to engage the church, more can always be done. Nondenominational, evangelical colleges and the academic work that takes place within them have often stood apart from denominational structures or local church bodies.[10] Mark Husbands notes, "As the history of Wheaton College illustrates. . .many evangelicals have been confessionally vague or even silent about the church—on occasion such neglect was deliberate; regardless, the ecclesiological vacuum has had severe consequences for subsequent generations of earnest, dutiful and intelligent Christians."[11] This ecclesiological vacuum will almost certainly hinder Old Testament theologians seeking to adapt to the concerns of a multiethnic church. Disconnection from local ecclesial concerns is somewhat mitigated by the participation of Old Testament theologians in those local bodies. Old Testament theologians teaching in the majority of colleges and seminaries in the United States and Europe will have less exposure to the concerns of the church in South America, Africa, China, and a host of other countries and contexts.

---

on the lived, Spirit-guided wisdom of the communion of saints, the whole people of God 'from every tribe and language and people and nation'" (Vanhoozer and Treier, *Theology and the Mirror of Scripture*, 126).

9. Kelsey's work points in this direction by highlighting the varying ways in which theologians use the Scriptures. Different types of biblical authority are used by different theologians suggesting that, in broader theological practice, there is no single concept of biblical authority (Kelsey, *Proving Doctrine*). Commenting on Kelsey's work, Vanhoozer notes, "Before using the Bible as authoritative, theologians make a judgment as to how the Bible will be brought to bear authoritatively: as doctrine, as myth, as history, as story, and so on . . . Kelsey's first achievement, then, is to have documented a number of different construals of Scripture, thus helping explain how the Bible is actually put to work as a theological authority" (Vanhoozer, *First Theology*, 29).

10. Old Testament theology done from within certain denominational frameworks may well have a stronger connection to a specific ecclesial body.

11. Husbands and Treier, *Community of the Word*, 10. Note the origin of Moody as described in George, *Guaranteed Pure*, as well as Hauerwas, *State of the University*, on the notion of the church community necessary to sustain the life of the mind in the university. Worthen, *Apostles of Reason* also has some interesting insights on this point.

In addition, the location of Old Testament scholarship within Western society has conditioned Old Testament theology toward more Western concerns. To some extent, this conditioning is appropriate given the context of most Old Testament theologians. It has, however, become more apparent that the context in which Old Testament theologians do their work is broader than the Western world. Old Testament theologians living in the West are not simply citizens of the United States, Britain, or Germany, but of the world. The growing awareness and increasing connection to the global church and the brothers and sisters in Christ who comprise it create a new environment in which the work of Old Testament theology is being done. This connection also represents an opportunity for Old Testament theology to listen differently to the word of God and to mine the Scripture for insights that may well have been hidden to Western eyes.

Certain aspects of evangelical history may also impede the development of a formative relationship between the field of Old Testament theology and the church. In *Guaranteed Pure*, Timothy George describes evangelicalism's shift away from a more "churchly orientation" toward a more individualistic notion of faith. This shift surely conditioned the de-centering of the church and tradition within evangelical thought.[12] The minimization of Christian identity rooted in the church "were orientations, not formal creeds." As George notes, "They comprised a set of starting assumptions that shaped religious belief and practice at a basic level."[13]

There certainly continue to be aspirations for stronger church-seminary partnerships. As Pamela Legg points out, "seminaries should be a major academic voice in the field and church, holding up the importance of Christian Education, exploring it in depth, offering new ideas for practitioners in the field, providing continuing education in the field for pastors and educators, and developing ongoing publications for academic engagement."[14] Such aspirations are certainly appropriate, yet within such aspirations, there does not appear to be a two-way influence between the church and the academe. The academic disciplines are not simply informing and influencing the church, but are being shaped by the church's diverse contexts and struggles. In other words, the academic disciplines do not stand alone.

12. George, *Guaranteed Pure*, 6.

13. Ibid.

14. Legg, "Work of Christian Education," 433. It is interesting to note that even in calling for greater engagement with the church, the academy's academic pursuits rise to the fore ignoring the actual participation of academic personnel in ministry as theologians on the front lines guiding from within the fray of ministry.

It is not as though the church and the academe have not sought to forge connections that would make the church an ever-present influence of academic life. Institutions of biblical and theological education have often been in the practice of hiring faculty members who are active members of a local congregation. Governing boards and institutional officers are also active in the church either professionally or as lay leaders. Admissions requirements for certain degree programs, like the Doctor of Ministry, often require applicants to have served in ministry prior to entry while others incorporate internship and practical ministry requirements to mitigate against graduating students with no sense of the church and its operations.

The strategies intended to retain a vital connection between academic institutions and church at large have generally been adapted to create or improve relationships with an increasingly multi-ethnic church. Diversifying governing boards, as well as faculty and student bodies, assumes, in part, that representation within an institution will provide the sort of connections needed to (re)orient the academe toward the perspectives and contexts of ethnic groups within the church. While increased diversity brings particular benefits to an institution and surely has a positive impact on a given institution's effectiveness in engaging a multi-ethnic church, such strategies may not address (1) the underlying dynamics of academia, (2) the relative rigidity of biblical and theological curricula and course content based on disciplinary norms, and (3) the sort of cultural capital valued in broader academic circles.

OLD TESTAMENT THEOLOGY AND
THE MULTI-ETHNIC CHURCH

For Old Testament theology to serve a multi-ethnic church in a more dynamic, embodied fashion, the church must exert a heavier influence on the academe to change the sort of capital valued within the academic field. As a field, Old Testament theology is in need of an ecclesially-oriented set of values that recognize Old Testament theology's situated nature within and for the church. More discrete local bodies and the broader body of Christ from around the world need to speak into the field of Old Testament theology to ensure that the field is not simply serving itself or a particular context, but is intentionally making space for those who would speak to the situation of specific local bodies around the world. In order to do so, it seems likely that the field of Old Testament theology will need to begin to view skills related to understanding contextual dynamics and the influence of historical, political, economic, and other factors on the life of the congregation as valuable forms of capital within Old Testament theology without allowing the norming norm of Scripture to fall from its place of primacy. In addition, the field of Old Testament theology will also likely need to begin to make room for the differing perspectives that will ultimately arise as the voices within Old Testament theology diversify.

In addition, Old Testament theology must consider the matter of distribution of theological scholarship and prestige within the academe. Western theological scholarship has most frequently been distributed through a process of peer reviewed academic journals, publishing houses, and presentation at theological society meetings, as well as the granting of doctoral degrees and the publication of dissertations. While teaching and Christian service are often taken into account in the evaluation of faculty, at many institutions, and within the scholarly guild more broadly, publication is an important measure of academic prowess. The fitness of these mechanisms for the development of a body of non-Western scholarship needs to be evaluated, particularly given the proliferation of more open, accessible platforms allowing electronic publication. Creating forums for scholarship that are influential in Old Testament theology, accessible to non-Western scholars, and utilized by students, faculty, ministry leaders, and interested lay leaders, will be essential if such scholars are to have a voice in shaping the field of Old Testament theology.

In developing a stronger focus on the church worldwide, the field of Old Testament theology may come to a greater awareness of its own contextual, situated nature. Old Testament theology is a field that exists within the context of global Christianity. While the history of Old Testament theology has been impacted by Western thinkers like Welhausen, Gunkel, Von Rad, and Childs, Old Testament theology is ultimately a field dedicated to hearing God through Scripture from and for particular ecclesial contexts. Old Testament theology is a field that exists to render intelligibly the God revealed in the Old Testament to the body of Christ while equipping the body of Christ with the resources to navigate faithfully the challenges life in a fallen world inevitably brings. In order to do so, Old Testament theology cannot be *constrained* by culturally situated patterns of thought, but must be open to the *incorporation* of such patterns of thought (whether Western or non-Western). Old Testament theology must seek out the wisdom of the church and its diverse members allowing that wisdom to reshape and refine the field of Old Testament theology.

Finally, the church must begin to recognize that service on governing boards, as administration or faculty, or otherwise participating in academic fields or institutions, is an act of service to the church. Churches would do well to support, guide, and engage those serving at Bible Colleges, Christian

Colleges and Universities, or Seminaries. At the same time, educational institutions need to encourage administration, faculty, and board members
to seek out the advice, counsel, and perceptions of the church and to allow such inputs to reshape institutional policy and practice, curriculum,
and other initiatives within the scope of the institution's mission. For Old
Testament theology (and Christian scholarship more generally) to flourish
as the non-Western church grows within a multiethnic world, the field of
Old Testament theology must develop a strong, reciprocal relationship with
local churches worldwide.

DISCUSSION QUESTIONS

1. What factors influence the way in which we read the Scriptures and
   develop theology from the Old Testament?

2. To what extent do factors related to an interpreter's background
   legitimately add to the development of Old Testament theology?
   What criteria might be used to determine whether one's background
   and experience are being used well in the interpretation of the Old
   Testament?

3. How might members of the church from different cultural contexts
   enhance the way the Old Testament is read?

BIBLIOGRAPHY AND RECOMMENDED READING

Barth, Karl. *God in Action: Theological Addresses.* Translated by E. G. Homrighausen
    and Karl J. Ernst. 1936. Reprint, Eugene, OR: Wipf & Stock, 2005.
Bourdieu, Pierre, and Loïc J. D. Wacquant. *An Invitation to Reflexive Sociology.* Chicago:
    University of Chicago Press, 1992.
Burt, Ronald S. *Brokerage and Closure: An Introduction to Social Capital.* Oxford:
    Oxford University Press, 2005.
George, Timothy F. W. *Guaranteed Pure: The Moody Bible Institute, Business, and the
    Making of Modern Evangelicalism.* Chapel Hill: University of North Carolina
    Press, 2015.
Hauerwas, Stanley. *The State of the University: Academic Knowledges and the Knowledge
    of God.* Illuminations—Theory and Religion. Malden, MA: Blackwell, 2007.
Husbands, Mark, and Daniel J. Trier. *The Community of the Word: Toward an Evangelical
    Ecclesiology.* Downers Grove, IL: InterVarsity, 2005.
Kelsey, David H. *Proving Doctrine: The Uses of Scripture in Modern Theology.* New York:
    T. & T. Clark, 1999.
Legg, Pamela M. "The Work of Christian Education in the Seminary and the Church:
    Then (1812) and Now (2012)." *Int* 66 (2012) 423–33.

Maton, Karl A. "A Question of Autonomy: Bourdieu's Field Approach and Policy in Higher Education." *JEP* 20 (2005) 687–704.

Vanhoozer, Kevin J. *The Drama of Doctrine: A Canonical Linguistic Approach to Christian Doctrine*. Louisville: Westminster John Knox, 2005.

———. *First Theology: God, Scripture and Hermeneutics*. Downers Grove, IL: InterVarsity, 2002.

Worthen, Molly. *Apostles of Reason: The Crisis of Authority in American Evangelicalism*. New York: Oxford University Press, 2014.

15

OLD TESTAMENT THEOLOGY
AND THE DIGITAL AGE

JAMES SPENCER

INTRODUCTION

Though scholars and thinkers differ in their opinions concerning the rise of digital natives and the benefits and drawbacks of digital technology use, it seems clear that the manner in which the internet and associated technologies are being used are influencing the way the next generation thinks and interacts.[1] As Marc Prensky notes, "research by social psychologists shows that people who grow up in different cultures do not just think about different things; they actually think differently."[2] The digital age has not only influenced the younger generations, but the cultural values and

---

1. "Digital natives" refers to those who have grown up exclusively in the era of digital technology. While writing one of the seminal works on the topic, Prensky notes, "as we move further into the 21st century when all will have grown up in the era of digital technology, the distinction between digital natives and digital immigrants will become less relevant" (Prensky, *From Digital Natives to Digital Wisdom*, 202).
2. Prensky, "Do They Really Think Differently?," 3.

behaviors tied to the use of technology are also requiring older generations to adapt and to think differently.[3]

Adapting to the digital world by changing the manner in which we think and interact has been met with a mixture of emotions ranging from lamentation to celebration. Some, if not most, thinkers have highlighted the potential negative impact of technology use though others desire a more balanced approach that retains the gains of the past while recognizing the gains of the future. Maryanne Wolf notes the similarity between the current transitions from a written to a digital culture and those from oral to written culture.[4] While recognizing the challenges that a digital shift bring, Wolf is less critical of that digital shift than she is concerned to preserve the benefits of a written culture.[5] Nicholas Carr is more critical of the digital shift, though he notes "you should be skeptical of my skepticism. Perhaps those who dismiss critics of the Internet as Luddites or nostalgists will be proved correct, and from our hyperactive, data-stoked minds will spring a golden age of intellectual discovery and universal wisdom."[6] While it is evident that Carr still has his doubts, other commentators take a more positive outlook on the potential benefits of technology for advancing human intelligence.

One such commentator is Clive Thompson who points to the use of technology in the world of chess moving from the initial defeat of grand masters by supercomputers to the eventual use of computer systems by human chess players to defeat the supercomputers. Thompson uses this latter event to illustrate the power and potential of human use of technology.[7] Others point to the more inherent advances in different forms of thinking skills such as those developed through "repeated exposure to computer games and other digital media," which are not as adequately developed through print media and linear thought processes.[8]

Whether this new rise of technology is bane, blessing, or something in between, it seems virtually impossible to avoid its influence. Given the brief sketch of opinions noted above concerning the way in which digital media

3. Kouloupoulos and Keldsen suggest that Generation Z be viewed "as a new set of behaviors and attitudes about how the world will work and how we will need to respond in order to stay current, competitive, and relevant . . . it doesn't matter when you were born, being part of Gen Z is a matter of adopting these behaviors" (Kouloupoulos and Keldsen, *The Gen Z Effect*, 4).

4. Wolf, *Proust and the Squid*, 69–72.

5. Ibid., 212ff.

6. Carr, "Is Google Making Us Stupid?"

7. Thompson, *Smarter Than You Think*.

8. Prensky, "Digital Natives, Digital Immigrants, Part II: Do They Really Think Differently?"

are influencing the manner in which we, particularly those among us who have grown up as "digital natives," think and act, it is important for those committed to the advancement of Old Testament theology to wrestle with the implications of the digital revolution for Old Testament theology.

INFORMATION AND OLD TESTAMENT THEOLOGY

The availability of vast amounts of information is one of the hallmarks of the digital age. Sifting through mountains of data on a daily basis can take its toll. We run the risk of "information overload" not because our brains get too full, but because our brains have difficulty processing, or prioritizing, the information. As Daniel Levitin notes,

> Our brains do have the ability to process the information we take in, but at a cost: We can have trouble separating the trivial from the important, and all this information processing makes us tired . . . Every status update you read on Facebook, every tweet or text message you get from a friend, is competing for resources in your brain with important things like whether to put your savings in stocks or bonds, where you left your passport, or how best to reconcile with a close friend you just had an argument with.[9]

The increase in information raises at least two potential challenges for Old Testament theology in the digital age.

First, the form of most Old Testament theology is not produced in a manner conducive to new media delivery systems such as Twitter, Instagram, Facebook, or even long form blogs or YouTube videos. Much of the audio and video content available online was produced for delivery in live classroom or conference venues, recorded, and then posted online. Compared to a TED Talk, a well-produced podcast, or even a home grown YouTube video or channel, Old Testament theology resources don't account fully for the habits of present-day media consumers.[10] Old Testament theology books (including the one you are reading right now) are generally written with a more academic readership in mind and, thus, conform to the style and form common within the guild.

Recognizing that the form of the Old Testament theology available online is not designed for the digital native, points to a second challenge, which is related to the purposes of Old Testament theology. If Old Testament

9. Levitin, *The Organized Mind*, 6–7.
10. Brandt, *The Rise of Writing*, 4.

theology is an activity intended to render God rightly from the Old Testament and to point the church to the Old Testament itself, shifts toward short form and visual media create an additional barrier for Old Testament theology. As Christians become more accustomed to assimilating information in a digital age, Old Testament theologians may need to adjust their own delivery to an audience that no longer has the inclination and/or capacity to sustain the sort of effort needed to read the Old Testament effectively. Biblical literacy in the digital age is not simply a matter of behavioral change. Instead, biblical literacy, like literacy more generally, is also influenced by the manner in which the "reading brain" is being displaced in the digital age.

Before the invention of the printing press and the widespread growth of societal literacy, much of the church could not have read the Scriptures even if they could have gained access to a printed Bible. The church may be entering a time in which the sort of literacy necessary to read the Scriptures cannot be assumed to be present and so may need to rethink the manner in which Scripture is taught.[11] This is not to say that the church should give up on asking individual believers to read the printed word. Bible reading in the digital age will, however, require the church to address both the discipline and capacity of individuals to read the Scriptures.

For instance, Patricia Greenfield notes, "Although the visual capabilities of television, video games, and the Internet may develop impressive visual intelligence, the cost seems to be deep processing: mindful knowledge acquisition, inductive analysis, critical thinking, imagination, and reflection."[12] More recent research on neuroplasticity suggests that the brain changes through a variety of stages including early childhood, adolescence, parenthood, and old age.[13] Far from being static, the brain is in regular flux, particularly in response to "learning, memory, and other experiences" which "probably produce widespread patterns of synaptic modification throughout entire networks of neurons in particular regions of the brain, depending on the type of experience."[14] One such experience that has been noted quite frequently is the potential impact of digital media and the internet on the brain. Nicholas Carr has been one of the more prolific critics of the digital age and the relatively unreflective manner in which it has been embraced: "What we're trading away in return for the riches of the Net. . .is what Karp

11. Wolf's treatment of the reading brain highlights the manner in which different activities impact the formation of the human brain (Wolf, *Proust and the Squid*). More recent work on neuroplasticity also suggests that adult brains are not immune. See Costandi, *Neuroplasticity*.

12. Greenfield, "Technology and Informal Education," 70.

13. Costandi, *Neuroplasticity*, 125–42.

14. Ibid., 66.

calls 'our old linear thought process.' Calm, focused, undistracted, the linear mind is being pushed aside by a new kind of mind that wants and needs to take in and dole out information in short, disjointed, often overlapping bursts."[15]

The digital age is raising questions concerning the human brain's ability to sustain modes of thought associated with "deep attention" while seeking to cope with and/or benefit from the Internet, which promotes "hyper attention."[16] Those interested in biblical literacy, as Old Testament theologians likely are, must take into account the challenges of cultivating sustained, deep thinking in relation to any topic, including Old Testament theology, in the digital age. While it is surely appropriate to suggest, as Berding seems to do at points, that reading the Scriptures is a matter of Christian discipline, we cannot neglect the shifts occurring in the professional and personal lives of believers that work to diminish the sort of thinking skills that are needed to reflect deeply on the Scriptures.[17]

OLD TESTAMENT THEOLOGY IN AN AGE OF ACCESS

Concerns about the written, or creative, side of literacy must also be added to the concerns about reading. Individuals and groups enjoy an unprecedented ability to publish personal blogs, launch podcasts, post videos on YouTube, Tweet, or garner support for biblically related projects via crowdsourcing sites like Kickstarter.com. Each of these platforms, and many others, provides the means for individuals to produce fresh works of biblical interpretation without jumping through the more traditional "hoops" like working with a publisher or submitting to a peer reviewed journal. In a way similar to the impact the invention of the printing press had on the accessibility of information and the expansion of reading literacy, the development of free online platforms have allowed individuals to produce and publish virtually infinite varieties of content for public consumption.

Andrew Keen laments the marginalization of "cultural gatekeepers" who "are necessary to help us to sift through what's important and what's not, what is credible from what is unreliable, what is worth spending our time on as opposed to the white noise that can be safely ignored."[18] Without the gatekeepers, individual readers must take on the responsibility of

15. Carr, *The Shallows*, 10.

16. For the distinction between deep and hyper attention, see Hayles, "Hyper and Deep Attention," 187–99.

17. Berding, *Bible Revival*.

18. Keen, *The Cult of the Amateur*, 45.

discerning the wheat from the chaff. Biblical literacy in the digital age will not only need to attend to understanding the biblical text, but to evaluating and making sense of the various interpretations of the biblical text and theological reflections on contemporary events offered online. Biblical literacy will increasingly need to intersect with information literacy. As the number of individuals commenting on Scripture and current events and issues increases, individual Christians and the church as a whole will need to learn well to discern the extent to which a particular voice represents a valid biblical and theological perspective.

Developing information literacy skills is complicated by the sheer volume of the material available and by the ways in which that material is organized. Social media, Google Books, and some Bible software programs are organized to allow for topical, key word, and affiliation searches that connect a variety of texts. More organic and, some would argue, more pernicious are the search filters that large search engines such as Google utilize to personalize search results.[19] These organizational strategies requires an expansion of informational literacy skills for users who must determine whether (a) the connections made are appropriate connections or (b) whether there are additional connections that might be significant, but not appearing in the search.

As Old Testament theologians think about both the ability to distribute and access information in the digital age, it will be important to recognize the potential drawbacks and benefits of such distribution and access. It is difficult to imagine that highly academic works of Old Testament theology will gain the sort of widespread readership that would provide a platform to influence broader Christian conversations, particularly if concerns about the loss of "deep attention" have any validity. Instead, short-form print, videos, and other such media will likely continue to be more widely consumed and serve as a means of shaping public and Christian opinion. Old Testament theologians will need to cultivate a viable, influential presence in the new media space while continuing to call the church back to deep reading of the Scriptures in print.[20]

19. Pariser, *The Filter Bubble*.

20. Baron argues for the importance of haptics for reading calling attention to both the emotive aspects of reading a book in physical form versus reading an e-book. See Baron, *Words Onscreen*, 139–49.

ADAPTING OLD TESTAMENT THEOLOGY
FOR THE DIGITAL AGE

If there is indeed potential for Old Testament theologians to have dimin-
ished influence in the digital age, it seems necessary for those within the
field to adapt in order to reach a digital generation more effectively. This
strategy cannot be boiled down to a focus on the number of retweets, likes,
or shares of a particular post. Defining influence solely in terms of volume
of distribution would seem to undercut Old Testament theology. Old Testament theology, by its very nature, assumes a deep reading of the Old Testament. At the same time, it seems unwise for Old Testament theologians to
maintain an isolationist mentality remaining cloistered in academic journals and societies or academic works. Instead, scholars would do well to
cultivate a clear understanding of media ecology, the way in which various
media fit within the broader ecosystem, and what different forms of media
require of those who engage with them.[21]

Suggesting that Old Testament theologians begin utilizing new media
outlets does not mean that the media used previously should be abandoned.
Old Testament theologians are in the business of communicating God's
word and equipping others to do the same. The vision is not to eliminate
highly academic works or to have Old Testament scholars abandon their
classrooms to become full-time bloggers. Instead, the idea is to participate
in new forms of societal discourse and to be Old Testament theologians in
the public square recognizing that the next generation of men and women
may well be less than likely or less than prepared to read academic works,
sit in a seminary classroom, or even attend a Sunday service. As the way
in which individuals consume content changes, Old Testament theologians
may well need to become savvy in the use of varied media to lead people into
the text of Scripture and toward an understanding of more robust theology.

CONCLUSION

It is certainly lamentable that believers do not spend more time reading
the word of God. It is also concerning that the increasing amount of information accessible with the tap of a finger threatens to crowd out time
that might otherwise be dedicated to reading the Scriptures. While it may

---

21. Commenting the relation between old and new media, Logan notes, "Understanding the interaction of a medium with other media has always been an important
part of the approach McLuhan pioneered, which is at the heart of media ecology. Understanding these interactions becomes even more critical with 'new media'" (Logan,
Understanding New Media, 8).

be possible to return to the golden age (if ever one truly existed) in which Christians read their Bible, memorized the word, and had conversations about the Scriptures, there are other avenues that might be explored. Turning the so-called distractions of social media and the internet into vehicles for compelling communications that will drive individuals toward deeper readings of Scripture and explorations into theology represents a very real opportunity for Old Testament theologians.[22]

We are entering an age in which the availability of the biblical text, commentaries, biblical and theological books, audio and video lectures, and bible study tools are sufficient to allow individual access to the Scriptures. Given the ongoing issue of biblical literacy and the ever-increasing volume of content available online, accessibility of content does not appear to be a significant factor in improving biblical literacy. What remains to be seen is whether a different orientation toward content, or a different means of content delivery, might have an impact and, if so, what impact it might have. Adapting the way Old Testament theology is conceived and communicated within a more participatory culture may have more positive results on biblical literacy than seeking to inspire individuals to read the Scriptures in print-based formats alone.[23] In the end, such adaptation, whatever forms it may take, must be judged, must remain faithful to the God who has revealed himself through the biblical text and communicate well God's word to God's people and to a watching world.

DISCUSSION QUESTIONS

1. How might the internet and the way that information is disseminated in a digital world impact biblical literacy?

2. How might Old Testament theologians become more influential through the use of new media? Are there any examples of Old Testament theologians using media effectively?

3. In what ways can Old Testament theologians balance the need for "deep thinking" with the realities of communicating information in today's world?

22. Note Dowling's more optimistic account of the possibility of deep reading in online environments within the context of participatory, discussion-based communities in Dowling, "Escaping the Shallows." While the internet has certainly changed individual reading habits, it is important to recognize that, despite the current trends, deep reading in the online environment is possible.

23. Note the model and accompanying examples and analysis in Jenkins and Kelley, *Reading in a Participatory Culture*.

BIBLIOGRAPHY AND RECOMMENDED READING

Baron, Naomi S. *Words Onscreen: The Fate of Reading in a Digital World*. New York: Oxford University Press, 2015.

Berding, Kenneth. *Bible Revival: Recommitting Ourselves to One Book*. Wooster, OH: Weaver, 2013.

Brandt, Deborah. *The Rise of Writing: Redefining Mass Literacy*. Cambridge: Cambridge University Press, 2015.

Carr, Nicholas. "Is Google Making Us Stupid?" In *The Composition of Everyday Life*, edited by John Mauk and John Metz, 355–62. Boston: Cengage Learning, 2016.

———. *The Shallows: What the Internet Is Doing to Our Brains*. New York: Norton 2011.

Costandi, Moheb. *Neuroplasticity*. MIT Press Essential Knowledge Series. Cambridge, MA: MIT Press, 2016.

Dowling, David. "Escaping the Shallows: Deep Reading's Revival in the Digital Age." *DHQ* 8 (2014). http://www.digitalhumanities.org/dhq/vol/8/2/000180/000180.html.

Greenfield, Patricia M. "Technology and Informal Education: What Is Taught, What Is Learned." *Science* 2 (2009) 69–71.

Hayles, Katherine H. "Hyper and Deep Attention: The Generational Divide in Cognitive Modes." *Profession* 13 (2007) 187–99.

Jenkins, Henry and Kelley, Wyn. *Reading in a Participatory Culture: Remixing Moby Dick in the English Classroom*. New York: Teachers College Press, 2013.

Keen, Andrew. *The Cult of the Amateur: How Blogs, MySpace, YouTube, and the Rest of Today's User-Generated Media Are Destroying Our Economy, Our Culture, and Our Values*. New York: Doubleday, 2008.

Koulopoulos, Tom, and Dan Keldsen. *The Gen Z Effect: The Six Forces Shaping the Future of Business*. New York: Bibliomotion, 2014.

Levitin, Daniel J. *The Organized Mind: Thinking Straight in the Age of Information Overload*. New York: Penguin, 2014.

Logan, Roberk K. *Understanding New Media: Extending Marshall McLuhan*. New York: Lang, 2010.

Pariser, Eli. *The Filter Bubble: How the New Personalized Web is Changing What We Read and How We Think*. New York: Penguin, 2012.

Prensky, Marc R. *From Digital Natives to Digital Wisdom: Hopeful Essays for 21st Century Learning*. Thousand Oaks, CA: Corwin, 2012.

———. "Digital Natives, Digital Immigrants, Part II: Do They Really Think Differently?" *On the Horizon* 9 (2001) 1–6.

Thompson, Clive. *Smarter Than You Think: How Technology Is Changing Our Minds for the Better*. New York: Penguin, 2013.

Wolf, Maryanne. *Proust and the Squid: The Story and Science of the Reading Brain*. New York: HarperCollins, 2007.

16

CONCLUSION
Methods for Biblical Interpretation

BRYAN C. BABCOCK

INTRODUCTION

Throughout this book we unpacked and explored several major themes in the Old Testament. To accomplish this task we completed an in-depth analysis of key passages and then demonstrated that the theme of each passage was developed and supported throughout the Old Testament and into the New Testament. Our study had two underlying goals: first, we wanted to help readers better understand the unity of the Bible, and second, we hoped to illuminate the methodology necessary for sound biblical inter-pretation (called *hermeneutics*).

In this final chapter we will outline our second goal about the process of biblical interpretation into twelve steps. The intent is to help the reader understand how to complete the task of interpretation and identify the meaning that God desired when inspiring the original author. Before we discuss the actual method of hermeneutics, we will first unpack it's meaning.

WHAT IS HERMENEUTICS?

Hermeneutics is defined as the art and science of biblical interpretation. The *science* of hermeneutics provides concrete methods of study that may easily be applied to any sort of literature. The *art* of hermeneutics requires more creativity. While the science of interpretation constrains this creativity, it must be allowed to play a significant role in the interpretive process.

In addition to art and science, which may be applied to non-Christian texts as well as to Scripture, there is also a spiritual component that, along with various other characteristics of Scripture, differentiates the practice of Christian hermeneutics from any other hermeneutic.

Hermeneutics is a transformative discipline whereby we open ourselves up to change. As William Klein states, "Any type of oral or written communication involves three expressions of meaning. (1) what the speaker or writer meant by what he or she said; (2) what the recipient actually understood by the statement; and (3) in some abstract sense, what meaning is actually encoded in the text or utterance itself."[1]

The methodology used in this book was designed to explore all three of these expressions of meaning with the scientific, artistic, and spiritual methodologies in mind. For the purposes of this book, our primary concern is what the biblical writer meant by what was recorded in the Bible.

The technical side is most evident in the use of the historical-grammatical approach to interpreting Scripture. This approach requires one to study words and clauses, to evaluate discourse, to delve into historical and cultural backgrounds, and to attend to genre and form.

In his 1947 book *The Idea of a University*, John Howard Newman states that the goal of a university education is "to open the mind, to correct it, to refine it, to enable it to know, and to digest . . . to give it application."[2] In this spirit, we encourage that your interpretations engage with diverse viewpoints in order to develop a significant biblical research tool: the ability to engage opinions different from your own to:

- understand them intellectually,

- evaluate them critically,

- and encounter them graciously.

One of the most important lessons you can learn as an interpreter is humility. As we come to another's work we must recognize that they are, like us, flawed. While we recognize those flaws, we should also engage them

---

1. William, *Introduction to Biblical Interpretation*, 8.
2. Newman, *Idea of a University*, 108.

in dialogue as we attempt to understand their positions and point of view. This sort of engagement will often help us to better understand ourselves, our beliefs, and our God.

The artistic movement of interpretation is more ambiguous than the technical side. This aspect includes the development of understanding. It will often require you to make difficult decisions about the meaning of words, the connections between phrases, and how a given passage relates to its historical-cultural background.

This artistic movement also includes the application of passages to various situations. Here you will be asked to interpret not only the biblical text, but life situations. The application of Scripture cannot be separated from the hermeneutical task. As Ernst Käsemann notes, "in the bodily obedience of the Christian, carried out as the service of God in the world of everyday, the lordship of Christ finds visible expression, and only when this visible expression takes personal shape in our lives, does the whole thing become credible as Gospel message."[3]

Last, but certainly not least, is the *spiritual movement*. Allowing the Spirit to engage in the process of interpretation is an indispensable part of interpretation. It will be important for you to engage in Christian practices that will help you experience God and to pull away from your own sinful habits. You will be asked to *recondition* your habits in order to more effectively hear the God who speaks in and through the biblical text.

HOW TO ANALYZE A BIBLICAL PASSAGE

The goal of building a methodology is to create "a careful system of hermeneutics [that] provides the means for the interpreter to arrive at the text's intention, to understand what God intended to communicate through human minds and hands."[4] To accomplish this task we need to complete several steps that help to ensure that we are minimizing our personal bias and truly exploring the meaning that God intended. The twelve steps below provide a starting point for sound biblical interpretation, and we hope that the described methodology helps you recreate the type of analysis found in this book.

Before we begin describing the methodology, let's spend a moment on our assumptions for the process of biblical interpretation. First, "the Bible is the inspired (God-breathed) Word of God and is therefore inerrant, infallible, clear, sufficient and authoritative in all the matters it addresses. The

3. Käsemann, "Apocalyptic," 135.
4. Klein, *Introduction to Biblical Interpretation*, 19.

crucial job of the interpreter of Scripture is to arrive at the meaning God intended when He breathed out Scripture through the human author. The meaning is single, definite and fixed."[5]

Second, the plain sense of Scripture is to be used when interpreting. "It is God who desired to give man his Word. He gave us his Word in order to communicate, not confound. We should seek to understand that communication plainly, for that is the normal way beings communicate."[6] The plain sense takes into account figures of speech, poetic language, and literary form.

Third, Scripture should be used to interpret Scripture since the Bible is its own best interpreter. Any conclusion regarding the meaning of a text that contradicts another passage of the Bible is *always* incorrect. This is one of the reasons that the prior chapters explore the interpretive conclusions throughout the balance of the Old Testament and into the New Testament.

Fourth, God's revelation of truth to mankind is progressive in nature. "To be able to consistently interpret plainly, it is imperative to recognize that revelation was given progressively. This means that in the process of revealing his message to humanity, God may add or even change in one era what he gave in another."[7] The interpreter must therefore understand that historical narrative is only *one part* of God's overall revelation. In determining application, one must keep in mind that revelation in the Old Testament may be changed by revelation in the New Testament.

Given the above assumptions, in the discussion below we can now provide an overview of the hermeneutic process.

Step One: Prayer

Prior to entering into a study of God's Word, it is important to prepare yourself through prayer. The goal of biblical interpretation is to uncover God's desired meaning and not the thoughts, biases, or desires of our own minds. The ministry of the Holy Spirit enables believers to understand the truth of the Bible (John 16:12–15; 1 Cor 2:9–16). Prayer evidences a humble and dependent reliance on God to open the interpreter's mind, eyes, and heart to his Word. In Ps 119:18 David prays, "Open my eyes that I may see wonderful things in your law."[8] After his resurrection, Jesus appeared to his disciples and "opened their minds so they could understand the Scriptures"

5. "Chicago Statement on Biblical Hermeneutics," 398.

6. Ryrie, *Basic Theology*, 131.

7. Ibid., 130.

8. All translations are original unless otherwise noted.

(Luke 24:45). Paul's prayer for the Ephesians is "that the God of our Lord Jesus Christ, the glorious Father may give you the Spirit of wisdom and revelation, so that you may know him better. I pray also that the eyes of your heart may be enlightened in order that you may know the hope to which he has called you, the riches of his glorious inheritance in the saints, and his incomparably great power for us who believe" (Eph 1:17–19). Paul is clear that divine enablement is needed to know God better. Therefore, prayer is the vital first step to any interpretation of Scripture.

Step Two: Read the Passage in Multiple Translations

This is accomplished in two ways. First, re-read the passage several times in your personal Bible. Read slowly and pay attention to punctuation, any important phrases, and repeated words. Then read the entire chapter where your passage is located. Note if any of the key phrases or repeated words from your passage are also found in the balance of the chapter. While reading the text, it is imperative that the interpreter "listens as carefully and competently as possible to the biblical witness, to use every available means to discover its truth claims by approaching the text as fairly as possible on its own terms and in view of its context."[9]

Second, pick several other translations and note where they differ.[10] Read parallel or complementary accounts of the narrative if available. For example, some narratives in Samuel or Kings have parallel or complementary accounts in Chronicles. Note the differences and similarities between these accounts. Begin to form questions to answer in your later research. For instance, how do the differences and similarities affect the meaning of my text?

Step Three: Review the Immediate Context of the Passage

Look carefully at the preceding verses and chapters. What events have preceded the present narrative? When the original author wrote the book (or chapter), to whom was he writing? What questions were they asking him? What was he trying to tell them? For instance, the first five books of the Bible were written by Moses to a group of people who left Egypt and were about to enter Canaan—a land promised to them by God. Therefore, we need to keep in mind that the book of Genesis is an etiology explaining who

---

9. Long, *Art of Biblical History*, 185.

10. A useful online tool is found at: www.biblegateway.com.

the Israelites are and how they initially arrive in Egypt. Understanding the immediate context of the book often helps us better understand the passage.

In addition, we want to determine where the present narrative falls in the timeline of the entire book. Look for recurring themes. How does the present narrative fit into the structure the author used to convey his purpose? Taking time to understand the overall "plot" of the story helps us understand the "scene—"essentially, seeing the forest and not getting lost in a grove of trees.

Step Four: Analyze the Meaning of Key Words

Word studies help us to determine the original meaning of a word in its context. Word studies should be performed:

- when you don't know or are uncertain about a word's meaning,
- when a word is particularly significant within a given passage,
- when you need to differentiate between two or more words in a passage (e.g., synonyms),
- when you are comparing the use of a word in two particular passages,
- when you need to clarify a passage that is unclear, and
- when different translations use different words to render the meaning of a given Greek or Hebrew word.

Note words that are unclear, repeated, unique, or theological. Are there words or phrases that contain a deeper meaning or fuller sense (*sensus plenior*) intended by God but not intended by the human author? Word studies are completed through the use concordances and can be completed using online tools.[11] Look for how the same Hebrew word is translated in other passages. This will help you understand the range of meaning and add a depth of understanding for your translation.

Seek to understand how the word is used elsewhere in the same book, other books with the same author, the rest of Old Testament, and in the New Testament. You might consult a Bible that cross references words or phrases. Be careful to note any additional insights this review provides. Note if there are other verses in the Bible that illuminate the present verse or narrative.

---

11. Online Concordance resources include: http://biblehub.com; and http://www.biblestudytools.com/concordances/. A concordance is an index that lists the various occurrences of a given word. Be sure to use an exhaustive concordance, which lists every occurrence of a given word.

Step Five: Explore the Grammar and Literary Genre

Understanding the genre of you passage is essential to understanding the meaning. If the passage is poetry, then we are likely to find vivid imagery, hyperbole, and metaphors. To take this poetic language literally would result in poor conclusions. Likewise, if the passage is narrative we need to determine whether it is a report, heroic narrative, prophet story, comedy, farewell speech, etc. Each of these have their own guidelines for grammar construction and each contains different types of information. Examine the literary components of setting, time, plot, and characterization. If this is an historical narrative, then we would want to focus on the life of the main character. We might then ask: How does the hero's life model a relationship with God and with other people? And what aspects of the original reader's worldview does it seek to critique or discredit? What values [does the] hero represent?

Be careful to note what the author is not saying. What details of the story have not been divulged? Why? How does the absence of certain details magnify the purpose and/or meaning of the text? Examine the perspective of the author or narrator. While the narrator is always omniscient, does he tell us everything, or must we be content with a limited knowledge of characters' thoughts and intentions? Does the narrator move in and out of time and space, or is the plot sequential in time? What was the narrator's intent or purpose in writing? Does the narrator insert his own observations or knowledge into the narrative?

Louis Berkhof notes that the biblical interpreter "must place himself on the standpoint of the author, and seek to enter into his very soul, until he, as it were, lives his life and thinks his thoughts. This means that he will have to guard carefully against the rather common mistake of transferring the author to the present day and making him speak the language of the twentieth century."[12]

Once you identify the genre of the passage, do some research to understand the guidelines for writing this genre in the first millennium BC. This time will be well spent as it will help to identify what items the author meant literally and which might be figurative or poetic.

Step Six: Research the Historical Context of the Passage

Understanding the historical context of the passage is truly central to understanding each passage. As an example, Ezekiel writes during the time of

---

12. Berkhof, *Principles of Biblical Interpretation*, 115.

the Babylonian exile. By understanding that Ezekiel (along with Isaiah and Jeremiah) lived during a time of extreme upheaval when people thought God had abandoned his people places the prophecies into perspective. Finally, Ezekiel's message is split between the impending wrath of God on the people of Judah and the future grace of God providing restoration. Understanding the historical events surrounding the time of the writing of the books adds perspective to the interpretation.

The first step in uncovering the historical context is to look within the Bible itself to determine the historical background of the narrative. "The principal resources for the historical interpretation of Scripture are found in the Bible itself."[13] The historical narratives are built on the foundation of the Pentateuch. "The Pentateuch contains much cultural background for the rest of the Bible."[14] It is essential that the interpreter becomes familiar with the whole Bible. "The more you are familiar with the whole Bible, the more you will have background knowledge to help you in interpretation."[15]

The next step is to analyze the historical, geographical, cultural, political, and religious components of the passage. Study aids such as a Bible dictionary, commentaries, cultural commentaries, and Bible atlases are helpful in this process. Questions to consider are: What is the historical context of the narrative? What geographical features exist in the narrative and how does understanding them illuminate the text? How does the culture of the ancient Near East affect my understanding of the text? "We are not to assume that what seems obvious to us as modern people is necessarily the meaning of the passage when seen in its total historical and literary context."[16]

When analyzing the political component, "the expositor should inform himself respecting the political organization of the nations that play an important part in it. Their national history, their relations with other nations, and their political institutions should be made the object of careful study. Particular attention must be devoted to the political changes in the national life of Israel."[17] It is also important for the interpreter to understand the present spiritual condition of Israel in the narrative. "The religious life of Israel did not always move on the same plane, was not always characterized by true spirituality. There were seasons of spiritual elevation, but these were soon followed by periods of moral and religious degradation."[18]

13. Ibid., 128.

14. Sterrett, *How to Understand Your Bible*, 80.

15. Ibid.

16. Long, *The Art of Biblical History*, 124.

17. Berkhof, *Principles of Biblical Interpretation*, 121.

18. Ibid., 123.

Finally, we should examine the perspective of the original hearers or readers of the narrative. "An intimate knowledge of the original readers will often illumine the pages of a writing addressed to them in an unexpected and striking manner."[19] What situation were the original hearers in? What would the narrative have meant to the original hearers or readers of the text?

Step Seven: Complete Research of Secondary Sources

Now that we understand the text in its context, we want to see what other scholars might have to add to our analysis. The study of the passage should include the review of several reputable commentaries or articles to glean additional insights into the meaning of the text. Some excellent commentary series include: Word Biblical Commentary, Apollos Old Testament Commentary, Expositors Bible Commentary, NIVAC, New International Commentary on the Old Testament, The Story of God Bible Commentary, and The Old Testament Library. Other excellent resources are: *The Bible Knowledge Commentary*, the *Believer's Bible Commentary*, *Anchor Bible Dictionary*, and *The Moody Bible Atlas*. Finally, don't forget to review some pastoral series like the MacArthur Bible Commentary and sermons by John Piper and John MacArthur.

As you explore what others write about your passage, see if they are asking the same questions you asked. Use their footnotes and endnotes to find more information. See if the theological conclusions of the pastor or commentary author agree or disagree with your faith tradition. If they are different, take the time to understand their point of view. Be sure to include some of the most insightful comments as quotes in your study. This lets your reader know what other scholars have to say and that you have done your background research!

Keep in mind that no one person has the correct interpretation of everything all the time. Consulting the interpretations of several scholars and/or pastors is advisable. Consult sources from church history. How has the narrative been interpreted traditionally throughout church history?

Step Eight: Analyze the Meaning of the Passage as Intended by the Original Author

Now it is time to bring steps 1–7 together and write a summary of the meaning of the passage. At this point in the analysis I stop and think about

19. Ibid., 125.

everything I have read and studied. Then I attempt to write a one sentence statement of the "big idea" of the passage. What is God trying to communicate to the original audience (not me—that comes later). "[A]ll the component parts of the narrative can work together to impress upon the reader a single major point. There is an overall drift or movement to a narrative, a kind of superstructure that makes the point, usually a single point."[20]

After identifying the big idea, write a few paragraphs summarizing the historical context of the passage, the author, and overall intent of the book. The study should then dive deeper into each verse of the passage. The review of each verse in the passage should include a paraphrase, where necessary, to illuminate its meaning in modern English. The analysis should conclude with a paragraph summarizing the big idea and supporting points. Think of this phase of the analysis as the point to take all your research and create a summary of your findings.

Step Nine: Explore the Identified Meaning in the Balance of the Old Testament

Having already analyzed the immediate context of the narrative within its book, determine the larger context of the passage in its relationship to the balance of the Old Testament. How does the present narrative contribute to the overall message of the Bible? Once you have identified the big idea, review other passages that mention, illustrate, or expand upon the same theme.

Through an analysis of similar biblical passages we can better understand God's working in the lives of his people over the course of time. We can see that God is unchanging and his message is unchanging. We are also better able to understand our initial passage through the lens of other passages. Keep asking what God is trying to communicate through these accounts.

Step Ten: Determine How This Theme Continues into the New Testament

Similar to step 9, we now turn to see if the theme of our passage is present in the New Testament. All too often Christians feel that the God of the New Testament and the God of the Old Testament are somehow different. Or that the Old and New Testaments offer a different message. This stage of the analysis helps us demonstrate that God exists in both testaments and that

20. Fee, *How to Read the Bible for All Its Worth*, 77.

his message is the same. The trajectories begun in Genesis continue through Revelation. By continuing our analysis into the New Testament, we are able to see the culmination of God's plan in Christ. This brings the exegetical analysis to completion.

Step Eleven: Develop a Theological Interpretation

Fee observes that "God is the hero of all biblical narratives."[21] Therefore, we now need to reflect upon the lasting takeaways from the passage within the context of the Bible. We should ask, what does the narrative reveal about God and His character or nature? To answer this question we can reflect upon the analysis illuminating facts in the passage that may have a typological significance. A type always prefigures some future reality. As such, are there events in the narrative that prefigure a future reality? We should also analyze Christological components of the narrative, if any are present. How do the events of the narrative point to the redemptive work or person of Christ?

Answering these questions allows us the opportunity to see if any universal (or theological) truths are found in our passage and confirmed in other supporting passages.

Step Twelve: Reflect upon Applications for the Modern Church

In keeping with Scripture's own stated purpose in 2 Tim 3:16–17, how does the passage teach, rebuke, correct, or train us in righteous living? Remember that Old Testament narratives do not always teach directly. "Do not be a monkey-see-monkey-do reader of the Bible."[22] The narratives tell a truthful story of how God acted in the lives of specific people during specific events in history. These events are unrepeatable. The interpreter should not assume that God expects us to do the same thing the Bible characters did.

When determining an application to a biblical passage, focus on what the passage teaches about the character and nature of God, since God never changes (Mal 3:6, Heb 13:8). What does this narrative teach that is truthful about God? In light of this truth about God and his nature, how should I respond to him? What does the narrative teach that is true about human nature? How has this narrative affected me personally? In light of Jas 1:22, how should I, or others, think or act differently based on the lesson of the narrative?

---

21. Ibid., 78.
22. Ibid., 85.

Long finds that "the biblical texts are more likely to yield their fruits when approached from various angles with a diversity of questions in mind."[23] In the same way, the twelve steps noted above probe the narrative from diverse angles in order to sharpen understanding. Interpreters of the Bible set out on an amazing journey designed to understand the singular meaning God intended when he breathed out Scripture through the original human author and how that meaning applies to our modern context. With God's help, much study of the Word, and the integration of principles of interpretation, we all should strive to be an interpreter "who correctly handles the word of truth" (2 Tim 2:15).

CONCLUSION: BIBLICAL TRAJECTORIES

As students of Scripture, we need to remember that interpretation is not a task that simply seeks a destination, but it is one that follows a particular path. As interpreters, we should be enjoying the trip. At the same time, we don't ignore the destination. We don't blindly follow any path that happens to be in front of us.

The title of this conclusion is "Interpretive Trajectories" rather than "Interpretive Destinations" for a reason. Interpretation is not concerned with reaching a destination with no regard to the journey it takes to get there, nor is it concerned with a journey that leads nowhere. Interpretation is concerned with purposeful, deliberate movement. It is concerned with an interpretive trajectory.

The trajectory of biblical interpretation points toward transformation. The biblical text stands as a witness calling humanity away from what it is and toward what it should be. The Bible does not ask us to leave the world behind, but to be different within it. It does not affirm us but rather challenges us to walk in a manner worthy of our calling.

In a process that is generally referred to as the hermeneutical spiral, interpreters read the text as they interact with the Spirit, other believers, and our life experiences. The diagrams below conceptualizes the relationship between the interpreter, the text, and the world. Though diagrams are often too simplistic, we hope that these will be useful as you think about interpretive trajectories.

The first concept is a circle. We begin by looking at the biblical text as a whole. We analyze the text and explore each part of the passage under study. After the analysis, we synthesize the pieces with a better understanding of the whole (see chart below). This creates a circle of analysis.

23. Long, *The Art of Biblical History*, 122.

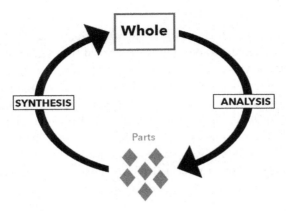

Our interpretation only begins with this initial circle. Grant Osborne writes that "biblical interpretation entails a 'spiral' from text to context, from its original meaning to its contextualization or significance for the church today . . . A 'spiral' is not a closed circle but rather an open-ended movement from the horizon of the text to the horizon of the reader."[24]

As such, our level of understanding increases with each repetition of this circle. The entry point is our preconceptions and preunderstandings of the passage and the Bible.[25] We then confront those preconceptions by examining the historical context, genre, grammar, context. Once the exegetical examination is complete we can then bring the passage back together as a whole with a deeper understanding. The spiral continues by repeating the cycle but now exploring new questions from biblical theology, systematic theology, and homiletics.

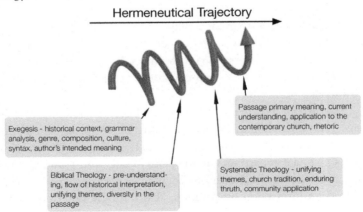

24. Osborne, *The Hermeneutical Spiral*, 6.

25. Duvall and Hays argue that we should hold on to our preunderstandings. Duvall, *Grasping God's Word*, 137–46.

Osborne argues that a spiral of interpretation is needed because "the sacred author's intended meaning is the critical starting-point, but not an end in itself. The task of hermeneutics must begin with exegesis, but is not complete until one notes the contextualization of that meaning for today."[26]

When we approach a passage, we should find ourselves confirming, questioning, or modifying our understanding of the text. This interaction with the Bible is followed by critical reflection on the Text in Community (TiC). Our reflection involves prayer and conversation with other believers about the passage. As we reflect critically on the text, we continue to Experience God in our lives (EG) by striving to live in accordance with his word.[27]

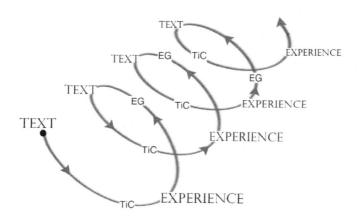

Ultimately, we return to the passage in order to hear God's voice again. As we visit the text this time, we have been changed by the sanctifying work of the Spirit, by our conversations with others, by our experiences, and by our reflection upon them. We approach the text with a new posture and a new outlook.

Osborne cautions that "doctrines should not be built upon a single passage, but rather should summarize all that Scripture says on that topic. If there are no clarifying passages (for example, on baptism for the dead in 1 Cor. 15:29 or a compartmentalized Hades in Luke 16:22–26), we must be careful about seeing a statement of dogma."[28] Osborne clarifies this point even more in his section on parables: "Do not base doctrines upon the

---

26. Ibid.

27. The abbreviations RT and RE follow Osborne.

28. Ibid., 11.

parables without checking corroborative details elsewhere. For instance, the parable of the rich man and Lazarus (Luke 16:19–31) is often taken as proof of a compartmentalized Hades. However, such a doctrine is not found in Jesus' teaching in Luke, and indeed nowhere else in Scripture. Therefore, the setting of the parable in Hades is local color rather than dogma and cannot be pressed too far."[29]

As we continue this sort of process throughout our lives and allow the Spirit to transform us into people who are growing in holiness:

- We will be able to hear God's voice in the text with greater accuracy and depth.
- We will be better able to stand as witnesses to a watching world.
- We will be more sensitive to the world around us and the practices necessary to distinguish ourselves from it.

Though other "interpretive trajectories," such as the search for truth or the defense of the faith, certainly exist, we are convinced that the transformative trajectory encompasses all others. We cannot afford to interpret Scripture without recognizing and seeking to be subject to and agents of its transformative functions of "teaching, reproof, correction, and training in righteousness" (2 Tim 3:16).

BIBLIOGRAPHY AND RECOMMENDED READING

Berkhof, Louis. *Priniciples of Biblical Interpretation.* Grand Rapids: Baker, 1950.

"Chicago Statement on Biblical Hermeneutics." *JETS* 25 (1982) 397–401.

Duvall, J. Scott, and J. Daniel Hays. *Grasping God's Word: A Hands-On Approach to Reading, Interpreting, and Applying the Bible.* 3rd ed. Grand Rapids: Zondervan, 2012.

Fee, Gordon D., and Douglas Stuart. *How to Read the Bible for All Its Worth.* Grand Rapids: Zondervan, 1982.

Howard, David M. *An Introduction to the Old Testament Historical Books.* Chicago: Moody, 2007.

Klein, William W., Craig L Blomberg, Robert L. Hubbard Jr. *Introduction to Biblical Interpretation.* Nashville: Nelson, 2004.

Long, V. Philips. *The Art of Biblical History.* Grand Rapids: Zondervan, 1994.

Osborne, Grant R. *The Hermeneutical Spiral: A Comprehensive Introduction to Biblical Interpretation.* Rev. and exp. ed. Downers Grove, IL: InterVarsity, 2006.

Ryrie, Charles C. *Basic Theology.* Chicago: Moody, 1999.

Sterrett, Norton T. *How to Understand Your Bible.* Downers Grove, IL: InterVarsity, 1978.

29. Ibid., 249.

Made in the USA
Monee, IL
13 October 2021